This book was made
possible by the
**Peggy V. Helmerich
Fund**

tulsa
LIBRARY TRUST

The History of Christianity

**Recent Titles in
Historical Facts and Fictions**

The Victorian World: Facts and Fictions
Ginger S. Frost

The Vikings: Facts and Fictions
Kirsten Wolf and Tristan Mueller-Vollmer

American Civil War: Facts and Fictions
James R. Hedtke

The Middle Ages: Facts and Fictions
Winston Black

The History of Christianity

Facts and Fictions

Dyron B. Daughrity

Historical Facts and Fictions

ABC-CLIO™

An Imprint of ABC-CLIO, LLC
Santa Barbara, California • Denver, Colorado

Library of Congress Cataloging-in-Publication Data

Names: Daughrity, Dyron B., 1973- author.
Title: The history of Christianity : facts and fictions / Dyron B. Daughrity.
Description: Santa Barbara : ABC-CLIO, 2019. | Series: Historical facts and fictions | Includes bibliographical references and index.
Identifiers: LCCN 2019010424 (print) | LCCN 2019012793 (ebook) | ISBN 9781440863387 (eBook) | ISBN 9781440863370 (print : alk. paper)
Subjects: LCSH: Church history.
Classification: LCC BR145.3 (ebook) | LCC BR145.3 .D383 2019 (print) | DDC 270—dc23
LC record available at https://lccn.loc.gov/2019010424

ISBN: 978-1-4408-6337-0 (print)
      978-1-4408-6338-7 (ebook)

23 22 21 20 19   1 2 3 4 5

This book is also available as an eBook.

ABC-CLIO
An Imprint of ABC-CLIO, LLC

ABC-CLIO, LLC
147 Castilian Drive
Santa Barbara, California 93117
www.abc-clio.com

This book is printed on acid-free paper ∞

Manufactured in the United States of America

This book is dedicated to the Pasadena Church of Christ
With profound respect, and true friendship
I am grateful for all you have been, all you are, and all you will be
We join hands and walk our path
Speak our truth
Offer our gifts
Keep embracing one another
As we have always done

Contents

Preface   ix

Acknowledgments   xi

Introduction: Did Jesus Christ Even Exist?   xiii

1. Jesus Was a Meek and Mild Carpenter   1

2. Early Christians Were Poor and Marginalized People   21

3. Early Christianity Was Bigoted toward Women   45

4. Constantine Was Insincere in His Christian Faith   69

5. Medieval Europe Was a Profoundly Christian Society   93

6. The Crusades Were a Series of Brutal, Unprovoked Attacks   119

7. Christianity Is Anti-Science   147

8. The United States Is Abandoning Christianity   175

9. Christianity Is Currently in Decline   199

Bibliography   221

Index   227

Preface

The Facts and Fictions series with ABC-CLIO is a fascinating approach to learning about history. Some of the volumes in the series (such as the *Vikings*, the *Civil War*, and the *Victorian World*) are rather narrow in their focus. Some, however, cover huge geographies and expanses of time, such as the volume on *Ancient Egypt* and the *History of Buddhism*. Such is the case with the present volume. I try to cover two thousand years of history in a few hundred pages. I have done my best to cover topics that illustrate the rich history of Christianity, but I am also careful to deal with topics that have been misunderstood—sometimes terribly—for much of Christianity's history.

The volume begins by asking whether Jesus Christ ever even lived. Chapter 1 deals with Jesus. Was he actually a meek and mild carpenter, or was he a strong Jewish leader? Chapters 2, 3, and 4 deal with early Christianity up to the time of Constantine. What was life like for early Christians? Were they poor and marginalized as often described? Or were they normal middle-class people? Then I take on the issue of women—one of the more important issues in Christianity today. The chapter on Constantine reviews whether the famous Roman emperor was a true Christian or if he was simply trying to pick a religion that would keep his empire together.

Chapters 5 and 6 are situated in the medieval era. We deal with a big theme in chapter 5: Was medieval Europe an extremely religious place, or not so much? Then we discuss the context of the Crusades.

Chapters 7, 8, and 9 present issues from the modern era: whether Christianity is anti-science, and, finally, we address the status of Christianity in the United States and the rest of the world. Is the Christian religion thriving today or is it losing steam?

I chose these topics because I think they give readers a good sense of the history of Christianity and cover some of the pivotal moments in the two-thousand-year history of the faith. The book is written in an accessible and (hopefully) engaging way so that even high school and college students will find it useful. The chapters also include excerpts of primary sources that will transport readers back to the era in which they emerged.

All Scripture quotations, unless otherwise indicated, are taken from the Holy Bible, New International Version®, NIV®. Copyright ©1973, 1978, 1984, 2011 by Biblica, Inc.™ Used by permission of Zondervan. All rights reserved worldwide. www.zondervan.com The "NIV" and "New International Version" are trademarks registered in the United States Patent and Trademark Office by Biblica, Inc.™

Acknowledgments

I must first acknowledge ABC-CLIO's history and religion editor, George Butler. I have not met him in the flesh, but we have a friendly and productive relationship via email. It was a happy day when he invited me to write this volume in an email dated Wednesday, August 16, 2017. He sent the invitation right as I was heading to Florence, Italy, to live for the academic year. I said yes, thinking I could do some writing while abroad. Alas, I was wrong. But as soon as I got back stateside, I hit it hard. I hope he is proud of this work being added to his innovative list in the Facts and Fictions series. George, I look forward to working with you again.

I extend a sincere thanks to another editor at ABC-CLIO, Robin Tutt. She is the kind of person I love to write for. She's quick with turnarounds, sharp, and ever the polite and friendly one in her communications.

Along with my colleagues and students at Pepperdine, we have come through a turbulent year with destructive fires, a mass shooting, and new leadership at our university. It looks like things are returning to normal, but our hearts are heavy due to the lives lost and the homes destroyed. My hope is that our recently elected president, Jim Gash, will enjoy enthusiastic support from our wonderful community here near the beaches of Malibu as we head into a new and exciting era. When times get tough, let us simply look out the window and be grateful for the place we are privileged to call home.

I must single out a few students who have helped me while I worked on this book project: Jared Sam Agtunong is my Hawaiian graduate assistant. It has been great to have him around. He helped me with grading, searched for many books, and became very familiar with the interlibrary loan system at Pepperdine. I should also mention Chase Manson and Bailey O'connor. They were in my church history class in the fall of 2018. I was impressed with their work and hired them to read portions of my book and offer feedback, which they did. Thanks to all three of you. I wish you the very best as you continue your studies.

I should mention several close colleagues in the Religion Division at Pepperdine: Randy Chesnutt, Ron Highfield, Dan Rodriguez, Nick Zola, Nick Cumming, Linda King, and Tim Willis. I must also thank my dear friends Jay Brewster and Brad Mancuso for being such constant sources of strength and fellowship.

As always, I acknowledge my loving family: my wife, Sunde; my son, Ross; and my daughters, Clare, Mande Mae, and Holly Joy. I do not know what you will do with all the books I plan to bequeath to you some-day, but I do hope you will treasure them and read them—certainly the ones I wrote! Sunde, you are the core that anchors all of us together. I am entirely unsure of what I would do without your stable, cheerful, support-ive presence in my life. Thank you for all you do. Kids, I cannot wait to see you each night after work to eat, dance, and listen to Foo Fighters with you. I am not quite as excited about Ariana Grande and Taylor Swift, but it's all about taking turns, right?

Mom and Dad—what can I say? You gave me an excellent founda-tion. I reflect upon that foundation whenever I finish another book. Your support for me, and pride in me, is palpable. I will never forget, Mom, when you gave me that booklet entitled "There is Greatness within You My Son." I hope there is some greatness in there, but my main hope is that there is goodness. You two raised me to be good . . . good to students, good to strangers, good to loved ones, and good to those who are less fortunate. I hope and pray I can model that goodness during the second half of my life.

Dyron B. Daughrity
Malibu, California
March 6, 2019

Introduction:
Did Jesus Christ Even Exist?

Before venturing into the facts and fictions related to the history of Christianity, we must tackle one central question that is crucial to a topic that takes us back two thousand years: Did Jesus ever even exist?

While there is some discussion about whether Jesus Christ actually ever existed, experts in the field do not doubt that he was a real person. Even some of the most skeptical Bible scholars, such as Bart Ehrman, go to great lengths to prove that, in fact, Jesus existed. In his 2013 book *Did Jesus Exist?*, Ehrman discusses how every week he receives emails from people asking whether Jesus ever existed. Some of these inquirers even use Ehrman as their authority, showing how Jesus never existed. The problem, however, is that Ehrman firmly believes that Jesus was a real person. How could people be so mistaken about such a basic fact? Could it be true that the most famous person in history never existed? Ehrman finally decided to engage this "Jesus never existed" scholarship, and, to his surprise, he found "a whole body of literature out there, some of it highly intelligent and well informed" (Ehrman 2013, 2).

After engaging the overwhelming amount of evidence and analyzing the sources, Ehrman's conclusion is resolute: "Jesus did exist, as virtually every scholar of antiquity, of biblical studies, of classics, and of Christian origins in this country and, in fact, in the Western world agrees." He compares those who doubt Jesus's existence to those who doubt the Holocaust, astronauts walking on the moon, or the assassination of American presidents. As he states it, they "simply *will* not be convinced" (Ehrman 2013, 5).

It should be pointed out that while Ehrman is one of the most respected New Testament scholars living today, he is not a Christian. He describes himself as "an agnostic with atheist leanings." But on the issue of Jesus's existence, he states unequivocally: "The reality is that whatever else you may think about Jesus, he certainly did exist" (Ehrman 2013, 4–5).

The existence of Jesus is not something that Bible scholars typically debate, since that issue is settled. What is still very much unsettled is the *interpretation* of Jesus. Throughout the centuries, Jesus has been portrayed in so many ways that it is often difficult to understand his life from a historical perspective. Was he a firebrand preacher or a meek and mild carpenter? Was he akin to a modern Catholic priest or closer to a Hebrew prophet from Old Testament times? Was he a difficult person, constantly getting into squabbles, or was he the friendly type who everyone wanted to associate with? Who was he? What was he like? And why did he make such an impact? Here we are two thousand years later, talking about this Galilean Jew who wandered around the countryside for one or two years, preaching and teaching, and managing to cause such a stir that people wanted him dead . . . while others believed him to be Lord of the universe (Sanders 1993, 13)!

C. S. Lewis made the famous "trilemma" argument that Jesus is one of three things: liar, lunatic, or Lord. Was Jesus simply lying to people when he told them he was "the way, the truth, and the life" (John 14:6)? Was he insane? In our heavily psychologized world, it might be thought that perhaps Jesus suffered from delusions of grandeur.

Lewis posed the argument that if Jesus was not lying, and if he wasn't insane, then he must be the Lord, just as his disciples claimed. His seemingly high standards of morality would have been at odds with the notion of him being a flagrant liar. Similarly, it is difficult to think of Jesus being insane if the Gospel records are historical in any sense. He was clearly a bright person, who was capable of impressing teachers and ordinary folks alike. He certainly conducted himself in such a way as to inspire a following . . . the largest following of any person in history! One would be hard pressed to find any human organization larger than the Christian religion—a movement that roughly one-third of humanity subscribes to. If he was a loon, then how could so many intelligent people today pray to him, follow his teachings, and proclaim him as uniquely connected to God?

Thus, Lewis concludes, Jesus must be who he said he is: Lord. By no means may we accept Jesus as just a moral teacher. Lewis warns, "That is the one thing we must not say." If Jesus was lying about his importance, then he would be truly diabolical, and if he was a lunatic, then we should be able to see through his exaggerated claims. If he was nuts, then the things he said of himself are "on a level with the man who says he is a poached egg" (Lewis [1952] 2001, 52).

But the central problem here is this: How seriously do we take the New Testament documents? Do we simply dismiss them as fiction? Or do we read them as fact? Right here is the big problem for modern readers. On the one hand, scholars tell us that Jesus was indeed real, that much of the New Testament is accurate, and that the places in the Bible were, indeed, real places. They tell us that the festivals and Roman leaders and Jewish rituals discussed in the New Testament are true, factual things. Herod the Great was real, and Pontius Pilate existed. Passover was a real festival that real Jews celebrated. Jews actually walked around the temple courts in Jerusalem discussing issues of religion. The Sea of Galilee—where Jesus spent so much time—is an actual place you can point to. Unlike stories found in folklore and myth, Bethlehem is a real place, with streets and shops. According to documented evidence, Bethlehem has been continuously inhabited since before the time of Jesus. All these years later, one can still visit Bethlehem and walk on those same streets just as Jesus did.

On the other hand, scholars also tell us that the Gospels were written by disciples who were faithful to Jesus. Perhaps they were a bit uncritical in their telling and recording of the stories about him. Perhaps they got carried away when they described Jesus's walking on water or rising up from the dead. Maybe the Gospel writers had various sources with them when they wrote their biographies that would later become so famous. Possibly, their accounts were not eyewitness accounts at all. They could have been writing "big fish" stories that got bigger with each passing year after Jesus's death. History is littered with examples of this tendency.

Maybe Jesus actually knew the Torah well, but, over time, people began to make up stories of him being a genius at the age of twelve, teaching rabbis in the temple. Maybe Jesus actually healed a few people, but, over time, the stories became inflated to the point that he became associated with resurrecting people—and himself—from the dead. Perhaps Jesus did feed a large group of people on one or two occasions, while over time the story escalated to him feeding thousands with only a few loaves of bread and a couple of fish. How can we ever know the truth? Where did this information come from? To what extent can it be considered historically reliable?

There are many theories about how the Gospel writers got their information. Were they eyewitnesses? Did they all borrow from Mark—who seems to be the earliest of the Gospel writers? Did they all have access to some mysterious document that we don't have access to today? Many scholars have proposed the "Q" theory—that Matthew, Mark, and Luke had access to some lost source that we don't have access to anymore. This would help to explain why these three Gospels share so much in common. However, nobody has ever found "Q." It is purely hypothetical. Increasingly, scholars are backing off that theory. And what about the Gospel of John? Why does it have such a drastically different tone than the synoptic Gospels?

Whether one believes in the religious teachings of the Gospels is a matter of conscience. Historians of religion do not typically venture into that territory. It is always up to the reader to decide whether Jesus is Lord, liar, or lunatic. There is some scholarly historical consensus on this point: much of what we see happening in the Gospels is based on true people, places, and things. Perhaps the Gospels contradict one another here and there in certain details, or report material differently from one another. They might even venture off into philosophical conjecture in places. But there is a lot of material in the Gospels that is accepted as true by people who spend their careers researching in this academic field.

There is a fair amount of agreement on the basic facts of Jesus's life:

- He was born around the year 4 BC, near the end of Herod the Great's life.
- He was raised mainly, or at least partly, in the small town of Nazareth, located in Upper Galilee, in northern Israel.
- His life was deeply impacted by Judaism, its teachings, texts, and rituals.
- He was baptized by John the Baptist, who was probably his cousin.
- He recruited disciples and taught them.
- He conducted a ministry of teaching and healing in the towns, villages, and countryside of Galilee.
- He taught extensively about Israel's God and God's kingdom.
- He was probably in his early thirties when he went to Jerusalem for the Passover festival. There was a disturbance surrounding his actions and teachings there that led to his condemnation. He was publicly interrogated by Jewish authorities and condemned to death by crucifixion, on the orders of Pontius Pilate—the prefect of the Roman province of Judaea.
- His followers fled out of fear. However, their fear turned to courage when they came to the conclusion that he had resurrected from the dead.
- His followers formed a community that commemorated his life and teachings, his death, and his purported resurrection. (Sanders 1993, 10–11)

If the basic, historical outline of the Gospels is essentially true, then this list is a reliable, albeit abbreviated, outline of the life of Jesus. One would be hard pressed to argue against the veracity of any of them.

N. T. Wright, a respected scholar of the New Testament, adds several other details about the life of Jesus to the list above (Wright 1996, 147–150). Most, if not all, of these facts are widely accepted by scholarly consensus:

- Jesus spoke Aramaic, as well as some Hebrew and some Greek.
- His teaching style involved parables as well as reinforcement through various acts that people described as miracles, particularly exorcisms and healings.
- He associated with—and, crucially, ate with—a wide variety of social classes, from the very poor and marginalized to the relatively wealthy and influential, a practice that caused offense and consternation to the Jewish religious establishment.
- He engaged in an itinerant ministry that took him into synagogues, private homes, the open countryside, and even into non-Jewish areas.
- He prayed often, both publicly and privately.
- His understanding of family was "puzzling and offensive" because of his teaching that people should forsake their families—if they must—for the sake of their devotion to him. (Wright 1996, 149)

These items are not creations of some secret society. They are not a conspiracy rooted in the Roman Catholic hierarchy to exert power over Roman subjects. They were not manufactured by Emperor Constantine in order to gain control of the minds of his empire.

No, these descriptions of Jesus and his life are not mere conjecture or biased assertions of the already devoted. Rather, it is the consensus of modern scholarship that these are historical facts. To the best of our knowledge, it appeared these things happened. These events were rooted in a real culture, situated in verifiable places that still exist to the present day.

Further Reading

Ehrman, Bart. 2013. *Did Jesus Exist?: The Historical Argument for Jesus of Nazareth*. New York: HarperOne.
Lewis, C. S. (1952) 2001. *Mere Christianity*. New York: HarperCollins.
Sanders, E. P. 1993. *The Historical Figure of Jesus*. London: Penguin.
Wright, N. T. 1996. *Jesus and the Victory of God*. Minneapolis, MN: Fortress.

1

Jesus Was a Meek and Mild Carpenter

What People Think Happened

When it comes to Jesus's disposition, personality, and profession, it is very difficult to know how accurate the Gospel writers were in their interpretation of Jesus. The facts go beyond subjective interpretation and are often verified by modern scholarship. Understanding Jesus's character is more difficult, since those who wrote the Gospels were obviously great admirers of his life and teaching. Nevertheless, it may be surprising to realize that the Gospels have a fair amount to say about how Jesus carried himself and how he handled the people with whom he interacted. Also, the pictures that are painted by the Gospel authors are rather consistent, taken as a whole.

It is difficult to summarize what the world's 2.5 billion Christians think about their Lord, but suffice it to say that the enduring picture of Jesus is one that emphasizes the good, the peaceful, and the compassionate. Jesus is history's leading icon for great ideals, such as self-sacrifice, empathic sensitivity to people, and, most of all, the Golden Rule—treating others the way you yourself want to be treated.

Throughout Christian history, Jesus has been depicted in various ways, probably most popularly as the man suffering an unjust death on a cross. The Roman Catholic Church, easily Christianity's largest denomination with 1.3 billion members, has adopted the symbol of the crucifix—Jesus on a cross—as its most important symbol. This was not always the case.

Christianity has numerous depictions of Jesus, such as the Good Shepherd, the Pantocrator (the ruler of all, used primarily by Eastern Orthodox Christians), the Sacred Heart (used commonly by Catholics), Christ the King, the Christ Child, the resurrected Christ in radiant white, and the broken body of Christ depicted famously by Michelangelo in his beautiful *Pietà* located near the entrance of St. Peter's Basilica in Rome.

What most of these depictions emphasize is the innocence and vulnerability of Christ. With the exception of the Pantocrator—which depicts Christ in a position of authority—Christ is typically portrayed to convey kindness, mercy, and meekness.

It is also commonly assumed that Jesus Christ was a carpenter prior to his earthly preaching ministry. There is a cottage industry of art based on Jesus's pre-ministry years, where he is depicted as faithfully working alongside his carpenter father, Joseph, in the woodshop. Many Protestant artists have run far with this theme, although Mel Gibson, a conservative Catholic, made much of this Jesus-as-carpenter idea in his blockbuster film *The Passion of the Christ* (2004). In that film, Jesus is depicted as a carpenter building a dining room table for a rich man. His mother objects that the table is too tall for people, given the fact that in antiquity, people tended to eat while sitting on the ground, reclining around a low table. Jesus informs her that he will make tall chairs. A bit annoyed, Mary replies, "This will never catch on."

Similarly, many fictional books have been written about Jesus, using his supposed carpenter years as a central assumption. A best-selling Protestant book of apologetics by Josh McDowell is entitled *More Than a Carpenter*. There are many others that continue with this theme such as *Lessons from the Carpenter* by Michael Brewer, *Wisdom of the Carpenter* by Ron Miller and Marcus Borg, and *Jesus: The Carpenter of Nazareth* by Robert Bird. A number of children's books continue this theme; for example, *The Impatient Carpenter: Hanging Out with Jesus* and *A Carpenter's Son: The Early Life of Jesus*.

How the Story Became Popular

The New Testament's depictions of Jesus are some of the best-known writings in the history of Western culture: the baby in the manger, the baptism by John the Baptist, the temptations in the wilderness, the Sermon on the Mount, Jesus walking on water, the raising of Lazarus, and, of course, the passion narrative.

The ones that have survived and thrived are those that present a Jesus who is open-minded, forgiving, and rather controlled. These gentler presentations make sense in the context of early Christianity, when Christianity's composition was changing from a Jewish faith to a mainly Gentile one. The church sought members, and a welcoming Lord figure proved attractive.

The story of Jesus is immersed in Judaism. As a baby, his parents presented him to God in the Jerusalem temple, with a sacrifice of two doves, as it was written, "Every firstborn male is to be consecrated to the Lord" (Luke 2:23–24). Jesus returned to the temple as a boy, perhaps multiple times. One account of his return to the Jerusalem temple is recorded in the Gospels. When Jesus was twelve, his family traveled there for the Passover festival. When the festival ended, the family was traveling home and realized Jesus was not with them. When they returned to the temple to find him, he was sitting with the teachers, "listening to them and asking them questions," and "everyone who heard him was amazed at his understanding and his answers" (Luke 2:46–47).

Jesus was steeped in Jewish culture. His parents were devoutly Jewish. His preaching and teaching ministry was to the Jews. He surrounded himself with Jewish disciples, notably the Twelve—all of them Jewish.

It was the apostle Paul who famously reached the Gentiles, or non-Jews. While it was the apostle Peter who was the one to first realize that Jesus's life and teachings were for all people everywhere (Acts 10:9–16), it was Paul who really made it happen. He traveled the Mediterranean region, preaching the gospel far and wide, planting Christian churches in several cities, like Corinth, Thessalonica, and Rome.

What is important about Paul's ministry is that he had to present a Jesus who was attractive to Gentiles. Up to Paul's time, the followers of Jesus remained a rather Jewish clique. For the Christian church to cross boundaries into the Gentile world, it needed a universal Christ rather than an insular Jewish Messiah. The word "Christ" is actually a Jewish concept that means "Messiah"—the "anointed one"—who would liberate the Jews from Roman oppression. For Christianity to cross cultural borders, it needed a way to jump that cultural fence, and this is where Paul's ministry excelled.

Paul's depiction of Jesus was a loving, caring, and humble man. In his letter to the Philippians, this is precisely the kind of Jesus that Paul preached, when he declared his hearers should behave like Jesus, showing "tenderness and compassion," and "in humility, value others above yourselves" (Philippians 2:1–3). Paul's Jesus was gentle. He emphasized the teachings and qualities of Jesus that would appeal to the Gentiles.

Paul's goal was to win people to the Christian cause, so he presented Jesus as the one who redeemed humanity out of love. And there are plenty of sources in the Gospels that match Paul's depiction of Jesus as a humble servant who humbly suffered for our sins.

For example, Jesus's Parable of the Lost Sheep in Luke 15 presents a shepherd who loves each individual sheep so much that he would leave the flock in order to search for and find one that got away and became lost. Jesus tells us, "And when he finds it [the lost sheep], he joyfully *puts it on his shoulders* and goes home" (Luke 15:5–6).

There is also a sermon from Jesus in John 10, wherein he declares himself "the good shepherd," who "lays down his life for the sheep." With tenderness, Jesus says, "I know my sheep and my sheep know me—just as the Father knows me and I know the Father—and I lay down my life for the sheep" (John 10:11–15).

These depictions of Jesus worked very well for the early Christian community because they appealed to virtually everybody. They made Jesus into a loving, caring figure who wanted to reach out to humans with tenderness and mercy. In the ancient catacombs in and around the city of Rome, we see Jesus depicted as a Good Shepherd on the walls. Over and over in antiquity, we find Christians identifying Jesus with a shepherd, carrying a sheep around his shoulders.

The Good Shepherd was probably the most common image for Christ in the earliest centuries of Christianity, as the cross was considered repulsive, due to its being the method of Jesus's persecution. Indeed, the earliest known evidence of a cross used for Christian symbolism is Constantine's (early fourth century) use of the labarum—a military flag with the Chi-Rho symbol on it. The Chi-Rho symbol was used by Constantine to represent Christ—whose name begins with the Greek letters Chi and Rho. The Chi in the Christogram soon became associated with the cross (Ferguson 1999, 303–304).

The Good Shepherd image, however, is "ubiquitous in early Christian art," and Christians "used it almost instinctively in funerary and liturgical contexts from an early date" (Ferguson 1999, 1055–1056).

The Good Shepherd and, later, the cross depicted a Jesus who was meek and mild. He was unjustly killed. He did not fight back. Indeed, as the book of Acts illustrates, Jesus "was led like a sheep to the slaughter, and as a lamb before its shearer is silent, so he did not open his mouth" (Acts 8:32). This is the Jesus that Gentiles were attracted to. The savior of the world died a cruel and unjust death. "In his humiliation he was deprived of justice" (Acts 8:33). And "by his wounds you have been healed . . . now you have returned to the Shepherd and Overseer of your souls" (1 Peter 2:24–25). This is the Jesus of the cross. This is the conception of Jesus that survives today in Christian art. This is the Christ we encounter when we enter St. Peter's basilica, or virtually any Catholic church for that matter. This is the sacrificial victim, the *hostia* (Latin for "sacrificial victim"), whose unjust death is commemorated and reinforced virtually every day across the Christian world in the sacrament of the Eucharist. This is the version of Jesus that has been vividly perpetuated in Christian art and theology for two millennia.

Perhaps no one captured the "meek and mild Jesus" more perfectly than the famous cofounder of the Methodist Church, Charles Wesley (1707–1788), one of Protestantism's most beloved hymn composers. Wesley not only wrote the famous hymn "Gentle Jesus, Meek and Mild" but he also wrote other hymns that presented Jesus in a similarly docile fashion: "Jesu, Gentle, Loving Lamb" and "Loving Jesus, Gentle Lamb."

But the meek and mild Jesus is an incomplete depiction, and we will soon see why.

On the matter of Jesus being a carpenter, this idea is rooted in the belief that Joseph, Jesus's earthly father, was a carpenter. Historically, all we have to support this long-standing, widespread belief is one biblical passage in Matthew 13:55, where someone comments about Jesus, "Isn't this the carpenter's son? Isn't his mother's name Mary?" There is also a parallel passage in Mark 6:3, where people in Jesus's hometown ask about Jesus, "Isn't this the carpenter?" The word for carpenter in these two passages has been studied extensively. It is the Greek word *tekton*, which has a range of meanings but most probably means "both mechanic in general and carpenter in particular" (Souvay 1913, 504). Another expert translates the term "tradesman," indicating a fairly broad range of possibilities for Joseph's line of work (Ferguson 1999, 629).

After investigating the history of the term *tekton* and its cognates in Greek literature, New Testament scholar George Wesley Buchanan has persuasively argued that Joseph was probably not a manual laborer but in all likelihood was a supervisor, a businessman, or a master. The term *tekton* is used by Homer in the *Iliad* to describe Harmon, who supervised the building of the Trojan ships. The text calls him the *tekton*, but he was not the one who actually built them with his hands. He was the supervisor who took charge of the massive building enterprise that resulted in the production of many vessels (Buchanan 1964, 202–204).

Buchanan argues, "If Jesus had been a carpenter who worked with his hands, then his home background was nowhere reflected in his teachings." He points out three passages that have something to do with building: (1) "the stone which the builders rejected" passage in Matthew 11:42; (2) the house whose foundation is built on the rock, not on sand (Luke 6:46–49); and (3) the man who wants to build a tower but has to first figure the cost in order to determine whether he can afford it (Luke 14:28–30). By contrast, the passages in the Gospels that reveal familiarity with the roles of a master, manager, landlord, king, landowner, householder, and other positions of wealth and authority are far more common and point to a familiarity with upper classes rather than an acquaintance with menial service (Buchanan 1964, 203). In the following chapter, we will expound this and related themes as we look more closely at the likely social status of the early Christians.

Nevertheless, the biblical record does tell us that Joseph and Jesus were craftsmen, and their identities are forever linked to those passages in Matthew 13:55 and Mark 6:3. The idea of them being craftsmen has survived to the present day, thanks to these two texts, various apocryphal texts, and innumerable artists who have depicted them in this light.

Arguably, the most important text for the Joseph-as-carpenter tradition is a Coptic (ancient Egyptian) story that has been dated to anywhere between the late fourth century and early seventh century. It is called *The History of Joseph the Carpenter*. The primary purpose of the text is to "uphold Mary's virginal conception of Jesus." However, there are other fascinating details that pertain more explicitly to Joseph. For example, Joseph is portrayed as an elderly widower with children from a previous marriage. This explains why Jesus is said to have brothers in the Gospels. If this apocryphal text is correct, then Jesus had no blood siblings. This would explain why the famous Latin scholar Jerome (AD 347–420) considered the "brothers" of Jesus to be, rather, "cousins." Thus, if Mary remained perpetually a virgin, and if Joseph was not Jesus's real father, then Jesus's blood relatives would be limited to his mother and her blood kin (Ferguson 1999, 630).

The History of Joseph the Carpenter tells us that Joseph lived to the ripe old age of 111 and was a practicing carpenter "to the very last day of his life" (v. 29). He had his own shop (v. 4) and "earned his living by the work of his hands; for, as the law of Moses had commanded, he never sought to live for nothing by another's labor" (v. 9). He remained robust and healthy to the very end, showing no signs of weakness, "nor had his sight failed, nor had any tooth perished from his mouth." Indeed, "like a boy he always in his business displayed youthful vigor, and his limbs remained unimpaired, and free from all pain" (v. 10).

While on his deathbed, according to the text, Joseph and Jesus had a long, touching conversation in which Joseph acknowledged the divinity of Jesus (v. 17). Joseph confessed to Jesus that he was sorry for ever doubting Mary's virginity during the time she was carrying Jesus in her womb. Mary and Jesus and Joseph's other children were all in the room during Joseph's final passage. Jesus held his hands for an hour, and while Joseph reached a point where he could not speak, he made it clear to Jesus that he wanted him to remain with him to the end. Jesus then put his hand on Joseph's breast and "perceived his soul now near his throat, preparing to depart from its receptacle" (v. 19). Jesus then asked God to send Michael and Gabriel to take away Joseph's soul to "the dwelling-place of the pious" (v. 23). Jesus later "embraced the body of my father Joseph, and wept over it" (v. 29).

We know *The History of Joseph the Carpenter* was read far and wide, due to the fact that it was translated into several languages. While scholars do not take it seriously as a historical source on the life of Joseph, it does illustrate the *tradition* that rose up around Joseph, as well as key ideas surrounding Jesus and his relationship with his earthly father, and many of the ideas preserved in that text have survived with us down to the present day, especially the Catholic notion of the perpetual virginity of Mary. But for our purposes here, we encounter in this fanciful text a Joseph who was very much a craftsman who practiced his carpentry with purpose up to the very end of his life.

PRIMARY DOCUMENTS

AN EXCERPT FROM *THE HISTORY OF JOSEPH THE CARPENTER*

The History of Joseph the Carpenter *is a text that was widely read and translated into various languages throughout church history. There is no consensus in the scholarship regarding its date, but it may have been written as early as the fourth century or as late as the seventh century. It may have been penned in Byzantine Egypt. This text emphasizes Mary's virginity, as well as Joseph's longevity and career as a carpenter. It played a major role in establishing some of the church tradition surrounding Joseph's life, death, and relationship to his family. For instance, Joseph is described as having numerous children, but from a previous marriage (he was a widower in the text); thereby upholding the perpetual virginity of Mary.*

4. Therefore they immediately sent out, and assembled twelve old men of the tribe of Judah. And they wrote down the names of the twelve tribes of Israel. And the lot fell upon the pious old man, righteous Joseph. Then the priests answered, and said to my blessed mother: Go with Joseph, and be with him till the time of your marriage. Righteous Joseph therefore received my mother, and led her away to his own house. And Mary found James the Less in his father's house, broken-hearted and sad on account of the loss of his mother, and she brought him up. Hence Mary was called the mother of James. Thereafter Joseph left her at home, and went away to the shop where he wrought at his trade of a carpenter. And after the holy virgin had spent two years in his house her age was exactly fourteen years, including the time at which he received her.

. . .

9. Now Herod died by the worst form of death, atoning for the shedding of the blood of the children whom he wickedly cut off, though there was no sin in them. And that impious tyrant Herod being dead, they returned into the land of Israel, and lived in a city of Galilee which is called Nazareth. And Joseph, going back to his trade of a carpenter, earned his living by the work of his hands; for, as the law of Moses had commanded, he never sought to live for nothing by another's labor.

10. At length, by increasing years, the old man arrived at a very advanced age. He did not, however, labor under any bodily weakness, nor had his sight failed, nor had any tooth perished from his mouth. In mind also, for the whole time of his life, he never wandered; but like a boy he always in his business displayed youthful vigor, and his limbs remained unimpaired, and free from all pain. His life, then, in all, amounted to one hundred and eleven years, his old age being prolonged to the utmost limit.

. . .

17. These are the words spoken by Joseph, that righteous old man. And I, going in beside him, found his soul exceedingly troubled, for he was placed in great perplexity. And I said to him: Hail! My father Joseph, you righteous man; how is it with you? And he answered me: All hail! My well-beloved son. Indeed, the agony and fear of death have already environed me; but as soon as I heard Your voice, my soul was at rest. O Jesus

of Nazareth! Jesus, my Savior! Jesus, the deliverer of my soul! Jesus, my protector! Jesus! O sweetest name in my mouth, and in the mouth of all those that love it! O eye which sees, and ear which hears, hear me! I am Your servant; this day I most humbly reverence You, and before Your face I pour out my tears. You are altogether my God; You are my Lord, as the angel has told me times without number, and especially on that day when my soul was driven about with perverse thoughts about the pure and blessed Mary, who was carrying You in her womb, and whom I was thinking of secretly sending away. And while I was thus meditating, behold, there appeared to me in my rest angels of the Lord, saying to me in a wonderful mystery: O Joseph, you son of David, fear not to take Mary as your wife; and do not grieve your soul, nor speak unbecoming words of her conception, because she is with child of the Holy Spirit, and shall bring forth a son, whose name shall be called Jesus, for He shall save His people from their sins. Do not for this cause wish me evil, O Lord! For I was ignorant of the mystery of Your birth. I call to mind also, my Lord, that day when the boy died of the bite of the serpent. And his relations wished to deliver You to Herod, saying that You had killed him; but You raised him from the dead, and restore him to them. Then I went up to You, and took hold of Your hand, saying: My son, take care of yourself. But You said to me in reply: Are you not my father after the flesh? I shall teach you who I am. Now therefore, O Lord and my God, do not be angry with me, or condemn me on account of that hour. I am Your servant, and the son of Your handmaiden; but You are my Lord, my God and Savior, most surely the Son of God.

. . .

19. My undefiled mother Mary, therefore, went and entered the place where Joseph was. And I was sitting at his feet looking at him, for the signs of death already appeared in his countenance. And that blessed old man raised his head, and kept his eyes fixed on my face; but he had no power of speaking to me, on account of the agonies of death, which held him in their grasp. But he kept fetching many sighs. And I held his hands for a whole hour; and he turned his face to me, and made signs for me not to leave him. Thereafter I put my hand upon his breast, and perceived his soul now near his throat, preparing to depart from its receptacle.

. . .

23. Therefore Michael and Gabriel came to the soul of my father Joseph, and took it, and wrapped it in a shining wrapper. Thus he committed

his spirit into the hands of my good Father, and He bestowed upon him peace. But as yet none of his children knew that he had fallen asleep. And the angels preserved his soul from the demons of darkness which were in the way, and praised God even until they conducted it into the dwelling-place of the pious.

. . .

29. Having thus spoken, I embraced the body of my father Joseph, and wept over it; and they opened the door of the tomb, and placed his body in it, near the body of his father Jacob. And at the time when he fell asleep he had fulfilled a hundred and eleven years. Never did a tooth in his mouth hurt him, nor was his eyesight rendered less sharp, nor his body bent, nor his strength impaired; but he worked at his trade of a carpenter to the very last day of his life; and that was the six-and-twentieth of the month Abib.

Source: Alexander Walker, trans., *The History of Joseph the Carpenter*, in *Ante-Nicene Christian Library: Translations of the Writings of the Fathers Down to A.D. 325*. Vol. 16, *Apocryphal Gospels, Acts, and Revelations*, edited by Alexander Roberts and James Donaldson (Edinburgh: T. & T. Clark, 1873), 62–77.

BIBLICAL PASSAGES SHOWING THE MEEKNESS OF JESUS

The following passages from the New Testament illustrate Jesus as being meek and humble. He is portrayed as a shepherd who lovingly looks after his sheep. The shepherd is always on the lookout in case one of his sheep may need help. Jesus is presented here as the friend to sinners. There is also an undertone of Jesus being the sacrificial lamb, who willingly offers himself up for the sins of humanity. This is a Jesus who allows himself to be mistreated and killed. The Philippians passage extends this understanding and presents Jesus as a suffering servant.

The Parable of the Lost Sheep (Luke 15:1–7)

Now the tax collectors and sinners were all gathering around to hear Jesus. But the Pharisees and the teachers of the law muttered, "This man welcomes sinners and eats with them." Then Jesus told them this parable: "Suppose one of you has a hundred sheep and loses one of them. Doesn't he leave the ninety-nine in the open country and go after the lost sheep until he finds it? And when he finds it, he joyfully puts it on his shoulders and goes home. Then he calls his friends and neighbors together and says, 'Rejoice with me; I have found my lost sheep.' I tell you that in the same way there will be more rejoicing in heaven over one sinner who repents than over ninety-nine righteous persons who do not need to repent."

The Good Shepherd and His Sheep (John 10:1–18)

"Very truly I tell you Pharisees, anyone who does not enter the sheep pen by the gate, but climbs in by some other way, is a thief and a robber. The one who enters by the gate is the shepherd of the sheep. The gatekeeper opens the gate for him, and the sheep listen to his voice. He calls his own sheep by name and leads them out. When he has brought out all his own, he goes on ahead of them, and his sheep follow him because they know his voice. But they will never follow a stranger; in fact, they will run away from him because they do not recognize a stranger's voice." Jesus used this figure of speech, but the Pharisees did not understand what he was telling them.

Therefore Jesus said again, "Very truly I tell you, I am the gate for the sheep. All who have come before me are thieves and robbers, but the sheep have not listened to them. I am the gate; whoever enters through me will be saved. They will come in and go out, and find pasture. The thief comes only to steal and kill and destroy; I have come that they may have life, and have it to the full.

"I am the good shepherd. The good shepherd lays down his life for the sheep. The hired hand is not the shepherd and does not own the sheep. So when he sees the wolf coming, he abandons the sheep and runs away. Then the wolf attacks the flock and scatters it. The man runs away because he is a hired hand and cares nothing for the sheep.

"I am the good shepherd; I know my sheep and my sheep know me—just as the Father knows me and I know the Father—and I lay down my life for the sheep. I have other sheep that are not of this sheep pen. I must bring them also. They too will listen to my voice, and there shall be one flock and one shepherd. The reason my Father loves me is that I lay down my life—only to take it up again. No one takes it from me, but I lay it down of my own accord. I have authority to lay it down and authority to take it up again. This command I received from my Father."

Philippians 2:5–8

Have the same mindset as Jesus Christ, who, being in very nature God, did not consider equality with God something to be used to his own advantage; rather, he made himself nothing by taking the very nature of a servant, being made in human likeness. And being found in appearance as a man, he humbled himself by becoming obedient to death—even death on a cross.

CHARLES WESLEY'S HYMN
"GENTLE JESUS, MEEK AND MILD"

Charles Wesley (1707–1788) was one of the greatest hymn writers in the history of Christianity. He is remembered today for his prolific output of hymns as well as his role in founding the Methodist movement at the University of Oxford in 1729. Later, his brother John Wesley and their friend George Whitefield joined the group, and it became one of the most important Protestant movements in the world and remains so today. Charles's hymns are known for their intimate approach to Jesus and their tender portrayal of Jesus as kind, compassionate, and rather docile.

Gentle Jesus, meek and mild,
Look upon a little child,
Pity my simplicity,
Suffer me to come to Thee.

Fain I would to Thee be brought;
Blessed Lord, forbid it not;
In the Kingdom of Thy grace
Give a little child a place.

Lamb of God, I look to Thee;
Thou shalt my example be;
Thou art gentle, meek, and mild;
Thou wast once a little child.

Fain I would be as Thou art;
Give me Thy obedient heart;
Thou art pitiful and kind,
Let me have Thy loving mind.

Loving Jesus, gentle Lamb,
In Thy gracious hands I am;
Make me, Savior, what Thou art;
Live Thyself within my heart.

Source: E. W. and J. Gall Inglis, *282 Hymns and Melodies for School and Family Use* (Edinburgh: Gall and Inglis, 1893), hymn number 143.

What Really Happened

There are many passages in the Gospels that show a different side to Jesus than the meek and mild one we have encountered in this chapter so far, and they have not been emphasized nearly as much in Christian art and literature. In all four Gospels, Jesus is rather frequently portrayed as being strong and powerful, to the point that people remarked how he taught with an unusually strong authority compared to other rabbis. In Matthew 7:29, just at the end of the Sermon on the Mount, we are told, "The crowds were amazed at his teaching, because he taught as one who had authority, and not as their teachers of the law."

On the other hand, Jesus could also become overwhelmed with sorrow. For example, when Jesus's good friend Lazarus died, the Gospel of John says, "Jesus wept" (John 11:35). When Jesus was about to be betrayed and killed, we see him in anguish, "overwhelmed with sorrow to the point of death," falling on his face in prayer, obviously with great emotion. Part of the problem was that Jesus kept asking his apostles to join him in prayer, but they kept falling asleep, at a time when he desperately wanted their company (Matthew 26:36–46).

At other times, Jesus could become agitated, frustrated, openly angry, and on one occasion he even makes a whip in order to drive the money-changers out of the temple courts, in the famous "cleansing the temple" scene that is recorded in all four Gospels. Just before he cleared the temple, he got so mad at a barren fig tree that he cursed it so that it would never bear fruit again. The fig tree didn't do anything wrong, however, since "it was not the season for figs" (Mark 11:13).

Perhaps the greatest example of Jesus having an outburst of emotion was when he launched his "Seven Woes" speech—a tirade against the teachers of the law and the Pharisees for behaving like hypocrites (Matthew 23:13–33). For example, in one of his invectives, he says, "You travel over land and sea to win a single convert, and when you have succeeded, you make them twice as much a child of hell as you are." In another, he says, "Woe to you . . . you hypocrites! You are like whitewashed tombs, which look beautiful on the outside but on the inside are full of the bones of the dead and everything unclean." He hurls insult after insult at them in this scene, saying: "you are the descendants of those who murdered the prophets," "you snakes," "you brood of vipers," "you hypocrites!" "On the outside you appear to people as righteous but on the inside you are full of hypocrisy and wickedness."

At one point, Jesus seems to have caused such a stir while preaching inside of a house that his family came to intervene, saying, "He is out of his mind." Others in the room accused Jesus of being "possessed by Beelzebul," saying his impressive miracles were actually due to demon possession. Jesus defended himself against these charges, and when asked if he was going to respond to his mother and brothers who were there to "take charge of him," he said, "Who are my mother and brothers? Here are my mother and my brothers! Whoever does God's will is my brother and sister and mother" (Mark 3:20–35). Jesus could be hard on his own family. In fact, at one point, he uttered the shocking words, "If anyone comes to me and does not hate father and mother, wife and children, brothers and sisters—yes, even their own life—such a person cannot be my disciple. And whoever does not carry their cross and follow me cannot be my disciple" (Luke 14:26–27). It was also in regard to family that Jesus uttered the words that continue to stump theologians to the present: "Do not suppose that I have come to bring peace to the earth. I did not come to bring peace, but a sword" (Matthew 10:34).

And finally, on the matter of Jesus being a carpenter, the evidence in the New Testament rather points to him being a learned teacher, a rabbi. The first Jewish teacher to be given the official title of rabbi was probably the great Yohanan ben Zakkai, who lived in the first century AD and was a contemporary to Jesus. Most scholars think the "office" of rabbi didn't officially begin until after the temple fell in AD 70. And the importance of rabbis increased dramatically once the temple was lost.

Thus, since Jesus was killed three or four decades before the fall of the Jerusalem temple, many scholars think he should not be considered an official rabbi. They argue that he was a particularly powerful teacher of the Jewish law.

It is clear from the Gospels that by the time of his ministry, Jesus was not engaged in carpentry; rather, his time was spent traveling around, teaching the Jewish law, while receiving support from various people along the way. In other words, Jesus was indeed a professional rabbi (meaning "teacher") during the years covered by the Gospels, as he received his livelihood from students.

On only one occasion was Jesus called a carpenter (Mark 6:3), and on one other occasion he is referred to the son of a carpenter (Matthew 13:55). But he is often called a rabbi throughout Matthew, Mark, and John. Luke chooses not to use the word "rabbi" for Jesus, since he had a "policy of omitting all Hebrew or Aramaic words from his Gospel" (Donaldson 1973, 289). The only exception is the word *amen*.

It seems everyone around Jesus called him "rabbi," including his disciples (John 4:31, Matthew 26:25), other Jewish leaders (John 3:2), people who Jesus healed (Mark 10:51), women who knew Jesus, such as Mary Magdalene (John 20:16), and the crowds who followed him around (John 6:25).

Jesus has many of the hallmarks of a rabbi when you look at his career and teaching style. For example, when he launches his ministry in Luke 4:14–30, we see him teaching in the synagogues, like a rabbi would do. He stood to read from the Isaiah scroll, where it says,

> The Spirit of the Lord is on me, because he has anointed me to proclaim good news to the poor. He has sent me to proclaim freedom for the prisoners and recovery of sight for the blind, to set the oppressed free, to proclaim the year of the Lord's favor. (Luke 4:18–19)

Immediately after reading this famous messianic passage, Jesus said, "Today this scripture is fulfilled in your hearing." Jesus was not only playing the part of a rabbi in this text, but he was taking it to the next level by insinuating he was the "anointed one," or the Messiah. Predictably, the people in the audience that day were "furious" by this claim and "drove him out of the town, and took him to the brow of the hill on which the town was built, in order to throw him off the cliff" (Luke 4:28–29).

Another rabbinic quality of Jesus was the nature of his teaching. He employed what one scholar, Jaroslav Pelikan, called a "rabbinic pedagogy." Pelikan repeats an old joke about a rabbi who was asked by his student, "Why is it that you rabbis so often put your teaching in the form of a question?" To which the rabbi answered, "So what's wrong with a question?" Jesus engaged in this kind of teaching, using questions to answer questions (Pelikan 1985, 13). For example, at one point in Matthew 21, the authority of Jesus was questioned while he was teaching in the temple courts. "By what authority are you doing these things? Who gave you this authority." To which Jesus responded, "I will also ask you one question. If you answer me, I will tell you by what authority I am doing these things." On that occasion, Jesus completely stumped them.

Perhaps Jesus's most archetypal rabbinical teaching device was his constant use of parables. As Matthew (13:34) points out, "Jesus spoke all these things to the crowd in parables; he did not say anything to them without using a parable." Jesus's extremely frequent use of the parable "makes sense only in the setting of his Jewish background" (Pelikan 1985, 13).

There are scholars today who tend to think that since Jesus was from Galilee, he was probably illiterate. This stems from the idea that northern Israel was considered a backward place. Even in the Bible (John 1:46), a disparaging comment is made about Jesus's hometown: "Nazareth! Can anything good come from there?" This adds fuel to the fire that Jesus could not have received good rabbinic training and may well have been illiterate.

However, the New Testament is clear that Jesus often read in public, as we saw when he read from Isaiah in Luke 4. Anyone who makes the argument that Galilee was a backward, illiterate place probably knows little about the history of rabbinic Judaism. The greatest rabbis of the age were from the same area Jesus was from. In fact, Yohanan ben Zakkai—the man recognized in Judaism as the very first official rabbi—was from Galilee. Zakkai is widely regarded as one of the most important rabbis of all time. As were some of the most celebrated rabbis of antiquity: Rabbi Hanina ben Dosa, Rabbi Haninah ben Teradion, and Rabbi Jose ben Abin. Assertions that Jesus was illiterate go against the evidence, as does the idea that Galilee was only for illiterates.

While it is possible, even likely, that Jesus worked with his father for some time, the Gospels point to a man highly trained in the Jewish tradition. We hear nothing of Joseph after Jesus's trip to Jerusalem when he was twelve years old; and it is possible that Joseph died when Jesus was a teenager or young man. Tradition lends some support to that idea. For example, the Roman Catholic Church has always taught that Joseph was much older than Mary. This might explain why the Gospels are silent about Joseph during Jesus's years of ministry.

Thus, the scholarly evidence points to Jesus being a Jewish rabbi, just as the Gospels say. In all likelihood, he was highly trained, with a clear ability to impress the people who heard him preach and teach. The famous scene of Jesus in the temple at the age of twelve, impressing the Jewish leaders, points to someone immersed in Torah study. An illiterate boy who spent all his time sawing wood doesn't make much sense in the light of the Gospels.

PRIMARY DOCUMENTS

BIBLICAL PASSAGES SHOWING THE FIERY SIDE OF JESUS AND THE PROBABILITY THAT HE WAS A TRAINED RABBI

The New Testament's depiction of Jesus is more complex than what many people imagine. In the Gospels, Jesus is often agitated, courageous, angry, and outspoken. He stands up for the oppressed and urges his followers to shake the dust from their feet when not accepted by people. He shouts at people at times and on one occasion even committed violence against religious leaders. He could be testy, yet the people around him tended to gravitate toward him. He was a lightning rod for criticism, though many people deeply respected his adept knowledge of the Torah. People usually addressed him as "rabbi," or "teacher."

Cleansing of the Temple (John 2:13–17)

When it was almost time for the Jewish Passover, Jesus went up to Jerusalem. In the temple courts he found people selling cattle, sheep and doves, and others sitting at tables exchanging money. So he made a whip out of cords, and drove all from the temple courts, both sheep and cattle; he scattered the coins of the money changers and overturned their tables. To those who sold doves he said, "Get these out of here! Stop turning my Father's house into a market!" His disciples remembered that it is written: "Zeal for your house will consume me."

Cursing of the Fig Tree (Mark 11:12–14)

The next day as they were leaving Bethany, Jesus was hungry. Seeing in the distance a fig tree in leaf, he went to find out if it had any fruit. When he reached it, he found nothing but leaves, because it was not the season for figs. Then he said to the tree, "May no one ever eat fruit from you again." And his disciples heard him say it.

The Seven Woes against the Religious Teachers (Matthew 23:13–33)

"Woe to you, teachers of the law and Pharisees, you hypocrites! You shut the door of the kingdom of heaven in people's faces. You yourselves do not enter, nor will you let those enter who are trying to.

"Woe to you, teachers of the law and Pharisees, you hypocrites! You travel over land and sea to win a single convert, and when you have succeeded, you make them twice as much a child of hell as you are.

"Woe to you, blind guides! You say, 'If anyone swears by the temple, it means nothing; but anyone who swears by the gold of the temple is bound by that oath.' You blind fools! Which is greater: the gold, or the temple that makes the gold sacred? You also say, 'If anyone swears by the altar, it means nothing; but anyone who swears by the gift on the altar is bound by that oath.' You blind men! Which is greater: the gift, or the altar that makes the gift sacred? Therefore, anyone who swears by the altar swears by it and by everything on it. And anyone who swears by the temple swears by it and by the one who dwells in it. And anyone who swears by heaven swears by God's throne and by the one who sits on it.

"Woe to you, teachers of the law and Pharisees, you hypocrites! You give a tenth of your spices—mint, dill and cumin. But you have neglected the more important matters of the law—justice, mercy and faithfulness. You should have practiced the latter, without neglecting the former. You blind guides! You strain out a gnat but swallow a camel.

"Woe to you, teachers of the law and Pharisees, you hypocrites! You clean the outside of the cup and dish, but inside they are full of greed and self-indulgence. Blind Pharisee! First clean the inside of the cup and dish, and then the outside also will be clean.

"Woe to you, teachers of the law and Pharisees, you hypocrites! You are like whitewashed tombs, which look beautiful on the outside but on the inside are full of the bones of the dead and everything unclean. In the same way, on the outside you appear to people as righteous but on the inside you are full of hypocrisy and wickedness.

"Woe to you, teachers of the law and Pharisees, you hypocrites! You build tombs for the prophets and decorate the graves of the righteous. And you say, 'If we had lived in the days of our ancestors, we would not have taken part with them in shedding the blood of the prophets.' So you testify against yourselves that you are the descendants of those who murdered the prophets. Go ahead, then, and complete what your ancestors started!

"You snakes! You brood of vipers! How will you escape being condemned to hell?"

Not Peace, but a Sword (Matthew 10:34–39)
"Do not suppose that I have come to bring peace to the earth. I did not come to bring peace, but a sword. For I have come to turn

> "'a man against his father,
> a daughter against her mother,
> a daughter-in-law against her mother-in-law—
> a man's enemies will be the members of his own household.'

"Anyone who loves their father or mother more than me is not worthy of me; anyone who loves their son or daughter more than me is not worthy of me. Whoever does not take up their cross and follow me is not worthy of me. Whoever finds their life will lose it, and whoever loses their life for my sake will find it."

Jesus Answers a Question with a Question (Matthew 21:23–27)

Jesus entered the temple courts, and, while he was teaching, the chief priests and the elders of the people came to him. "By what authority are you doing these things?" they asked. "And who gave you this authority?"

Jesus replied, "I will also ask you one question. If you answer me, I will tell you by what authority I am doing these things. John's baptism—where did it come from? Was it from heaven, or of human origin?"

They discussed it among themselves and said, "If we say, 'From heaven,' he will ask, 'Then why didn't you believe him?' But if we say, 'Of human origin'—we are afraid of the people, for they all hold that John was a prophet."

So they answered Jesus, "We don't know."

Then he said, "Neither will I tell you by what authority I am doing these things."

Further Reading

Buchanan, George Wesley. 1964. "Jesus and the Upper Class." *Novum Testamentum* 7:3 (June): 195–209.

Donaldson, James. 1973. "The Title Rabbi in the Gospels: Some Reflections on the Evidence of the Synoptics." *Jewish Quarterly Review* 63:4 (April): 287–291.

Ehrman, Bart, and Zlatko Plese. 2013. *The Other Gospels: Accounts of Jesus from Outside the New Testament.* Oxford: Oxford University Press.

Ferguson, Everett, ed. 1999. *The Encyclopedia of Early Christianity.* 2nd ed. New York: Routledge.

Pelikan, Jaroslav. 1985. *Jesus through the Centuries.* New Haven, CT: Yale University Press.

Souvay, Charles. 1913. "Joseph." In *The Catholic Encyclopedia.* Vol. 8. New York: Encyclopedia Press.

Vermes, Geza. 1981. *Jesus the Jew.* Minneapolis, MN: Fortress.

Walker, Alexander, trans. 1873. "The History of Joseph the Carpenter." In *Ante-Nicene Christian Library: Translations of the Writings of the Fathers Down to A.D. 325.* Vol. 16, *Apocryphal Gospels, Acts, and Revelations,* edited by Alexander Roberts and James Donaldson. Edinburgh: T. & T. Clark.

2

Early Christians Were Poor and Marginalized People

What People Think Happened

Where should we place the blame for this misconception that the early Christians were poor and marginalized people? Is it because of the beatitudes? Jesus seemed to have a preferential option for the poor in both renditions of the Beatitudes, found in Matthew 5 and Luke 6. In Luke's account, we see Jesus not only extending a preference for the poor but also exhibiting antipathy toward the rich: "Woe to you who are rich, for you have already received your comfort" (Luke 6:24). Was Jesus opposed to rich people? Is there a conflict between being a person of means and being a Christian at the same time?

The traditional story is that the earliest Christians were a poor, despised, and socially marginalized people. This idea may be rooted in the very origins of the Jesus narrative. Mary and Joseph *must have been* poor because they could not even get a room at the inn, thus they had to stay in an animal stable, accompanied by shepherds—the country bumpkins of their day. It seems certain they were a rather hapless people.

Further, when they presented Jesus in the Jerusalem temple, all they could afford was a pair of doves to sacrifice to the Lord (Luke 2:24). This seems to imply that they were poor, based on the passage from Leviticus that poor people could offer two doves or pigeons if they could not afford a lamb:

> These are the regulations for the woman who gives birth to a boy or a girl. But if she cannot afford a lamb, she is to bring two doves or two young

pigeons, one for a burnt offering and the other for a sin offering. In this way the priest will make atonement for her, and she will be clean. (Leviticus 12:7b–8)

It seems fairly straightforward. Mary and Joseph were poor. They were marginalized people, unable to get a room for childbirth, and surrounded by rural folk. They presented a sacrifice that was required of the have-nots.

The early church community seems to have consisted of social rejects. The apostles were poor and disenfranchised people. Fishermen, uneducated, down on their luck disciples would have had no problem following Jesus. They had nothing better to do other than spend the day fishing, so why not follow Jesus and wander around the countryside? An appropriately employed person would have no such ability.

Adolf Deissmann, a prominent scholar of the early twentieth century, described early Christianity as

> a movement among the weary and heavy-laden, men without power or position, "babes," as Jesus Himself calls them, the poor, the base, the foolish, as St. Paul with a prophet's sympathy describes them. . . . The profane historians of the world contemporary with Primitive Christianity were thoroughly aristocratic spirits . . . looking down and not up at the world. The insignificant, despised movement that followed the appearance of Jesus, the unknown Galilean, could not attract the attention of these historians of state affairs, nor, if it had attracted their attention, could it have seemed interesting to them. (Deissmann 1927, 466)

The early Christians were social rejects, according to this view, capable of nothing other than religious zealotry. They were barely noticeable due to their being part of the lowest of the low classes: slaves, fishermen, farmers, and itinerant preachers.

Further, we are told that during the early centuries of Christianity the followers of Jesus were a people on the run, struggling to escape persecution. Several of the emperors in the first three centuries AD—Nero, Trajan, Severus, Decius, Valerian, and, most infamously, Diocletian—were happy to see Christians persecuted, denied basic freedoms, and even in some cases hunted and killed. Public executions in the first three centuries of Christianity were common and served as a warning that following Christ came with considerable risk, even potentially requiring one to pay the ultimate price.

Weren't these Christians in the first few centuries social rejects? Poor, disenfranchised, slaves, humble . . . the sort of people we read about in the beatitudes. After all, the apostle Paul made it clear that the members of the church at Corinth were powerless and marginal in society. He writes, "Not many of you were wise by human standards; not many were influential; not many were of noble birth. But God chose the foolish things of the world to shame the wise; God chose the weak things of the world to shame the strong" (1 Corinthians 1:26b–27).

How the Story Became Popular

In the late nineteenth century, the writings of the German theorists Karl Marx (1818–1883) and Friedrich Engels (1820–1895) were beginning to gain traction. Their work reached full bloom in the early twentieth century, especially after the 1917 socialist revolution in Russia. While known primarily for their economic theories, both Marx and Engels were avid writers on religion, and their works have become foundational in the field of Religious Studies. Their theory of religion argues that religion keeps people in a state of docility, preventing them from rebelling against the upper classes. In their view, religion keeps people focused on unreal things, such as God, angels, heavenly places, and reuniting with loved ones after death. It prevents working-class people from facing their despicable existence and demanding change from those currently in power.

In other words, religion is like an opiate. It keeps people in a foggy state of acceptance, in spite of the fact that they might be experiencing life-threatening injury. While they are actually suffering, religion—"the opiate of the masses"—masks their pain and dulls them into submission. Religion is for people who have little to hope for in the present life, so they remain focused on life after death. Like opium, it provides them with vivid hallucinations and pain relief. According to Marxism, religion is a form of escapism; it prevents people from facing reality. Further, Marx argued that if we were to rid ourselves of the drug, we would start a revolution and fix society's problems. Religion is, therefore, the primary culprit of human suffering because it stifles the revolution. Religion tricks us into thinking we'll be okay . . . someday . . . when we all leave this world and enter the eternal bliss of heaven. These are the reasons why Marx and Engels considered religion to be so insidious.

This critique of religion by Marx and Engels had a powerful impact in the twentieth century as the field of Religious Studies began to mature. Religious Studies is very different from the field of Theology. Scholars of

Religious Studies approach religion much like a scientist would approach his or her science. You look at facts in an empirical way; you don't appeal to gods or scripture. You operate by the scientific principles of experimentation and falsification.

The field of Theology, however, is a discipline for people intending to join the clergy and usually takes place underneath the authority of the church. The classic explanation of theology is "faith seeking understanding." Faith is assumed. Then the quest toward understanding that faith ensues. But faith is a foundation.

The writings of Marx and Engels were of particular import for those who studied religion in the scientific and sociological sense, although their extremely influential views have become standard fare in many theological programs, too. Their theories have bequeathed to the social sciences a powerful critique of religion. In one of Marx's most revealing and poignant statements that could serve as a summary of his entire work, he wrote, "The criticism of religion is the premise of all criticism" (Marx [1844] 1964, 41).

In 1894–1895, Friedrich Engels penned an enormously influential essay entitled *On the History of Early Christianity* that summarized the most mature work of the two socialist pioneers. That essay makes the assertion that "early Christianity has notable points of resemblance with the modern working-class movement" (Engels [1895] 1964, 316).

Engels and Marx convinced generations of scholars that Christianity was an archetypal Communist movement, and they found their scriptures to prove it. Who could deny that the early Christians had striking parallels to the vision of Marx and Engels in the *Communist Manifesto*? Acts 2:44–47 paints the early Christians as living a kind of socialist utopian existence:

> They devoted themselves to the apostles' teaching and to fellowship, to the breaking of bread and to prayer. Everyone was filled with awe at the many wonders and signs performed by the apostles. All the believers were together and had everything in common. They sold property and possessions to give to anyone who had need. Every day they continued to meet together in the temple courts. They broke bread in their homes and ate together with glad and sincere hearts, praising God and enjoying the favor of all the people. And the Lord added to their number daily those who were being saved.

The only problem for Marx and Engels, however, was that the early church believed in God. Not only God; they believed that Jesus Christ was God's one and only son, and they also believed in the promise of the Holy Spirit. Marx and Engels made no such claims. Their parallels were strictly in terms of economics and social class.

The views of Marx and Engels left a stamp on the academy for generations. Already by 1931, a highly popular textbook was echoing their views that early Christian converts

> were drawn in an overwhelming majority from the lowest classes of society. Then as now the governing classes were apprehensive of a movement which brought into a closely knit and secret organization the servants and slaves of society. At that time Christianity was regarded by an upper-class Roman much as an upper-class American would regard a society which united for secret meetings and eternal brotherhood the lowliest toilers of America, which, it was universally believed, made incest and murder a regular part of its meetings, and whose members refused to salute the flag, and, in most cases, to serve in the army. (Goodenough 1970, 37)

We can see from the above quotation that, in this textbook, the early Christians were portrayed as, clearly, coming from the margins of society: the slaves, the "lowliest toilers," and the unpatriotic.

Scholars typically refer to early Christianity as a marginalized sect of Judaism. They were despised and rejected by the main, until they were able to grow large enough to gain a measure of stability. It is a process found within the development of virtually all religions. If they can survive the early, chaotic days when it seems everything works against their ability to organize, then they stand a chance of growing large enough to sustain themselves, and eventually move into a new phase: that of being a church.

Ernst Troeltsch (1865–1923) was an influential German scholar who studied the social dynamics of Christianity throughout the history of its development. According to Troeltsch, all religions begin as sects. As they mature, they become bona fide churches. Christianity fits the typology well: it began as a Jewish sect and then evolved into a proper church. However, embedded within Christianity is a sectarian tendency that continues to create new religious movements that are inspired by Jesus and his earliest followers. Troeltsch understood the early Christian community to be a "lower class" sect—an ascetic community resistant to social development and economic advancement. On these matters, he wrote the following:

> The sects . . . are connected with the lower classes, or at least with those elements in Society which are opposed to the State and to Society; they

work upwards from below, and not downwards from above. . . . The asceticism of the sects . . . is merely the simple principle of detachment from
the world, and is expressed in the refusal to use the law, to swear in a court
of justice, to own property, to exercise dominion over others, or to take
part in war. The sects take the Sermon on the Mount as their ideal; they
lay stress on the simple but radical opposition of the Kingdom of God to
all secular interests and institutions. They practice renunciation only as a
means of charity, as the basis of a thoroughgoing communism of love. . . .
The ascetic ideal of the sects consists simply in opposition to the world and
to its social institutions. . . . Since the sect-type is rooted in the teaching of
Jesus, its asceticism also is that of primitive Christianity and of the Sermon
on the Mount . . . it is still the continuation of the attitude of Jesus towards
the world. The concentration on personal effort, and the sociological connection with a practical ideal, makes an extremely exacting claim on individual effort, and avoidance of all other forms of human association. . . .
The sect maintains the original radicalism of the Christian ideal and its
hostility towards the world. . . . The sect . . . starts from the teaching and
the example of Jesus, from the subjective work of the apostles and the pattern of their life of poverty. (Troeltsch 1931, 2:331–343)

Troeltsch first published this theory in 1911, but it proved highly convincing to the scholarly community, who accepted it as a kind of dogma
about the rise of religions. Christianity serves as one of the archetypal
examples that confirm Troeltsch's theories. Christianity began as a persecuted sect. They were a meek and mild group with almost no power. But
they survived. And eventually grew to the point that they became appealing to the noble classes and eventually the emperor himself.

By the 1950s, it was a rather established view that "Jesus, the figure
around whom Christianity centered, was of humble birth. . . . He chose
for his intimates men from the humble walks of life and had few friends
among the influential" (Latourette [1953] 1975, 33–34).

The idea that earliest Christianity may have had people of means in its
ranks seemed lost on most, except for the most careful of readers who read
between the lines of the Gospels and the Epistles. Perhaps hiding in plain
sight—right there in the Bible—was a segment of the Christian church
that was rather stable in a financial, materialistic sense. Could it be possible that some of the early Christians were wealthy? Influential? Perhaps
even connected to some of the highest echelons of Greco-Roman society?
Or are we to assume that out of nowhere Constantine decided to follow
the faith of slaves and rejects. Perhaps Christianity was never confined to

the lowest of the low. Perhaps from its earliest days, it had movers and shakers within its ranks. That would seem to make more sense for why this faith progressively captivated the world of antiquity.

PRIMARY DOCUMENTS

BIBLICAL PASSAGES SHOWING THE MEEK AND MILD VERSION OF JESUS

The meek and mild depiction of Jesus is certainly not without evidence. The readings included here provide that evidence. In the Beatitudes, Jesus even praises meekness, saying the meek will inherit the earth. He praises peacemakers and blesses those who are persecuted for righteousness. The Lukan version of the Beatitudes shares some ideas with Matthew, but overall it has a different tone. Luke has Jesus blessing the "poor" and not just the "poor in spirit." Luke always has an economic concern in his writings that is not nearly as developed in the other Gospel writers. Luke's Jesus also condemns the rich, which might tell us as much about Luke as about Jesus. The infancy story of Jesus in Luke presents us with a most beautiful, touching, tender look at a meek and humble family bringing their firstborn son into the world. This is the Jesus who is probably best known today: quiet, humble, a baby who is defenseless. We see a couple who is poor. They are not even influential enough to get a room; they were rejected from the inn. The Pauline reading from 1 Corinthians betrays a poor and uninfluential group of people—the early Christians—who had very little to boast about because of their humble roots. Paul tells them that if they have something to boast about, they can boast in their allegiance to Christ. He tells us that very few of the Corinthian Christians came from established backgrounds. They were poor, marginal people.

The Beatitudes (Matthew 5:3–12)

Blessed are the poor in spirit, for theirs is the kingdom of heaven.
Blessed are those who mourn, for they will be comforted.
Blessed are the meek, for they will inherit the earth.
Blessed are those who hunger and thirst for righteousness, for they will be filled.
Blessed are the merciful, for they will be shown mercy.
Blessed are the pure in heart, for they will see God.
Blessed are the peacemakers, for they will be called children of God.

Blessed are those who are persecuted because of righteousness, for
theirs is the kingdom of heaven.

Blessed are you when people insult you, persecute you and falsely say
all kinds of evil against you because of me.

Rejoice and be glad, because great is your reward in heaven, for in
the same way they persecuted the prophets who were before you.

The Beatitudes (Luke 6:20–26)

Blessed are you who are poor, for yours is the kingdom of God.

Blessed are you who hunger now, for you will be satisfied.

Blessed are you who weep now, for you will laugh.

Blessed are you when people hate you, when they exclude you and
insult you and reject your name as evil, because of the Son of Man.

Rejoice in that day and leap for joy, because great is your reward in
heaven. For that is how their ancestors treated the prophets.

But woe to you who are rich, for you have already received your
comfort.

Woe to you who are well fed now, for you will go hungry.

Woe to you who laugh now, for you will mourn and weep.

Woe to you when everyone speaks well of you, for that is how their
ancestors treated the false prophets.

The Birth of Jesus (Luke 2:1–21)

In those days Caesar Augustus issued a decree that a census should be
taken of the entire Roman world. (This was the first census that took place
while Quirinius was governor of Syria.) And everyone went to their own
town to register.

So Joseph also went up from the town of Nazareth in Galilee to Judea,
to Bethlehem the town of David, because he belonged to the house and
line of David. He went there to register with Mary, who was pledged to be
married to him and was expecting a child. While they were there, the time
came for the baby to be born, and she gave birth to her firstborn, a son.
She wrapped him in cloths and placed him in a manger, because there was
no guest room available for them.

And there were shepherds living out in the fields nearby, keeping watch
over their flocks at night. An angel of the Lord appeared to them, and the
glory of the Lord shone around them, and they were terrified. But the
angel said to them, "Do not be afraid. I bring you good news that will
cause great joy for all the people. Today in the town of David a Savior has

been born to you; he is the Messiah, the Lord. This will be a sign to you: You will find a baby wrapped in cloths and lying in a manger."

Suddenly a great company of the heavenly host appeared with the angel, praising God and saying, "Glory to God in the highest heaven, and on earth peace to those on whom his favor rests."

When the angels had left them and gone into heaven, the shepherds said to one another, "Let's go to Bethlehem and see this thing that has happened, which the Lord has told us about."

So they hurried off and found Mary and Joseph, and the baby, who was lying in the manger. When they had seen him, they spread the word concerning what had been told them about this child, and all who heard it were amazed at what the shepherds said to them. But Mary treasured up all these things and pondered them in her heart. The shepherds returned, glorifying and praising God for all the things they had heard and seen, which were just as they had been told.

On the eighth day, when it was time to circumcise the child, he was named Jesus, the name the angel had given him before he was conceived.

"Not Many Were of Noble Birth" (Apostle Paul in 1 Corinthians 1:26–31)

Brothers and sisters, think of what you were when you were called. Not many of you were wise by human standards; not many were influential; not many were of noble birth. But God chose the foolish things of the world to shame the wise; God chose the weak things of the world to shame the strong. God chose the lowly things of this world and the despised things—and the things that are not—to nullify the things that are, so that no one may boast before him. It is because of him that you are in Christ Jesus, who has become for us wisdom from God—that is, our righteousness, holiness and redemption. Therefore, as it is written: "Let the one who boasts boast in the Lord."

FRIEDRICH ENGELS, *ON THE HISTORY OF EARLY CHRISTIANITY* (1894–1895)

Friedrich Engels (1820–1895) was the son of a wealthy textile businessman who owned companies in both England and Prussia. Engels worked closely with Karl Marx to develop theories of economics, chiefly the idea that the upper classes exploit the lower classes to the detriment of everybody. He and Marx penned the famous Communist Manifesto, *which impacted numerous fields of thought and was implemented by many national governments throughout the twentieth century and beyond.*

The history of early Christianity has notable points of resemblance with the modern working-class movement. Like the latter, Christianity was originally a movement of oppressed people; it first appeared as the religion of slaves and emancipated slaves, of poor people deprived of all rights, of peoples subjugated or dispersed by Rome. Both Christianity and the workers' socialism preach forthcoming salvation from bondage and misery; Christianity places this salvation in a life beyond, after death, in heaven; socialism places it in this world, in a transformation of society. Both are persecuted and baited, their adherents are despised and made the objects of exclusive laws, the former as enemies of the human race, the latter as enemies of the state, enemies of religion, the family, social order. And in spite of all persecution, nay, even spurred on by it, they forge victoriously, irresistibly ahead. Three hundred years after its appearance Christianity was the recognized state religion in the Roman World Empire, and in barely sixty years socialism has won itself a position which makes its victory absolutely certain.

> **Source:** Friedrich Engels, *On the History of Early Christianity*. First published in *Die Neue Zeit*, 1894–1895. Translation by the Institute of Marxism-Leninism, 1957. Available at the Marxists Internet Archive, https://www.marxists.org/archive/marx/works/1894/early-christianity/index.htm.

KARL KAUTSKY, *FOUNDATIONS OF CHRISTIANITY* (1925)

Karl Kautsky (1854–1938) was a Czech scholar and journalist who applied the teachings of Marx in his historical, political, and philosophical writings. His ideas on early Christianity were very popular and translated into numerous languages. His understanding of the early Christians as a proletarian community proved to be very influential on generations of scholars. In his view, the early Christians were the archetypal communists.

This proletarian character of early Christianity is not the least of the reasons for our being so poorly informed on this early phase. Its first advocates may have been very eloquent persons, but they were not versed in reading and writing. These arts were far stranger to the habits of the masses of the people of those days than they are now. For a number of generations the Christian teaching of the history of its congregation was limited to oral transmission, the handings down of feverishly excited, incredibly credulous persons, reports of events that had been witnessed only by a small circle, if they ever really took place at all. . . . Only when more educated persons, of a higher social level, turned to Christianity, was a beginning made in the written fixation of its traditions, but even in this case the purpose was not historical so much as controversial, to defend certain views and demands.

. . .

[I]t is nevertheless very important to have definite information concerning the nature of the primitive Christian congregation.

. . .

In the first place, there is a savage class hatred against the rich.

This class hatred is clearly apparent in the Gospel of Saint Luke, which was written early in the Second Century, particularly in the story of Lazarus, which we find in this Gospel alone. . . . In this passage, the rich man goes to Hell and the poor man into Abraham's bosom. . . . The rich man is condemned for the simple reason that he is a rich man. The same Gospel has Jesus say: "How hardly shall they that have riches enter into the Kingdom of God, for it is easier for a camel to go through a needle's eye than for a rich man to enter into the Kingdom of God." Here also the rich man is condemned because of his wealth, not because of his sinfulness. . . . The reader will observe that to be rich and enjoy one's wealth is regarded as a crime, worthy of the most cruel punishment.

. . .

Few are the occasions on which the class hatred of the modern proletariat has assumed such fanatical forms as that of the Christian proletariat. . . . The first Christians were not capable of making such a clear and calm statement of the case. But their short observations, exclamations, demands, imprecations, clearly indicate in every case the uniformly communistic character of the first stage of the Christian congregation.

Source: Karl Kautsky, *Foundations of Christianity: A Study in Christian Origins* (New York: International Publishers, 1925), 325, 326, 327, 328, 329, 334.

PHILIP SCHAFF, *HISTORY OF THE CHRISTIAN CHURCH* (1858)

Philip Schaff's (1819–1893) seven-volume History of the Christian Church *shaped generations of theologians and church historians and is still in use today. In this reading on the social conditions of the Christians in Rome in the first century, Schaff betrays a sense of ambivalence about the social class of the early Christians. Early on, he describes the Christians at Rome as rather poor and marginal, but as the piece reads on, he highlights exceptions to this depiction. By the end of the reading, one begins to wonder whether his earlier assertion—that the Roman Christians were lower class—even holds up. This piece was chosen to show that although nineteenth-century scholars often characterized the early Christians as poor and marginalized, they were fully aware of numerous exceptions to this stereotype.*

The great majority of the Christians in Rome, even down to the close of the second century, belonged to the lower ranks of society. They were artisans, freedmen, slaves. The proud Roman aristocracy of wealth, power, and knowledge despised the gospel as a vulgar superstition. The contemporary writers ignored it, or mentioned it only incidentally and with evident contempt. The Christian spirit and the old Roman spirit were sharply and irreconcilably antagonistic, and sooner or later had to meet in a deadly conflict. But, as in Athens and Corinth, so there were in Rome also a few honorable exceptions.

Paul mentions his success in the praetorian guard and in the imperial household. . . . Pomponia Graecina, the wife of Aulus Plautius, the conqueror of Britain, who was arraigned for "foreign superstition" about the year 57 or 58 . . . was probably the first Christian lady of the Roman nobility. . . . A generation later two cousins of the Emperor Domitian (81–96), T. Flavius Clemens, consul (in 95), and his wife, Flavia Domitilla, were accused of "atheism," that is, of Christianity, and condemned, the husband to death, the wife to exile. Recent excavations in the catacomb of Domitilla, near that of Callistus, establish the fact that an entire branch of the Flavian family had embraced the Christian faith. Such a change was wrought within fifty or sixty years after Christianity had entered Rome.

Source: Philip Schaff, *History of the Christian Church*. Vol. 1, *Apostolic Christianity, A.D. 1–100* (New York: Charles Scribner's Sons, 1920), 373–375.

What Really Happened

Most scholars of early Christianity now believe that the early Christians came largely from middle and upper classes. Yes, there were poor Christians, but it is erroneous to think the majority of them were poor.

Eminent historian Peter Brown has researched extensively on this topic. His writings show how early Christians were cognizant of the poor, and they tried to help them. If Christians were so often urged to help the poor, then it is unlikely that they were all poor themselves. A far better explanation is that Christians were in most cases people of means, and they took a leading role in helping the lower strata of society. The frequent mandate for Christians to give alms demonstrates that Christians were people who *could* give alms; whereas, the poor would be unable to feed themselves, much less sustain others. Giving alms and helping the most vulnerable people in society was something that the Christians did with vigor.

Brown explains that Christians went to great lengths to not just care for the poor but also to "maintain solidarity" with the poor. Most Christians in the first two centuries of Christianity were "respectable, middling persons, such as had always found a social niche for themselves in large cities like Rome and Carthage." They were people of some means. Their wealth and influence ascended remarkably over the generations, greatly impacting the social landscape of the Christian community. Early Christians gained many respectable and influential converts along the way, to the point that "by 300 AD, many Christians were already wealthy, cultivated, and even powerful" (Brown 2015, 34–41).

A common misconception is that Christianity was a religion for the poor and marginalized well up until Constantine's rule in the early 300s. However, Brown reverses this script: "After the conversion of Constantine in 312, the poor now flooded the churches. They needed charity on a far greater scale than previously" (Brown 2015, 43).

There are many examples in antiquity—going back to the New Testament itself—of Christians using their own wealth to provide social uplift to the people around them. This was a critical part of being a Christian. For example, in Galatians 2, Paul reflects on his first meetings with the apostles "who were held in high esteem"—like James, Peter, and John. Once they recognized Paul's gifts and his desire to preach the gospel to the Gentiles, they had one very simple request for him: "All they asked was that we should continue to remember the poor, the very thing I had been eager to do all along" (Galatians 2:10). This clearly indicates that the apostles were not from "the poor" classes, but rather from a higher class that had access to resources—enough resources to help the less fortunate.

As we discussed in chapter 1, it is very unlikely that Jesus was but a simple carpenter. While it is possible that his father had a business, and Jesus may have worked with him, there is far more evidence to indicate that Jesus was trained as a rabbi. There is little doubt that Jesus was an immensely gifted and learned religious scholar, capable of holding his own in argumentation with Jewish leaders even as a youth when he and his family visited the Jerusalem Temple.

By the time we read of Jesus's ministry, it is all too clear that he was highly trained in the Torah, was truly competent in rhetoric, and was familiar with leading services in the synagogue. The Gospels also show us a Jesus who easily befriended the upper classes of society such as tax collectors, teachers of the law, Roman centurions, synagogue rulers, and wealthy laypeople such as Susanna and Joanna—a woman described as the wife of Chuza, who managed Herod Antipas's household (Luke 8:3). Yes, Jesus was financially supported by a woman from the highest echelon of Jewish society.

It is also fairly obvious that in the Gospels "the majority of Jesus's teachings were directed toward the upper economic class with whom Jesus associated" (Buchanan 1964, 209). It is very possible that he associated with upper classes so much because he was one of them. In fact, Jesus was often derided for socializing with the wealthy, especially the wretched tax collectors who had become rich by fleecing the people. In 2 Corinthians 8:9, we read the following from the apostle Paul, "For you know the grace of our Lord Jesus Christ, that though he was rich, yet for your sake he became poor, so that you through his poverty might become rich." This passage is often thought to be metaphoric in nature, or perhaps refer to Jesus being rich while in heaven—prior to his coming to earth. However, some scholars take this passage at face value and assert that Jesus probably came from wealth.

Hiding in plain sight are also clues that Jesus's disciples were not poor and downtrodden, but rather were men and women of means. The apostles James and John were successful enough in their family fishing business to own their own boats and hire servants to do the labor (Mark 1:19–20). The apostle Matthew was a publican—a public contractor who helped in the collection of taxes. Zacchaeus was another tax collector of high standing who followed Jesus. Tax collectors were powerful men, among the most influential members of Roman civil society. This is why they were despised. Another wealthy disciple of Jesus was Joseph of Arimathea, mentioned in Matthew 27:57–59. The text tells us that he was rich and had a personal relationship with Pilate—the Roman governor of Judea who condemned Jesus to death. Joseph provided a "new tomb" for Jesus's body. This was not a hole in the ground. It was cut out of rock. This was how the wealthy took care of their dead.

The apostle Paul was a Jew who held Roman citizenship; he was from a family "of wealth and standing" (Nock 1938, 21). He was trained by Gamaliel—perhaps the most important Jewish rabbi of that era. Paul was extremely gifted. Not only a man of arts and letters, he also ran a tent-making business on the side (Acts 18:3).

The apostle Paul was a highly literate man, capable of penning master-pieces, such as the Epistle to the Romans—one of the greatest letters of antiquity. He could argue with philosophers and could recruit new con-verts from the wealthy strata of society, such as Lydia—a woman of means who sold purple fabric. We are told in Acts 16 that she was a homeowner with a house large enough for her own household as well as Paul and his travel companions. Lydia is often regarded as the first documented convert to Christianity in Europe. Thus, Christianity in Europe began not with a marginal group of social rejects, but with the conversion of a wealthy landowner who owned a lucrative textile business.

A careful reading of the New Testament provides ample examples of well-to-do and influential Christians actively participating in the early Christian narratives. We have been taught to notice the poor and mar-ginalized in the early church, rather than the people who had political or economic power. For instance, in Acts 19:22, we encounter a man named Erastus who is identified as one of Paul's helpers. That same Erastus is mentioned in Romans 16:23 as being the city treasurer for Corinth—one of the most important cities of Roman Greece.

In a careful study of Paul's social circle, historian Wayne Meeks notes that the apostle Paul mentions around eighty of his acquaintances in the New Testament. Regarding their social status, we have helpful clues for about thirty of them. These clues give us a fair understanding of Paul's circles of friends and acquaintances (Meeks 1983, 55ff).

- Euodia and Syntyche (Philippians 4:2) were Greek women with names that indicate they were "among the merchant groups."
- Tertius (Romans 16:22) was probably a professional scribe.
- Luke (Colossians 4:14), the writer of the Gospel, was a medical doctor.
- Gaius (Romans 16:23) had a house that was large enough to host Paul and the entire local church in Corinth. Meeks writes, "He is evidently a man of some wealth" (1983, 57).
- Crispus (Acts 18:8) is called "the synagogue leader" and, according to Meeks, "he not only has high prestige in the Jewish community but is also probably well to do" (1983, 57).

- Erastus, as mentioned earlier, "was probably a Corinthian freedman who had acquired considerable wealth in commercial activities" (Meeks 1983, 59).

- Prisca and Aquila are mentioned several times in Paul's writings. They were tentmakers, like Paul, who enjoyed "relatively high" levels of wealth. They traveled often, hosted churches in their homes in three cities, and enthusiastically supported Paul's ministry with their finances. Interestingly, Prisca "has higher status than her husband" (Meeks 1983, 59).

- Philemon, the slave owner and namesake for the New Testament letter, was wealthy with a large house. He hosted the church in his home and supported evangelists financially.

- Phoebe (Romans 16:1–2) was "the patroness of many Christians," including Paul. She was "an independent woman" who probably traveled for business. She "has some wealth" and is also one of the leaders of the church in Cenchreae (Meeks 1983, 60).

- Mark's mother (Acts 12:12) had a house of her own that was large enough to host the substantial church in Jerusalem.

- Barnabas (Acts 4:36–37) was "reasonably well-to-do" and sold one of his farms and put the money at the apostles' feet.

- Apollos, mentioned frequently in the New Testament, was a scholar and skilled rhetorician who traveled widely, indicating some level of wealth.

- Jason (Acts 17:5–9) owned a home and was wealthy enough to post bond for himself and others in order to get out of jail.

- In Philippians 4:22, we are told that members of Caesar's own household had converted to the Christian faith!

- The Narcissus mentioned in Romans 16:11 was probably the same person who served as emperor Claudius's private secretary. "No one in Rome was so powerful and so intimate with the emperor as a certain Narcissus . . . it seems likely that these were the very two persons whose households are mentioned here by the apostle [Paul]" (Harnack 1908, 45).

And there are many other New Testament examples that show how Christianity appealed to upper classes as much or more as it did to the lower classes.

Why did the old view persist for so long—that Christianity was mainly for the poor, marginalized, and unlearned? One of the first scholars to really take notice of these facts hiding in plain sight was the Australian scholar E. A. Judge. His pioneering work in the 1960s on the social setting of the early Christians deeply impacted the field to the point that, as early as 1983, scholars such as Abe Malherbe, could refer to a "new consensus" happening in the field.

> It appears from the recent concern of scholars with the social level of early Christians, that a new consensus may be emerging. This consensus, if it is not premature to speak of one, is quite different from the one represented by Adolf Deissmann, which has held sway since the beginning of the century. The more recent scholarship has shown that the social status of early Christians may be higher than Deissmann [and others] had supposed. (Malherbe 1983, 31)

While there is no doubt that early Christianity appealed to the poor—the evidence is clear in both the Gospels as well as the Epistles—there is no longer any reason to suppose that Christianity was primarily for the poor and marginalized.

Christianity seems to have been a movement that had a fair number of members from all strata of society. This would explain why Paul (1 Corinthians 11:22) exhorts the Corinthian Christians to stop dividing themselves into what appears to be social groups when they gather for the Lord's Supper. "Do you despise the church of God and shame those who have nothing?" In other words, it is likely that the rich were avoiding the poor. Followers of Jesus, however, were to be unified (John 17), regardless of social class or anything else. The same idea comes out in James's epistle, when he writes extensively in chapter two about how the poor were being dishonored in the church.

PRIMARY DOCUMENTS

BIBLICAL PASSAGES

Divisions in the Church at the Lord's Supper (1 Corinthians 11:17–22)
This first reading simply shows that the early church was not a unified bunch. In fact, there were divisions, and those divisions are often described in the New Testament. In this case of the Lord's Supper, the divisions appear to be socioeconomic in nature.

In the following directives I have no praise for you, for your meetings do more harm than good. In the first place, I hear that when you come together as a church, there are divisions among you, and to some extent I believe it. No doubt there have to be differences among you to show which of you have God's approval. So then, when you come together, it is not the Lord's Supper you eat, for when you are eating, some of you go ahead with your own private suppers. As a result, one person remains hungry and another gets drunk. Don't you have homes to eat and drink in? Or do you despise the church of God by humiliating those who have nothing? What shall I say to you? Shall I praise you? Certainly not in this matter!

Prejudice against the Poor in the Early Church (James 2:1–9)
Traditionally, the book of James is thought to have been written by the brother of Jesus. This would make sense because so much of James resembles the teachings of Jesus, including this reading on how the poor should be treated with dignity.

My brothers and sisters, believers in our glorious Lord Jesus Christ must not show favoritism. Suppose a man comes into your meeting wearing a gold ring and fine clothes, and a poor man in filthy old clothes also comes in. If you show special attention to the man wearing fine clothes and say, "Here's a good seat for you," but say to the poor man, "You stand there" or "Sit on the floor by my feet," have you not discriminated among yourselves and become judges with evil thoughts?

Listen, my dear brothers and sisters: Has not God chosen those who are poor in the eyes of the world to be rich in faith and to inherit the kingdom he promised those who love him? But you have dishonored the poor. Is it not the rich who are exploiting you? Are they not the ones who are dragging you into court? Are they not the ones who are blaspheming the noble name of him to whom you belong?

If you really keep the royal law found in Scripture, "Love your neighbor as yourself," you are doing right. But if you show favoritism, you sin and are convicted by the law as lawbreakers.

TERTULLIAN'S DEFENSE OF CHRISTIANITY (APPROXIMATELY AD 155–240)

Tertullian wrote long defenses of Christianity because "Christians are counted as public enemies" and "enemies of the state." In this section of his Apologeticus—*written in AD 197—we see him arguing that the Christian community is no threat because its lifestyle is above reproach. He also points out that Christianity has grown in all classes and places to the point that it is rather futile to keep persecuting it so harshly. Christians could now be found in all areas of society, even the "palaces, senate, forum." Persecuting them would only hurt the empire. Besides, as he famously states in chapter 50, "The oftener we are mown down by you, the more in number we grow; the blood of Christians is seed." In this reading, we also see Tertullian showing how wealthier Christians served the needs of the poorer members of the faith. The last section of this reading shows how Christians were contributors to society, and that meant financial contributors as much as anything else. Indeed, according to Tertullian, Christians clearly out-gave non-Christians.*

How often you inflict gross cruelties on Christians, partly because it is your own inclination, and partly in obedience to the laws! How often, too, the hostile mob, paying no regard to you, takes the law into its own hand, and assails us with stones and flames! . . . We are but of yesterday, and we have filled every place among you—cities, islands, fortresses, towns, market-places, the very camp, tribes, companies, palaces, senate, forum—we have left nothing to you but the temples of your gods. . . . You would have to seek subjects to govern. You would have more enemies than citizens remaining. For now it is the immense number of Christians which makes your enemies so few—almost all the inhabitants of your various cities being followers of Christ. Yet you choose to call us enemies of the human race.

. . .

There is no buying and selling of any sort in the things of God. Though we have our treasure-chest, it is not made up of purchase-money, as of a religion that has its price. On the monthly collection day, if he likes, each puts in a small donation; but only if it be his pleasure, and only if he be able: for there is no compulsion; all is voluntary. These gifts are, as it were, piety's deposit fund. For they are not taken thence and spent on feasts, and drinking-bouts, and eating-houses, but to support and bury poor people, to supply the wants of boys and girls destitute of means and parents, and of old persons confined now to the house; such, too, as have suffered shipwreck; and if there happen to be any in the mines, or banished to the islands, or shut up in the prisons, for nothing but their fidelity to the cause of God's church, they become the nurslings of their confession.

. . .

We call each other brethren. . . . One in mind and soul, we do not hesitate to share our earthly goods with one another. All things are common among us but our wives.

. . .

But we are called to account as harm-doers on another ground, and are accused of being useless in the affairs of life. How in all the world can that be the case with people who are living among you, eating the same food, wearing the same attire, having the same habits, under the same necessities of existence? We are not Indian Brahmins or Gymnosophists, who dwell in the woods and exile themselves from ordinary human life. . . . So we sojourn with you in the world, abjuring neither forum [meeting hall], nor shambles [butcher], nor bath, nor booth, nor workshop, nor inn, nor weekly market, nor any other places of commerce. We sail with you, and fight with you, and till the ground with you; and in like manner we unite with you in your traffickings—even in the various arts we make public property of our works for your benefit. How it is we seem useless in your ordinary business, living with you and by you as we do, I am not able to understand.

. . .

Our compassion spends more in the streets than yours does in the temples.

Source: From *Apologeticus*, sections 35–42, in *The Writings of Quintus Sept. Flor. Tertullianus.* Vol. 1 (Edinburgh: T & T Clark, 1869), 116–126.

ADOLF VON HARNACK, *ON THE INWARD SPREAD OF CHRISTIANITY* (1908)

Harnack was an eminent scholar ahead of his time. In this reading, he shows his awareness that the early Christian community was not just made up of poor and marginalized people. Rather, quite early on, Christians could be found "among the aristocratic, the cultured, the wealthy, and the official classes" (Harnack 1908, 33–52).

The officials of the Christian church frequently belonged to the lowest class. Even Paul, however, implies that some people who were wise and mighty and of good birth had become Christians. And this is borne out by the book of Acts. The proconsul Sergius Paulus was brought over to the faith in Cyprus (13:7–12), Dionysius the Areopagite in Athens (17:34), and "not a few women of good position" in Thessalonica (17:4). . . . Pliny informs Trajan that "many of all ranks" in Bithynia [modern Turkey] had gone over to the Christian sect. In Rome a distinguished lady, Pomponia Graecina, was converted, followed not long afterwards by the consul Titus

Flavius Clemens and his wife Domitilla. These and similar results must ere long have attracted a large number of adherents to the local Christian church from the better classes.

Hermas frequently has occasion to mention the rich members of the church, and his reproofs of their conduct are severe. . . . Marcion, too, was so well off that he could present the church of Rome with 200,000 sesterces. The age of Commodus [emperor from AD 177 to 192] marks a distinct stage in the movement. . . . Apollonius at Rome . . . indeed was in likelihood a senator. . . . Tertullian narrates how the pagans complained of people "of all ranks" going over to Christianity. . . . Similar testimony is borne by Clement and Origen.

. . .

The civil service, too, was widely permeated by Christianity. The "Octavius" of Minucius Felix plunges us into that circle at an early stage in the history of the faith, while the second rescript issued by Valerian in 258 against the Christians takes notice of none but the upper classes and the members of Caesar's household, outside the clergy: "Senators and prominent men and Roman knights are to lose their position, and moreover be stripped of their property; if they still persist in being Christians after their goods have been taken from them, they are to be beheaded. Matrons are to be deprived of their property and banished into exile. But members of Caesar's household are to have their goods confiscated and be sent in chains by appointment to the estates of Caesar." The rescript shows, more clearly than any single passage could, the extent to which Christianity had already spread among the upper classes.

. . .

We can see, then, how even prior to Constantine the Christian religion had made its way into the government service, just as it had found an entrance, thanks to Clement and Origen, into the world of learning. . . . We also know a whole series of names of orators and grammarians who came over to Christianity. . . . [Emperor] Diocletian [reigned from AD 284 to 305] had a Latin orator and a grammarian summoned from Africa to Nicomedia, when it was discovered that both were Christians.

. . .

The really decisive factor was the development of Christian learning at Alexandria and Caesarea. It adhered to the church. But it won over the educated classes to Christianity, and provided the Neoplatonist philosophers with serious rivals.

. . .

Some of the Syrian royal ladies were favorably disposed to Christianity. . . . Philip the Arabian . . . was claimed ere long as a secret Christian. . . . Under Diocletian (whose wife and daughter were Christians) the court at Nicomedia consisted largely of Christians. The early rescripts of Diocletian were specially designed to purge the court of them.

Source: Adolf von Harnack, *The Mission and Expansion of Christianity in the First Three Centuries*. Vol. 2, translated by James Moffatt (London: Williams and Norgate, 1908), 34–51.

Further Reading

Brown, Peter. 2015. *The Ransom of the Soul: Afterlife and Wealth in Early Western Christianity*. Cambridge, MA: Harvard University Press.

Buchanan, George Wesley. 1964. "Jesus and the Upper Class." *Novum Testamentum* 7:3 (June): 195–209.

Deissmann, Adolf. 1927. *Light from the Ancient East*. London: Hodder and Stoughton.

Engels, Friedrich. (1894–1895) 1964. "On the History of Early Christianity." In *On Religion*, edited by Karl Marx and Friedrich Engels, 316–347. New York: Schocken Books.

Goodenough, Erwin R. 1970. *The Church in the Roman Empire*. New York: Cooper Square Publishers. Originally published: New York: Henry Holt and Company, 1931.

Judge, E. A. 1960. *The Social Pattern of the Christian Groups in the First Century*. London: Tyndale Press.

Kautsky, Karl. 1953. *Foundations of Christianity*. Translated by Henry Mins. New York: Russell & Russell. Originally published as *Foundations of Christianity: A Study of Christian Origins*. New York: International Publishers, 1925.

Latourette, Kenneth Scott. (1953) 1975. *A History of Christianity: Beginnings to 1500*. New York: HarperSanFrancisco.

Malherbe, Abraham. 1983. *Social Aspects of Early Christianity*. 2nd ed. Philadelphia: Fortress.

Marx, Karl. (1844) 1964. "Contribution to the Critique of Hegel's Philosophy of Right." In *On Religion*, edited by Karl Marx and Friedrich Engels, 41–58. New York: Schocken Books.

Meeks, Wayne. 1983. *The First Urban Christians: The Social World of the Apostle Paul*. New Haven, CT: Yale University Press.

Nock, Arthur Darby. 1938. *St. Paul*. New York: Harper.

Schaff, Philip. 1953. *History of the Christian Church*. Vol. 1, *Apostolic Christianity, A.D. 1–100*. Grand Rapids, MI: Eerdmans, 1953. Originally published in 1858, revised in 1882, third revision in 1890. The Eerdmans version is a reproduction of the 1910 edition published by Charles Scribner's Sons.

Tertullian. 1872. "Apology." In *Ante-Nicene Christian Library*. Vol. 11, *The Writings of Tertullian*. Vol. 1, edited by Alexander Roberts and James Donaldson. Edinburgh: T. & T. Clark.

Troeltsch, Ernst. 1960. *The Social Teaching of the Christian Churches*. 2 vols. New York: Harper & Row. Earlier English translation: London: George Allen & Unwin Ltd., 1931. Original German was published in 1911 as *Die Soziallehren der christlichen Kirchen und Gruppen*.

Von Harnack, Adolf. 1908. *The Mission and Expansion of Christianity in the First Three Centuries*. Vol. 2. 2nd ed. New York: G. P. Putnam's Sons.

3

Early Christianity Was Bigoted toward Women

What People Think Happened

Some people look at the history of Christianity and think that it is and always has been a thoroughly patriarchal religion. They have their standard citations; for example, the fact that the Eastern Orthodox and Roman Catholic churches still disallow women from serving in the priesthood. Only in the last century or so have we seen women become ordained regularly in the Protestant churches. While a few Protestant groups ordained women as pastors as early as the nineteenth century—as in the case of the Salvation Army, which has ordained women since its founding in 1865—it was far more typical for Protestants to begin ordaining women only in the last half of the twentieth century. There are many Protestant churches, however, that still do not ordain women to the preaching ministry, especially if that means they are placed in a position of authority over a man.

In the New Testament, there are passages that have been interpreted as being quite limiting to the role of women in the Christian faith. In recent generations, the apostle Paul has received much criticism for his seemingly patriarchal views, especially among feminists and progressive Christians. Some of these critiques are justifiable, but others are much more comprehensible when seen in the larger context of the Greco-Roman world.

While female ordination is increasing, it is still much more common for Christians to worship in venues where men are in charge. The patriarchal nature of Christianity gets reified into the consciousness of many Christians today who are used to seeing women making great gains in the workforce and public sphere. However, when these people go to church, they encounter what is, at least ostensibly, a patriarchal setting.

Some suggest that the Bible reinforces the stereotype that early Christianity was bigoted toward women by often referring to "brothers" without mentioning "sisters." Prayers in the Bible are addressed to God the Father, not God the Mother. Of course, Jesus was male, as were all twelve of the apostles. Jesus did not marry. Paul was single, and he encouraged Christians to remain single if they possibly could. However, if Christians "burn with passion," then they should go ahead and get married according to Paul in 1 Corinthians 7:9. Passages like these seem to relegate women to the source of lust in the worst case, but in the best case, they are seen as a remedy for men's passions. In either case, however, celibacy seems to be the preferred practice for a man or a woman.

There is a widespread idea that since early Christianity was based on Judaism, it inherited the view that women caused "the Fall" in early Genesis and are therefore to be blamed for original sin. However, while it is true that the apostle Paul—the New Testament's most prolific writer—reinforces this interpretation of the Adam and Eve narrative, it is also true that women in the early church seemed not to be too repelled by Paul's ideas. As this chapter will reveal, women were particularly eager to join the faith, they contributed significantly to the growth of early Christianity, and in many cases they had real power.

How the Story Became Popular

Embedded in the New Testament are two distinct ways of reading the passages explicitly pertaining to women, their rights and opportunities, as well as their roles in the church. One way is the egalitarian view, summarized by Paul in his letter to the Galatians (3:23–29). That passage indicates that the old law placed limitations on people, depending upon their status in life: Jew or Greek, slave or free, male or female. But Paul seems to indicate that in Christianity people are freed from the restrictions of the law, and, therefore, this dualistic understanding of humanity is abolished. In other words, all Christians are equal because they are under the new covenant rather than the old one.

The other major interpretation is one that subordinates women to men in certain spheres of life. It is often known as complementarianism. This view holds that while women and men are fundamentally equal before God in terms of worth or dignity, they have different, complementary roles in both church and family. Thus, wives are subordinate to the authority of their own husband. Women are to be equally respected in the church, but they may not teach or hold authority over believing men. Women serve the family and the church in capacities different from men. While women were a critical part of Jesus's ministry, they were not chosen to serve in his inner circle—the apostolate. This is the chief reason why Roman Catholics and Eastern Orthodox Christians still do not ordain women into the priesthood.

In the New Testament, there are explicit passages that uphold notions of male headship, both in the family as well as in the leadership of the church. Some of these ideas are clearly rooted in the Genesis creation narrative, which identifies Adam as the first one created, and then Eve—who is created from Adam's rib in order to be his helper. Therefore, the familial hierarchy is something not unique to Christianity, but rooted in the Israelite conception of gender roles, particularly within marriage.

In the early centuries of Christianity, the widespread practice of women refraining from public and vocal leadership in the churches continued. For example, the church father Tertullian (160–220) argued around the year AD 207 in his treatise *On the Veiling of Virgins*, chapter 9, "It is not permitted to a woman to speak in the church; but neither is it permitted her to teach, nor to baptize, nor to offer, nor to claim to herself a lot in any manly function, not to say in any sacerdotal office."

By the time of the Council of Nicaea in AD 325, it was becoming rather fixed belief that female leaders in the church were not to be considered clergy, but rather laity. In Canon 19 of the Council, there is a clear reference to the office of "deaconess," which is mentioned by Paul in Romans 16:1. In the biblical passage, Paul commends "our sister Phoebe, a deaconess." However, the word used for deaconess is "diakonon," which translates directly into English as "minister" or "servant" but in some cases gets transliterated into "deacon"—an officially ordained office within the church. Bishops at the Council of Nicaea interpreted Romans 16:1 to say that female servants in the church are not to be considered clergy because they were not formally ordained with the laying on of hands: "Likewise in the case of their deaconesses, and generally in the case of those who have been enrolled among their clergy, let the same form be observed. And we mean by deaconesses such as have assumed the habit, but who, since they have no imposition of hands, are to be numbered only among the laity." What the bishops at Nicaea likely had in mind is that while deacon ordination in the book of Acts (chapter 6) involved the "laying on of hands," there is no evidence that Phoebe underwent such a process.

By the Council of Chalcedon in AD 451, the matter had been further settled in Canon 15, "No woman under forty years of age is to be ordained a deacon, and then only after close scrutiny. If after receiving ordination and spending some time in the ministry she despises God's grace and gets married, such a person is to be anathematized along with her spouse." It seems that the office of deaconess declined precipitously after Chalcedon, and further councils at Epaone in 517 and at Orleans in 533 completely abolished the office of deaconess (Ferguson 1999, 322).

The question of whether women can become priests in the Roman Catholic or Eastern Orthodox churches seems settled for the time being. There has never been much contest regarding women priests. In the Roman Catholic churches, the latest definitive statement on this matter was in the 1976 document *Inter Insigniores*, which declared that "the Church, in fidelity to the example of the Lord, does not consider herself authorized to admit women to priestly ordination. . . . It is a position which will perhaps cause pain but whose positive value will become apparent in the long run, since it can be of help in deepening understanding of the respective roles of men and of women." Recent popes such as John Paul II, Benedict XVI, and Francis have upheld this position.

The ordination of women as deacons in the Orthodox and Roman Catholic churches, however, is a discussion that is still very much alive. In 2016 and 2017, Pope Francis held several discussions on the matter and even appointed a commission of twelve—six men and six women—to study the issue afresh. While no significant changes have happened yet, some have found his openness to be meaningful and promising. The Orthodox churches have also been grappling with this issue ever since the Patriarch of Alexandria appointed deaconesses in the Democratic Republic of the Congo in 2017. The fallout from that event is ongoing, with prominent players on either side.

Most mainline Protestant denominations now have female deaconesses, priests, and even bishops. Several denominations have had females in the church's highest position such as the Episcopal Church of the United States (Katharine Jefferts Schori), the Christian Church Disciples of Christ (Sharon Watkins and Teresa Hord Owens), and the Evangelical Lutheran Church in America (Elizabeth Eaton).

Today, many people believe that the church is finally coming around. They are modernizing and are extending proper respect for the leadership gifts that women are able to contribute. But there is an abiding sense that Christianity has always been a patriarchal religion—from its very inception—and only now is it proving itself to be the welcoming place that it always should have been. This is not an accurate depiction, however. Of course, women in the church is a complex, two-thousand-year story, but the next section of this chapter reveals that Christianity was quite welcoming to women in its early years. In fact, were it not for the influx of women into the early church, it would not have grown to become the dominant religion of the Roman Empire in less than three centuries.

PRIMARY DOCUMENTS

BIBLICAL PASSAGES ON THE ROLE OF WOMEN

Genesis 3:1–13, 16

In this passage of Genesis, we see the earliest roots of male and female roles in the Judeo-Christian tradition. This reading deals with what is typically termed "the Fall" as it recounts how the serpent tempted Adam and Eve to sin against God by eating fruit from the tree that God specifically told them to avoid.

Now the serpent was more crafty than any of the wild animals the Lord God had made. He said to the woman, "Did God really say, 'You must not eat from any tree in the garden'?"

The woman said to the serpent, "We may eat fruit from the trees in the garden, but God did say, 'You must not eat fruit from the tree that is in the middle of the garden, and you must not touch it, or you will die.'"

"You will not certainly die," the serpent said to the woman. "For God knows that when you eat from it your eyes will be opened, and you will be like God, knowing good and evil."

When the woman saw that the fruit of the tree was good for food and pleasing to the eye, and also desirable for gaining wisdom, she took some and ate it. She also gave some to her husband, who was with her, and he ate it. Then the eyes of both of them were opened, and they realized they were naked; so they sewed fig leaves together and made coverings for themselves.

Then the man and his wife heard the sound of the Lord God as he was walking in the garden in the cool of the day, and they hid from the Lord God among the trees of the garden. But the Lord God called to the man, "Where are you?"

He answered, "I heard you in the garden, and I was afraid because I was naked; so I hid."

And he said, "Who told you that you were naked? Have you eaten from the tree that I commanded you not to eat from?"

The man said, "The woman you put here with me—she gave me some fruit from the tree, and I ate it."

Then the LORD God said to the woman, "What is this you have done?"

The woman said, "The serpent deceived me, and I ate."

. . .

To the woman he [God] said,

"I will make your pains in childbearing very severe;
with painful labor you will give birth to children.
Your desire will be for your husband,
and he will rule over you."

1 Timothy 2:9–15

This passage is from a letter written by Paul and addressed to Timothy. The context is Paul giving advice to Timothy on how to minister effectively in the church. This particular reading has been controversial in recent decades due to its explicit teaching that women should be silent and submissive in the Christian assembly. Paul bases his logic on the Adam and Eve narrative.

I also want the women to dress modestly, with decency and propriety, adorning themselves, not with elaborate hairstyles or gold or pearls or expensive clothes, but with good deeds, appropriate for women who profess to worship God.

A woman should learn in quietness and full submission. I do not permit a woman to teach or to assume authority over a man; she must be quiet. For Adam was formed first, then Eve. And Adam was not the one deceived; it was the woman who was deceived and became a sinner. But women will be saved through childbearing—if they continue in faith, love and holiness with propriety.

1 Corinthians 11:2–16

This passage is from Paul's first letter to the church at Corinth. He outlines his understanding of male headship, basing it on the Genesis story of the creation of Adam and Eve. Paul reasons that man's authority is rooted in the fact that

Eve came from Adam's side. Interlaced throughout are Paul's instructions on head coverings—these teachings illustrate Paul's idea that women and men have differing but complementary roles.

I praise you for remembering me in everything and for holding to the traditions just as I passed them on to you. But I want you to realize that the head of every man is Christ, and the head of the woman is man, and the head of Christ is God. Every man who prays or prophesies with his head covered dishonors his head. But every woman who prays or prophesies with her head uncovered dishonors her head—it is the same as having her head shaved. For if a woman does not cover her head, she might as well have her hair cut off; but if it is a disgrace for a woman to have her hair cut off or her head shaved, then she should cover her head.

A man ought not to cover his head, since he is the image and glory of God; but woman is the glory of man. For man did not come from woman, but woman from man; neither was man created for woman, but woman for man. It is for this reason that a woman ought to have authority over her own head, because of the angels. Nevertheless, in the Lord woman is not independent of man, nor is man independent of woman. For as woman came from man, so also man is born of woman. But everything comes from God.

Judge for yourselves: Is it proper for a woman to pray to God with her head uncovered? Does not the very nature of things teach you that if a man has long hair, it is a disgrace to him, but that if a woman has long hair, it is her glory? For long hair is given to her as a covering. If anyone wants to be contentious about this, we have no other practice—nor do the churches of God.

1 Corinthians 14:34–35
This passage, also in 1 Corinthians, is probably the most concise and forceful summary of the complementary understanding of gender roles in the church. It has been a subject of heated debate in recent decades as more denominations open themselves to the ordination of women into Christian ministry.

Women should remain silent in the churches. They are not allowed to speak, but must be in submission, as the law says. If they want to inquire about something, they should ask their own husbands at home; for it is disgraceful for a woman to speak in the church.

Ephesians 5:21–33

This passage, written by the apostle Paul to the church in Ephesus, defines what is meant by "biblical headship" in the Christian family. Again, it contains a logic that is rooted in Genesis, in this case the Adam and Eve story, in Genesis 2:24.

Submit to one another out of reverence for Christ.

Wives, submit yourselves to your own husbands as you do to the Lord. For the husband is the head of the wife as Christ is the head of the church, his body, of which he is the Savior. Now as the church submits to Christ, so also wives should submit to their husbands in everything.

Husbands, love your wives, just as Christ loved the church and gave himself up for her to make her holy, cleansing her by the washing with water through the word, and to present her to himself as a radiant church, without stain or wrinkle or any other blemish, but holy and blameless. In this same way, husbands ought to love their wives as their own bodies. He who loves his wife loves himself. After all, no one ever hated their own body, but they feed and care for their body, just as Christ does the church—for we are members of his body. "For this reason a man will leave his father and mother and be united to his wife, and the two will become one flesh." This is a profound mystery—but I am talking about Christ and the church. However, each one of you also must love his wife as he loves himself, and the wife must respect her husband.

1 Corinthians 7:1–11

This passage, also from Paul to the church in Corinth, outlines the sexual obligations between husbands and wives. Paul's logic is that while celibacy is preferred—exemplified in his own life as well as in the life of Christ—Christians should go ahead and marry if they find themselves consumed with lust. The passage concludes with advice on divorce.

Now for the matters you wrote about: "It is good for a man not to have sexual relations with a woman." But since sexual immorality is occurring, each man should have sexual relations with his own wife, and each woman with her own husband. The husband should fulfill his marital duty to his wife, and likewise the wife to her husband. The wife does not have authority over her own body but yields it to her husband. In the same way, the husband does not have authority over his own body but yields it to his wife. Do not deprive each other except perhaps by mutual consent and for a time, so that you may devote yourselves to prayer. Then come together again so that Satan will not tempt you because of your lack of self-control. I say this as a concession, not as a command. I wish that all of you were as I am. But each of you has your own gift from God; one has this gift, another has that.

Now to the unmarried and the widows I say: It is good for them to stay unmarried, as I do. But if they cannot control themselves, they should marry, for it is better to marry than to burn with passion.

To the married I give this command (not I, but the Lord): A wife must not separate from her husband. But if she does, she must remain unmarried or else be reconciled to her husband. And a husband must not divorce his wife.

Acts 6:1–6

This passage describes a biblical example of deacon ordination. It has often been used to deny the ordination of women deacons, since Phoebe—the "deaconess" mentioned in Romans 16:1—does not seem to have experienced the "laying on of hands" process that came to be linked with ordained ministry in the church. Advocates of female ordination argue that it is likely that Phoebe did in fact receive the laying on of hands; otherwise she would not have been called a deaconess. Obviously, the matter is by no means settled.

In those days when the number of disciples was increasing, the Hellenistic Jews among them complained against the Hebraic Jews because their widows were being overlooked in the daily distribution of food. So the Twelve gathered all the disciples together and said, "It would not be right for us to neglect the ministry of the word of God in order to wait on tables. Brothers and sisters, choose seven men from among you who are known to be full of the Spirit and wisdom. We will turn this responsibility over to them and will give our attention to prayer and the ministry of the word."

This proposal pleased the whole group. They chose Stephen, a man full of faith and of the Holy Spirit; also Philip, Procorus, Nicanor, Timon, Parmenas, and Nicolas from Antioch, a convert to Judaism. They presented these men to the apostles, who prayed and laid their hands on them.

CATECHISM OF THE CATHOLIC CHURCH: THE SACRAMENT OF HOLY ORDERS

The Catechism of the Catholic Church *is a summary of Catholic Church teaching for children and adult converts to the faith. Its history goes back to the early church when people who prepared for baptism were required to understand the fullness of their Christian commitment. The Roman Catechism was an influential catechism published in 1566 in the aftermath of the Council of Trent and represents a formalizing of the Catholic Church's official catechism. Various catechisms have been published since, but in 1992 the* Catechism of the Catholic Church *was published under the authority of Pope John Paul II and has quickly become the most important summary of teaching for the Catholic faithful. In this reading, we see the church's explanation for having men only serve as priests. Interestingly, Catholic churches in the West may not normally have married men as priests unless they are converts from Anglican or Orthodox churches who already had a wife. Catholic churches in the East, however, are allowed to have married priests.*

V. WHO CAN CONFER THIS SACRAMENT?

1575 Christ himself chose the apostles and gave them a share in his mission and authority. Raised to the Father's right hand, he has not forsaken his flock but he keeps it under his constant protection through the apostles, and guides it still through these same pastors who continue his work today. Thus, it is Christ whose gift it is that some be apostles, others pastors. He continues to act through the bishops.

1576 Since the sacrament of Holy Orders is the sacrament of the apostolic ministry, it is for the bishops as the successors of the apostles to hand on the "gift of the Spirit," the "apostolic line." Validly ordained bishops, i.e., those who are in the line of apostolic succession, validly confer the three degrees of the sacrament of Holy Orders.

VI. WHO CAN RECEIVE THIS SACRAMENT?

1577 "Only a baptized man (*vir*) validly receives sacred ordination." The Lord Jesus chose men (*viri*) to form the college of the twelve apostles, and the apostles did the same when they chose collaborators to succeed them in their ministry. The college of bishops, with whom the priests are united in the priesthood, makes the college of the twelve an ever-present and ever-active reality until Christ's return. The Church recognizes herself to be bound by this choice made by the Lord himself. For this reason the ordination of women is not possible.

1578 No one has a *right* to receive the sacrament of Holy Orders. Indeed no one claims this office for himself; he is called to it by God. Anyone who thinks he recognizes the signs of God's call to the ordained ministry must humbly submit his desire to the authority of the Church, who has the responsibility and right to call someone to receive orders. Like every grace this sacrament can be *received* only as an unmerited gift.

1579 All the ordained ministers of the Latin Church, with the exception of permanent deacons, are normally chosen from among men of faith who live a celibate life and who intend to remain *celibate* "for the sake of the kingdom of heaven." Called to consecrate themselves with undivided heart to the Lord and to "the affairs of the Lord," they give themselves entirely to God and to men. Celibacy is a sign of this new life to the service of which the Church's minister is consecrated; accepted with a joyous heart celibacy radiantly proclaims the Reign of God.

1580 In the Eastern Churches a different discipline has been in force for many centuries: while bishops are chosen solely from among celibates, married men can be ordained as deacons and priests. This practice has long been considered legitimate; these priests exercise a fruitful ministry within their communities. Moreover, priestly celibacy is held in great honor in the Eastern Churches and many priests have freely chosen it for the sake of the Kingdom of God. In the East as in the West a man who has already received the sacrament of Holy Orders can no longer marry.

> **Source:** United States Conference of Catholic Bishops, *Catechism of the Catholic Church*, 1993. Available at http://www.vatican.va/archive/ccc_css/archive/catechism /p2s2c3a6.htm. © Libreria Editrice Vaticana. Used by permission.

INTER INSIGNIORES: ON THE QUESTION OF ADMISSION OF WOMEN TO THE MINISTERIAL PRIESTHOOD

This Declaration was published in 1976 for His Holiness Pope Paul VI by the Sacred Congregation for the Doctrine of the Faith. It provides an authoritative stance still upheld by the Roman Catholic Church today on the issue of women ordination, with broader implications for women in church life.

For some years now various Christian communities stemming from the sixteenth-century Reformation or of later origin have been admitting women to the pastoral office on a par with men. This initiative has led to petitions and writings by members of these communities and similar groups, directed toward making this admission a general thing; it has also led to contrary reactions. This therefore constitutes an ecumenical problem, and the Catholic Church must make her thinking known on it, all the more because in various sectors of opinion the question has been asked whether she too could not modify her discipline and admit women to priestly ordination.

. . .

The Catholic Church has never felt that priestly or episcopal ordination can be validly conferred on women. A few heretical sects in the first centuries, especially Gnostic ones, entrusted the exercise of the priestly ministry to women: This innovation was immediately noted and condemned by the Fathers, who considered it as unacceptable in the Church.

. . .

Jesus Christ did not call any women to become part of the Twelve.

. . .

The apostolic community remained faithful to the attitude of Jesus towards women.

. . .

The practice of the Church therefore has a normative character: in the fact of conferring priestly ordination only on men, it is a question of unbroken tradition throughout the history of the Church, universal in the East and in the West, and alert to repress abuses immediately. This norm, based on Christ's example, has been and is still observed because it is considered to conform to God's plan for his Church.

. . .

Women who express a desire for the ministerial priesthood are doubtless motivated by the desire to serve Christ and the Church. And it is not surprising that, at a time when they are becoming more aware of the discriminations to which they have been subjected, they should desire the ministerial priesthood itself. But it must not be forgotten that the priesthood does not form part of the rights of the individual, but stems from the economy of the mystery of Christ and the Church. The priestly office cannot become the goal of social advancement: no merely human progress of society or of the individual can of itself give access to it: it is of another order.

What Really Happened

Jesus's interactions with females were progressive for his time, especially his interactions with marginalized women. For example, he healed a woman who had been bleeding for twelve years. This was forbidden in Judaism according to the Torah, as women were considered unclean when they were bleeding, and anyone who touched them would be considered unclean (Leviticus 15:25–27). He spoke with widows, a Samaritan woman, and a Syrophoenician woman. It was rather scandalous for Jesus to freely interact with women like this because it was outside the norms of acceptable social behavior of a Jewish rabbi. But Jesus treats them with obvious dignity. He also interacts freely with female members of his inner circle, including the sisters Mary and Martha (Luke 10:38–42). In the case of Mary, Jesus commends her for sitting and listening to his teaching, an act that would have been seen as disruptive to normative Jewish society because of taboos against women being involved in the teaching and learning of the Torah.

While Jesus is often heralded as a great emancipator of women, the apostle Paul usually bears the blame for placing restrictions on women's roles both in the church and in the Christian home. Scholars, however, are not convinced that Paul was trying to limit women's roles, or to subordinate them to men. Paul writes often of women and mentions their leadership roles in texts that have often been dismissed or overlooked.

In 1 Corinthians 11, Paul explicitly recognized the gift of prophecy in certain women in the church. This would not have been surprising, since prophetesses are found in the Old Testament as well: Miriam (Exodus 15:20), Deborah (Judges 4:4), Huldah (2 Kings 22:14), and others. In the New Testament, Anna prophesied when Jesus was presented at the temple (Luke 2:36). The book of Acts speaks of women prophesying at Pentecost, and the apostle Peter references Joel's prediction about the last days, "I will pour out my Spirit on *all* people. Your sons *and daughters* will prophesy" (Acts 2:17). Some prophetesses became popular indeed in the early centuries of Christianity, such as Maximilla and Priscilla. They were two of the leaders of the Montanist movement—a Christian sect in second-century Phrygia that placed a large emphasis on the spontaneity of the Holy Spirit.

Early church writings often seem to contain a spirit of egalitarianism within them. In Galatians 3:28, Paul states rather forcefully, "There is neither Jew nor Gentile, neither slave nor free, nor is there male and female, for you are all one in Christ Jesus." This passage is probably the most referenced one for those who argue for gender egalitarianism in the church. There is plenty of indirect evidence showing Paul's reliance upon women in his ministry. For example, Paul tells us that his travel companions Priscilla and Aquila—a husband wife team—were of tremendous help to him in his ministry (Acts 18:18, Romans 16:3). They were both competent teachers and on one occasion helped the well-known preacher Apollos to understand the gospel "more adequately" (Acts 18:26). In Philippians 4:2–3, Paul mentions two women—Euodia and Syntyche—as having worked side by side with him in the cause of the gospel.

In Romans 16, Paul sends greetings to sixteen women and eighteen men, showing just how involved the women were in the leadership of the church at Rome. Paul refers to one of the women—Junia—as an apostle (v. 7). As discussed earlier, there is controversy over whether Paul thought Phoebe was an official deacon in the church (v. 1). Either way, she was important enough for Paul to single her out for recognition; she is the first person mentioned in his long list of people in Romans 16.

It seems fairly clear that in its earliest centuries, "Christianity was laid hold of by women in particular, and also that the percentage of Christian women, especially among the upper classes, was larger than that of Christian men." Importantly, we know that "women who read the Bible are frequently mentioned," a practice that was typically forbidden in Judaism (Harnack 1908, 73).

Women were just as likely to suffer a martyr's death as were men during the Roman persecutions. The famous martyrdoms of Blandina (in Lyon, France, in AD 177), Perpetua, and Felicity were a source of courage to those facing a similar fate. Blandina was a mere teenager at her death. She was put into a net and killed publicly by a wild bull.

Probably the most celebrated female martyrs in Christian history are Perpetua and Felicity, killed on the same day in Carthage in AD 203. Perpetua was twenty-two years old and nursing a baby. Felicity was Perpetua's servant. A wild cow was set loose on the women. After giving each other the kiss of peace, a swordsman thrust them through the ribs. Perpetua survived for a time. However, she eventually put the sword to her own throat because the young gladiator dispatched to kill her was a novice and was reluctant to finish the deed.

Why would women choose to die like this? Why would they even join a faith entrenched in patriarchalism? And why were more women joining the new faith than men? A theological response would be that these women felt the teachings of Jesus Christ and the apostles to be true. But a more scientific response would require us to look at humanistic motivations, rather than only theological ones.

In many cases, women who converted to Christianity received some real advantages over their pagan counterparts, which could explain why so many women—especially women of wealth—joined the Christian movement in its early years.

For example, the Roman Empire had more adult men than women, and that difference is probably largely explained by infant exposure, a practice that was more commonly directed at baby girls than boys. Jews did not partake in the practice, and even received the praise of Aristotle, who thought they were the only group of people who forbade it. Abortion was also widely practiced in the Roman Empire, but here again Jews refused to conform to societal standards. This commitment to raising all children "was transmitted to the Christians" (Harris 1994, 2–4, 15–17).

One important Christian writer, Justin Martyr, in his *First Apology*, opposed child exposure in particular, saying it was a wicked practice, a "sin against God," because more times than not it led to these baby girls—and boys too—being raised solely for prostitution. Many were raised for other forms of slavery as well. Most of them died due to the elements, while some were eaten by wild animals, especially dogs (Harris 1994, 8).

While there was a devaluing of females in the Roman population, particularly among the unfree majority, Christians were different. Statistical analyses of death inscriptions in the Roman Empire have revealed the Christians to be a people very "peculiar . . . and sets them apart from the earlier non-Christian populations of the city." What was so "peculiar" about Christians? According to Brent Shaw, they always had equal numbers of females as males (like Jews did). They did not have complex families—various wives, with numerous stepchildren, and complications from divorces—as they valorized the nuclear family and worked hard to keep families intact. Indeed, "Christians emphasized the downward links with the children more than their pagan predecessors, and seem to have narrowed the preferential gap between sons and daughters" (Shaw 1996, 107–110).

Another possible reason that women joined the Christian church is because they did not have to marry so young. "The general age at marriage was higher for Christians." This was especially the case for Christian girls, who married a full three years later than did their pagan counterparts. Most girls married in their teen years, but many pagan girls married at age twelve or even younger. One thing is clear: when Christianity began to dominate, the age of marriage rose considerably. This must have been welcomed for those girls who no doubt dreaded being given away for marriage just as puberty began to happen, and often before (Hopkins 1965, 320).

Women also may have been lured to Christianity because of the security of their marriage and the treatment they received in marriage. While divorce was fairly common and accepted in Judaism as well as in Greco-Roman society, Jesus taught strongly against it. In Matthew 19:3–9, he stated that divorce is only acceptable when there has been a sexual violation of the marriage vows. Jesus also frowned upon remarriage in that passage. Biblical passages like these demonstrate why most Christian nations didn't legalize divorce until the twentieth century. Who hasn't heard his words at a wedding: "Therefore what God has joined together, let no one separate" (Matthew 19:6). Those must have been refreshing words for women in a society that allowed men to discard wives without any real consequences.

The apostle Paul—sometimes called a misogynist—was no less stringent in his teachings in favor of women. In Ephesians 5, he commands women to submit to their own husband, but he also commands the men to "love your wives, just as Christ loved the church and gave himself up for her. . . . In this same way, husbands ought to love their wives as their own bodies." Paul is far from being a chauvinist in this passage, and in other passages, such as 1 Corinthians 7:11, where he says, "A husband must not divorce his wife."

Not only were Christian marriages more secure than pagan ones, but Christian men were far more likely to remain faithful to their spouse due to the strong teachings against adultery in the Judeo-Christian scriptures. Not only do the Ten Commandments forbid adultery, but Jesus and Paul routinely condemn it. Jesus even condemns lusting after another (Matthew 5:28). Christian men—not just the women—were taught to honor their marital vows and keep the marriage bed pure, "for God will judge the adulterer and all the sexually immoral" (Hebrews 13:4).

Sociologist Rodney Stark brilliantly lays out numerous reasons for high Christian growth rates—leading to the Christian faith's numerical dominance in the Roman Empire. His argument is that "Christianity was unusually appealing because within the Christian subculture women enjoyed far higher status than did women in the Greco-Roman world at large"

(Stark 1996, 95). Not only did Christians not abort their children but also forbade the common practice of child exposure. Abortion was dangerous and brutal in those times and often left women infertile at an early age. One of the earliest Christian texts, the *Didache*—written in the first century AD—explicitly condemns these practices: "Thou shalt not procure abortion, nor commit infanticide" (2:2). Child-exposure death was an outcome that worked against pagan birth rates.

Christians neither aborted, nor struggled with infertility that often resulted from botched abortions, nor did they practice child exposure. This would have worked in favor of the numerical rise of Christianity. Christian women also were attracted to Christianity because their female children were valued and taken care of. They welcomed pregnancy. This, combined with the higher age of marriage for Christians, was attractive, leading to a preference for Christianity over the pagan religious options. Christian women had more stable marriages, they raised all their children, they had higher fertility rates, and—importantly—they often converted their unbelieving husbands to their faith. All of these factors would have boosted Christian growth rates relative to the declining fertility rates that Roman people were experiencing at the time.

Christians were expected to treat women well. In 1 Timothy 5:2, Paul instructs that Christian men should treat "older women as mothers and younger women as sisters, with absolute purity." James, the brother of Jesus, wrote, "Religion that God our Father accepts as pure and faultless is this: to look after orphans and widows in their distress and to keep oneself from being polluted by the world" (James 1:27).

In the first part of this chapter, we pointed out that there are two ways to interpret the teachings of the Bible on the role of women in the church. One is the complementarian view that men and women each have their defined roles, and it is men who should lead in the church. The other view, dealt with in the second half of this chapter, is the egalitarian view, which sees no distinction between males and females, as Paul wrote in Galatians. I hope this chapter has established that early Christianity was quite favorable toward women, rather than bigoted toward them.

Before ending this chapter, we must draw attention to a Protestant woman in the seventeenth century who changed the game for female leadership in the church: Margaret Fell (1614–1702), one of the founders of the movement we know today as the Quakers. She is often known as the Mother of the Quakers, although her movement is officially known as the Society of Friends, which she established with George Fox in England.

Margaret Fell penned a treatise in 1666 entitled "Womens Speaking Justified, Proved and Allowed of by the Scriptures." This text laid the groundwork for the dismantling of "women's silence" in many Protestant churches. The arguments used today for justifying female clergy and female preaching are rooted in Fell's powerful text. Once Fell opened up the possibility for female leadership in the church, others followed in her wake. And while female ordination was not common until the twentieth century, the dam had been breached. In 1848, at Seneca Falls, New York, a famous gathering of Christian feminists took place that pronounced "the speedy overthrow of the male monopoly of the pulpit." Just a few years later, in 1853, Oberlin College and Seminary in Ohio, started accepting female candidates for study and ordination. Antoinette Brown was the first female graduate from Oberlin and was ordained in the Congregational church (Ruether 1987, 231).

PRIMARY DOCUMENTS

BIBLICAL PASSAGES

Matthew 19:1–9
In this passage Jesus teaches strongly against divorce. His teaching would have been extraordinary in Roman society as well as in Jewish society.

When Jesus had finished saying these things, he left Galilee and went into the region of Judea to the other side of the Jordan. Large crowds followed him, and he healed them there.

Some Pharisees came to him to test him. They asked, "Is it lawful for a man to divorce his wife for any and every reason?"

"Haven't you read," he replied, "that at the beginning the Creator 'made them male and female,' and said, 'For this reason a man will leave his father and mother and be united to his wife, and the two will become one flesh'? So they are no longer two, but one flesh. Therefore, what God has joined together, let no one separate."

"Why then," they asked, "did Moses command that a man give his wife a certificate of divorce and send her away?"

Jesus replied, "Moses permitted you to divorce your wives because your hearts were hard. But it was not this way from the beginning. I tell you that anyone who divorces his wife, except for sexual immorality, and marries another woman commits adultery."

Luke 10:38–42

This passage in Luke shows Jesus commending a woman who chose to listen to him teach. This would have been controversial because it was not at all common for women to study the Torah alongside rabbis and other men.

As Jesus and his disciples were on their way, he came to a village where a woman named Martha opened her home to him. She had a sister called Mary, who sat at the Lord's feet listening to what he said. But Martha was distracted by all the preparations that had to be made. She came to him and asked, "Lord, don't you care that my sister has left me to do the work by myself? Tell her to help me!"

"Martha, Martha," the Lord answered, "you are worried and upset about many things, but few things are needed—or indeed only one. Mary has chosen what is better, and it will not be taken away from her."

Galatians 3:23–29

This passage in Galatians is famous among those who embrace the "egalitarian" understanding of gender roles in the Christian era. Paul claims there is neither male nor female now that the Messiah has come. This would have been extremely controversial in Judaism, since the roles of men and women were (and still are in Orthodoxy) so different.

Before the coming of this faith, we were held in custody under the law, locked up until the faith that was to come would be revealed. So the law was our guardian until Christ came that we might be justified by faith. Now that this faith has come, we are no longer under a guardian.

So in Christ Jesus you are all children of God through faith, for all of you who were baptized into Christ have clothed yourselves with Christ. There is neither Jew nor Gentile, neither slave nor free, nor is there male and female, for you are all one in Christ Jesus. If you belong to Christ, then you are Abraham's seed, and heirs according to the promise.

THE MARTYRDOM OF BLANDINA

Blandina (c. 162–177) is unknown to history outside of this incident. She was a teenager whose courage in the arena was impressive. She was probably a slave. Her torture and public execution were particularly brutal. She was lashed with the whip, placed on the hot grate, forced to watch her friends die to various tortures,

was put into a net, and thrown before wild beasts. In the end, she was "sacrificed,"
or had her throat sliced by a gladiator. This text shows the tenacity of women to
remain committed to the Christian faith even during the worst of times. It also
shows how women were dignified and even revered in early Christian texts.

For while we all trembled, and her earthly mistress, who was herself also
one of the witnesses, feared that on account of the weakness of her body,
she would be unable to make bold confession, Blandina was filled with
such power as to be delivered and raised above those who were torturing
her by turns from morning till evening in every manner, so that they
acknowledged that they were conquered, and could do nothing more to
her. And they were astonished at her endurance, as her entire body was
mangled and broken; and they testified that one of these forms of torture was sufficient to destroy life, not to speak of so many and so great
sufferings.

. . .

Blandina was suspended on a stake, and exposed to be devoured by the
wild beasts who should attack her. And because she appeared as if hanging
on a cross, and because of her earnest prayers, she inspired the combatants
with great zeal. For they looked on her in her conflict, and beheld with
their outward eyes, in the form of their sister, him who was crucified for
them, that he might persuade those who believe in him, that everyone who
suffers for the glory of Christ has fellowship always with the living God.

As none of the wild beasts at that time touched her, she was taken
down from the stake, and cast again into prison.

. . .

On the last day of the contests, Blandina was again brought in, with Ponticus, a boy about fifteen years old. They had been brought every day to
witness the sufferings of the others, and had been pressed to swear by the
idols. But because they remained steadfast and despised them, the multitude became furious, so that they had no compassion for the youth of the
boy nor respect for the sex of the woman.

Therefore, they exposed them to all the terrible sufferings and took them
through the entire round of torture, repeatedly urging them to swear, but
being unable to effect this; for Ponticus, encouraged by his sister so that
even the heathen could see that she was confirming and strengthening
him, having nobly endured every torture, gave up the ghost.

But the blessed Blandina, last of all . . . after the scourging, after the wild beasts, after the roasting seat, she was finally enclosed in a net, and thrown before a bull. And having been tossed about by the animal, but feeling none of the things which were happening to her, on account of her hope and firm hold upon what had been entrusted to her, and her communion with Christ, she also was sacrificed. And the heathen themselves confessed that never among them had a woman endured so many and such terrible tortures.

Source: Eusebius, *Church History Book V*, translated by Arthur Cushman McGiffert, in *Nicene and Post-Nicene Fathers*, Second Series, Vol. 1, edited by Philip Schaff and Henry Wace (Buffalo, NY: Christian Literature Publishing Co., 1890). Available at http://www.newadvent.org/fathers/250105.htm.

JUSTIN MARTYR, "GUILT OF EXPOSING CHILDREN"

Justin Martyr (c. 100–165) was a Christian convert from Samaria who staunchly defended Christian morality and criticized the morality of the culture around him. In this reading, from his First Apology, *he critiques the Roman practice of child exposure, which he found to be reprehensible because it leads to a whole host of problems over time such as incest, slavery, sexual vice, and other "unmentionable iniquities."*

But as for us, we have been taught that to expose newly-born children is the part of wicked men; and this we have been taught lest we should do any one an injury, and lest we should sin against God, first, because we see that almost all so exposed (not only the girls, but also the males) are brought up to prostitution. And as the ancients are said to have reared herds of oxen, or goats, or sheep, or grazing horses, so now we see you rear children only for this shameful use; and for this pollution a multitude of females and hermaphrodites, and those who commit unmentionable iniquities, are found in every nation. And you receive the hire of these, and duty and taxes from them, whom you ought to exterminate from your realm. And anyone who uses such persons, besides the godless and infamous and impure intercourse, may possibly be having intercourse with his own child, or relative, or brother. And there are some who prostitute even their own children and wives, and some are openly mutilated for the purpose of sodomy; and they refer these mysteries to the mother of the gods, and along with each of those whom you esteem gods there is painted a serpent, a great symbol and mystery. Indeed, the things which you do openly and with applause, as if the divine light were overturned and extinguished, these you lay to our charge; which, in truth, does no harm to us who shrink from doing any such things, but only to those who do them and bear false witness against us.

Source: Justin Martyr, *The First Apology*, translated by Marcus Dods and George Reith, in *Ante-Nicene Fathers*, Vol. 1, edited by Alexander Roberts, James Donaldson, and A. Cleveland Coxe (Buffalo, NY: Christian Literature Publishing Co., 1885). Available at http://www.newadvent.org/fathers/0126.htm.

MARGARET FELL, "WOMENS SPEAKING JUSTIFIED, PROVED AND ALLOWED OF BY THE SCRIPTURES"

Margaret Fell's bombshell treatise, first published in London in 1666, was truly a watershed moment in the history of Christianity. The arguments put forward for female leadership in the church today are but a repeat of what she advances here. This text proved pivotal due to its erudition, clarity, and powerful use of persuasion. It is still unsurpassed in its potency of argument. Only her conclusion is quoted here, as it reiterates some of the points she makes throughout, yet with great eloquence.

And so let this serve to stop that opposing Spirit that would limit the Power and Spirit of the Lord Jesus, whose Spirit is poured upon all flesh, both Sons and Daughters, now in his Resurrection; and since that the Lord God in the Creation, when he made man in his own Image, he made them *male* and *female*; and since that Christ Jesus, as the Apostle saith, was made of a Woman, and the power of the Highest overshadowed her, and the holy Ghost came upon her, and the holy thing that was born of her, was called *the Son of God*, and when he was upon the Earth, he manifested his *love*, and his *will*, and his *mind*, both to the Woman of *Samaria*, and *Martha*, and *Mary* her Sister, and several others, as hath been shewed; and after his Resurrection also manifested himself unto them first of all, even before he ascended unto his Father. *Now when Jesus was risen, the first day of the week, he appeared first unto Mary Magdalene*, Mark 16. 9. And thus the Lord Jesus hath manifested himself and his Power, without respect of Persons, and so let all mouths be stopt that would limit him, whose Power and Spirit is infinite, that is pouring it upon all flesh.

And thus much in answer to these two Scriptures, which have been such a stumbling block, that the ministers of Darkness have made such a mountain of; But the Lord is removing all this, and taking it out of the way.

Source: Margaret Fell, *Womens Speaking Justified, Proved, and Allowed of by the Scriptures.* Edited by Mary Mark Ockerbloom (London, 1666). Available at https://digital.library.upenn.edu/women/fell/speaking/speaking.html.

Further Reading

Balsdon, J. P. V. D. 1963. *Roman Women: Their History and Habits.* New York: John Day.

Boak, Arthur E. R. 1955. *Manpower Shortage and the Fall of the Roman Empire in the West.* Ann Arbor: University of Michigan Press.

Brooten, Bernadette. 1982. *Women Leaders in the Ancient Synagogue.* Chico, CA: Scholars.

Brunt, P. A. 1971. *Italian Manpower, 225 B.C.–A.D. 14.* Oxford: Oxford University Press.

Ferguson, Everett, ed. 1999. *Encyclopedia of Early Christianity.* 2nd ed. New York: Routledge.

Frend, W. H. C. 1984. *The Rise of Christianity.* Philadelphia: Fortress Press.

Gorman, Michael J. 1982. *Abortion and the Early Church.* Downers Grove, IL: InterVarsity.

Harnack, Adolf von. 1908. *The Expansion of Christianity in the First Three Centuries.* Vol. 2. New York: Putnam's Sons.

Harris, W. V. 1994. "Child-Exposure in the Roman Empire." *Journal of Roman Studies* 84: 1–22.

Hopkins, M. K. 1965. "The Age of Roman Girls at Marriage." *Population Studies* 18:3: 309–327.

Kertzer, D. I., and R. P. Sallers. 1991. *The Family in Italy from Antiquity to the Present.* New Haven, CT: Yale University Press.

Kraemer, Ross Shepard. 1992. *Her Share of the Blessings: Women's Religions among Pagans, Jews, and Christians in the Greco-Roman World.* Oxford: Oxford University Press.

Lefkowitz, Mary R., and Maureen B. Fant. 2005. *Women's Life in Greece and Rome: A Source Book in Translation.* 3rd ed. Baltimore: Johns Hopkins University Press.

Lindsay, Jack. 1968. *The Ancient World: Manners and Morals.* New York: Putnam's Sons.

Parkin, Tim G. 1992. *Demography and Roman Society*. Baltimore: Johns Hopkins University Press.

Percival, Henry. 1900. "First Council of Nicaea, A.D. 325." In *Nicene and Post-Nicene Fathers*, edited by Philip Schaff and Henry Wace. Buffalo, NY: Christian Literature Publishing Co.

Pomeroy, Sarah B. 1975. *Goddesses, Whores, Wives, and Slaves: Women in Classical Antiquity*. New York: Schocken Books.

Rawson, Beryl, ed. 1986. *The Family in Ancient Rome*. Ithaca, NY: Cornell University Press.

Riddle, John M. 1994. *Contraception and Abortion from the Ancient World to the Renaissance*. Cambridge, MA: Harvard University Press.

Ruether, Rosemary Radford. 1987. "Christianity." In *Women in World Religions*, edited by Arvind Sharma. Albany, NY: SUNY Press.

Sharma, Arvind, and Katherine Young, eds. 1999. *Feminism and World Religions*. Albany, NY: SUNY Press.

Shaw, Brent. 1996. "Aspects of Mortality in Imperial Rome." *Journal of Roman Studies* 86: 100–138.

Stark, Rodney. 1996. *The Rise of Christianity*. San Francisco: HarperCollins.

Tertullian. 1885. "On the Veiling of Virgins," translated by S. Thelwall. In *Ante-Nicene Fathers*. Vol. 4, edited by Alexander Roberts, James Donaldson, and A. Cleveland Coxe. Buffalo, NY: Christian Literature Publishing Co.

4

Constantine Was Insincere
in His Christian Faith

What People Think Happened

Constantine the Great (AD 272–337), the first Christian emperor of the Roman Empire, has sparked endless debate among historians for hundreds of years. Some of the most vexing questions have circled around the sincerity of his Christian convictions. One historian put it this way: "There is perhaps no more robustly discussed issue connected with Constantine than the nature of the conversion and the nature of the visions connected with the conversion. The range of opinion is vast" (Potter 2013, 329).

On the surface, it appears that Constantine became a Christian and did more for Christianity than virtually any ruler in history. During his rule (AD 306–337), Christianity's fortunes changed dramatically. What was once a persecuted faith suddenly became the preferred faith of the Roman Empire due to a series of events that still inspire many Christians but also cause others to doubt the genuineness of Constantine's Christian faith.

Constantine was a supremely gifted warrior, and in the year 312, before going to war against his co-emperor Maxentius at the famous Battle of the Milvian Bridge, he had a vision that changed the course of Western history. The Milvian Bridge still stands over the Tiber River, in the northern part of the city of Rome. It was there that the religious contours of Western civilization took a sudden shift as the Christian faith was endowed with legal status the following year in 313 with the famous Edict of Milan—a document that allowed Christians the opportunity to practice their faith freely and without being molested. What has stumped historians, however, is whether Constantine actually became a Christian himself or whether he was just using Christianity politically, in order to bolster his own grasp at power.

Crucial to the story is a controversial vision that Constantine had. At some point before the Milvian Bridge battle, possibly the night before—on October 27, 312—Constantine had a vision that has captivated the interest of historians ever since. Historian Peter Leithart writes, "Over the centuries, this has been *the* 'Constantinian question.' . . . What, if anything, happened to Constantine on the night before the Battle of the Milvian Bridge" (Leithart 2010, 72)? Did he have a conversion experience akin to Paul's blinding light on the road to Damascus? Did he and his soldiers actually see a cross in the sky with the following words inscribed on it: "By this, conquer"? Was the incident just another of Constantine's visions? After all, he was prone to this sort of thing, and mystical experiences were common in that era.

Here's where charges of Constantine's insincerity come to light. It is argued that Constantine never really cared about Jesus Christ as his personal Lord; rather, what he cared about was politics. In his calculations, Christianity was gaining an undeniable foothold in his empire. The Christian church was growing exponentially and any leader who opposed it would have to use a heavy hand indeed to rein it in, or else he would have to live in constant tension with a sizable—and growing—percentage of souls in his empire.

The charge goes like this . . . Constantine was first and foremost an astute politician. He was supremely tactical in his thinking. He realized he could use this once-persecuted faith to his benefit. Potentially, he could even gain the mantle of this faith and serve as its great champion, since Christian growth rates were soaring as Constantine was coming to power. By calling the Council of Nicaea and presiding over it, Constantine could bend Christianity to his will, subject the faith to his own authority, and use the Christian hierarchy as pawns in his game of thrones.

The pressing issue here is one of motive. Was Constantine simply using the Christian church to fulfill a personal quest for absolute power? Or was he convinced that Christianity was true: a legitimate faith worthy of his devotion. If indeed he thought Christianity was true, then it would be quite natural for him to protect it, indeed, even propagate it across his empire.

Crucially, if Christianity were worthy of his loyalty, then, ostensibly, Constantine would want to convert to the faith himself. Historians tell us that he postponed his baptism until just before his death. Skeptics say that is evidence of an insincere conversion, which is really not a conversion at all. He was merely pretending, or perhaps safeguarding his soul just in case the religion was true. In other words, he refused to get baptized during mid-life because he did not ultimately believe in it. Besides, if Constantine were smart, he would realize that non-Christians in his empire might turn against him if he publicly confessed Christ as Lord through initiatory baptism . . . whether sincere or not.

Thus, what we are left with is a cynical perspective on Constantine. Ever the politician, his Christianity was a mere political ploy. He used it. The bishops were his puppets so he could maintain authority over an empire that was turning Christian anyway. Can't beat 'em? Then join 'em. Cynics argue that Constantine was never a Christian in the true sense of the term. His understanding of Christianity was not true Christianity at all. It was, rather, the "Constantinianization" of Christianity. It was his tool, his appropriation of the faith. Wielding this tool smartly and effectively meant he could retain the mantle of the great Roman Empire.

How the Story Became Popular

Shortly after Constantine's death in 337, one of his later successors, Julian the Apostate (Roman Emperor from AD 361 to 363), questioned the entire conversion story, preferring to characterize Constantine "as an insincere and self-indulgent tyrant" (Stark 2011, 169). Julian is not remembered well in the annals of Christian history. His nickname, the apostate, suits him well as he was the last non-Christian emperor of the Roman Empire. He went to great lengths to dissolve the influence of Christianity, and he worked mightily to restore the traditional religions of Rome's past. His attempt to push back the clock failed, as Christianity continued to expand right across the empire. It is probably apocryphal that a Christian killed Julian, but it would be safe to say that not many of them grieved his death. He tried to weed out Christianity from the influential classes and reinstate paganism as the state religion, but it backfired badly, as Roman religion was very diverse. There were many religions, and the followers believed vastly different things and practiced their faiths in a multitude of ways. His idea to create one Roman religion out of many proved incomprehensible to most people and may in fact have helped the cause of Christianity, which although not united (there were various Christian factions), it at least had a central narrative based on the life of Christ.

The next major figure to question the sincerity of Constantine's Christian conversion was Zosimus, a historian who lived from around 460 to 520. Like Julian, Zosimus was a pagan who despised the Christian religion. He viewed the Christianization of the Roman Empire as a cause for its fall. He despised Constantine and his decision to embrace Christianity, and he offered words of praise for the apostate Julian.

Zosimus was extremely critical of Constantine, characterizing him as "untrustworthy in alliances, addicted to luxury, wasteful in finance, and destructive of the empire's security." Zosimus's influence on subsequent non-Christian historians continued for centuries. For example, the French writer Voltaire found Zosimus to be a useful ally in his own trenchant broadsides of Christianity. Indeed, Voltaire considered Constantine to be a tyrant and a murderer, who would easily butcher those around him—even family members—in order to preserve his death grip on power. This is the kind of thinking that served as fuel for Dan Brown's best-selling novel *The Da Vinci Code*, which painted Constantine in a particularly unfavorable light. According to Brown, Constantine exalted Jesus to a divine status in order to serve the needs of his own political machinations. In truth, Brown claims, Constantine was really a pagan who never divorced himself from his loyalty to old pagan gods. Oh, and Constantine was also responsible for compiling the Christian canon at the Council of Nicaea—which he had complete control over. Of course, that is all nonsense (Leithart 2010, 80).

Indeed, Constantine has been one of history's great "whipping boys," and he receives his strikes from both Christians and non-Christians. While many non-Christians see him as ruining the great Roman Empire, many Christians view him as fatally undermining the authenticity of the church due to his grand institutionalization of the faith. Francis of Assisi accused Constantine's efforts of leading to a corrupt and degenerate church. John Wycliffe and Jan Hus also echoed Assisi here. The Radical Reformers in particular understood Constantine's move toward caesaropapism to be a lamentable development in church history that had the effect of hijacking the faith for over a millennium—until the truth arrived—which for them meant the disentanglement of church from state. This way of thinking culminated in the work of the influential Mennonite theologian John Howard Yoder (1927–1997), who called Constantinianism "an eschatological heresy," which can ultimately become "demonic," since it mingles worldly power with the church. "Constantinian Christianity succumbs to the original temptation of Satan, to seize godlikeness and try to wrest control of history from God. . . . Anti-Constantinian Christians obey Jesus [i.e., not the government], come what may" (Leithart 2010, 9, 306–307, 313).

It was the famous British historian and politician Edward Gibbon (1737–1794) who really "blackened the name of the first Christian emperor" of the Roman Empire in his six-volume masterpiece *The History of the Decline and Fall of the Roman Empire*, published between 1776 and 1788. His "brilliant indictment of Christianity" has proven to be long-lasting, as historians have struggled to overcome his conviction that Constantine was essentially insincere in his Christian faith. As one historian puts it, "Gibbon's reading of Constantine's character . . . allows no other interpretation than a late, insincere conversion" (Jordan 1969, 93–94).

Gibbon's dominance over the story of Rome's decline and fall has profoundly colored how we understand Constantine and his era. First off, it should be noted that Gibbon was openly hostile to the Christian religion in his writings. And, in his view, Constantine's decision to partner with the faith was extremely misguided, it was a tragic decision that had horrible consequences for the future of the Roman Empire.

One of Constantine's most egregious mistakes was to move the capital of the empire east to Byzantium, the sign of "a pusillanimous emperor willing to sacrifice the old Rome in order to erect a monument to his own glory." But none of his mistakes compared with his abysmal decision to link Rome and Christ. It was a decision rooted in Constantine's "boundless ambition" and ultimately led to the empire's collapse. This is why Gibbon assails Constantine's motives: his decision to link Christianity and Rome was hypocritical. It was insincere, solely for "personal glory." One historian writes, "Gibbon's Constantine was converted to Christianity only after weighing the advantages and disadvantages of the move. He desired the Empire, and he was willing to do whatever was necessary to secure it." So he "became" a Christian, although he postponed baptism until his deathbed. This "insidious" act was meant to clean the slate of a murderous and defiled life so that Constantine the Great could still enjoy the benefits of a heavenly paradise and would not have to be accountable for his crimes and sins (Jordan 1969, 76–93).

Gibbon's grilling of Constantine was persuasive to generations of historians, such as the great Swiss historian Jacob Burckhardt (1818–1897). In his influential book *The Age of Constantine the Great*, Burckhardt reached conclusions similar to Gibbon: Constantine's lust for power overrode any semblance of religiosity, since "such a man is essentially unreligious, even if he pictures himself standing in the midst of a churchly community."

Indeed, he was a "murderous egoist" who, thankfully, stopped the persecution of Christians . . . "but we are not obliged to share that elation after a millennium and a half." To further complicate matters, Burckhardt argued, Constantine meddled in church affairs, to the point of defining doctrine, indeed, even the Trinity—as he is often accused of doing by pressing for the term *homoousios* (of the same essence) to be used to define Christ's relationship with God (Burckhardt [1880] 1949, 292–293, 315).

PRIMARY DOCUMENTS

JULIAN THE APOSTATE'S *THE CAESARS*

Julian the Apostate ruled the Roman Empire from 361 to 363 and was the last emperor from Constantine's line. His marriage was childless, and his death ended the Constantinian dynasty. Raised a Christian, he "apostatized" around the age of twenty. He became a passionate advocate for Greek and Roman religion and eventually worked hard to suppress Christianity and reinstate paganism. His short reign and violent death in battle against the Sassanid Persians lent credibility to the idea that Christianity was the superior faith. The Caesars, written in the first year of his reign, is a fictional, comical sketch describing a contest taking place among the Roman Emperors in the presence of the Greco-Roman gods. In this work, Julian insults many of his predecessors. At the end of the document, he takes aim at Constantine, assailing his motives for baptism into the Christian faith.

As for Constantine, he could not discover among the gods the model of his own career, but when he caught sight of Pleasure, who was not far off, he ran to her. She received him tenderly and embraced him, then after dressing him in raiment of many colors and otherwise making him beautiful, she led him away to Incontinence. There too he found Jesus, who had taken up his abode with her and cried aloud to all comers: "He that is a seducer, he that is a murderer, he that is sacrilegious and infamous, let him approach without fear! For with this water will I wash him and will straightway make him clean. And though he should be guilty of those same sins a second time, let him but smite his breast and beat his head and I will make him clean again."

Source: Julian. Vol. 2, *Orations 6–8. Letters to Themistius, to the Senate and People of Athens, To a Priest. The Caesars. Misopogon,* translated by Wilmer C. Wright, Loeb Classical Library 29 (Cambridge, MA: Harvard University Press, 1913), 341–415. This quotation is found on p. 413.

ZOSIMUS, *NEW HISTORY*

Zosimus (460–520) was an early Byzantine historian. Like Julian the Apostate, he thought Constantine's embrace of Christianity was an enormous mistake that hastened the fall of Rome. His views are useful to historians because they represent an oppositional understanding of Constantine and the rise of Christianity. In this piece, Zosimus portrays Constantine's character as ruthless and vile, and his conversion as naïve. In this reading, Constantine killed his son and mother-in-law. Afterwards, his guilty conscience caused him to listen to a Spanish reprobate named Aegyptius, who told him about Christian baptism cleansing all sin, no matter how wicked. Constantine fell for this man's words, became a Christian, and began demeaning the Greco-Roman religions.

Now that the whole empire had fallen into the hands of Constantine, he no longer concealed his evil disposition and vicious inclinations, but acted as he pleased, without control. He indeed used the ancient worship of his country; though not so much out of honor or veneration as of necessity. Therefore, he believed the soothsayers, who were expert in their art, as men who predicted the truth concerning all the great actions which he ever performed. But when he came to Rome, he was filled with pride and arrogance. He resolved to begin his impious actions at home. For he put to death his son Crispus, styled (as I mentioned) Caesar, on suspicion of debauching his mother-in-law Fausta, without any regard to the ties of nature. And when his own mother Helena expressed much sorrow for this atrocity, lamenting the young man's death with great bitterness, Constantine under pretense of comforting her, applied a remedy worse than the disease. For causing a bath to be heated to an extraordinary degree, he shut up Fausta in it, and a short time after took her out dead. Of which his conscience accusing him, as also of violating his oath, he went to the priests to be purified from his crimes. But they told him, that there was no kind of lustration that was sufficient to clear him of such enormities. A Spaniard, named Aegyptius, very familiar with the court-ladies, being at Rome, happened to fall into converse with Constantine, and assured him, that the Christian doctrine would teach him how to cleanse himself from all his offences, and that they who received it were immediately absolved from all their sins. Constantine had no sooner heard this than he easily believed what was told him, and forsaking the rites of his country, received those which Aegyptius offered him; and for the first instance of his impiety, suspected the truth of divination. For since many fortunate occurrences had been thereby predicted to him, and really had happened according to such prediction, he was afraid that others might be told something which should fall out to his misfortune; and for that reason applied himself to the abolishing of the practice. And on a particular festival, when the army was to go up to the Capitol, he very indecently reproached the solemnity, and treading the holy ceremonies, as it were, under his feet, incurred the hatred of the senate and people.

Source: Zosimus, *New History*, Book 2 (London: W. Green and T. Chaplin, 1814). Translator is anonymous. Available at http://www.tertullian.org/fathers/zosimus02 _book2.htm.

EDWARD GIBBON, THE CONVERSION OF CONSTANTINE

Edward Gibbon's (1737–1794) famous six-volume masterpiece on the fall of the Roman Empire has been revered by historians since its publication. It is truly a tour de force. In this reading, we see the careful attention Gibbon gave to Constantine's conversion to Christianity. We also see Gibbon's mastery of the sources, as well as his cautious approach. Gibbon was no friend to Christianity, but in some ways his restraint comes through as well. In addition to the conversion, we also read Gibbon's telling of the Milvian Bridge battle as well as his interpretation of how it impacted Constantine's interaction with his Empire.

In the consideration of a subject which may be examined with impartiality, but cannot be viewed with indifference, a difficulty immediately arises of a very unexpected nature; that of ascertaining the real and precise date of the conversion of Constantine. The eloquent Lactantius, in the midst of his court, seems impatient to proclaim to the world the glorious example of the sovereign of Gaul; who, in the first moments of his reign, acknowledged and adored the majesty of the true and only God. The learned Eusebius has ascribed the faith of Constantine to the miraculous sign which was displayed in the heavens whilst he meditated and prepared the Italian expedition. The historian Zosimus maliciously asserts, that the emperor had imbrued his hands in the blood of his eldest son, before he publicly renounced the gods of Rome and of his ancestors. The perplexity produced by these discordant authorities is derived from the behavior of Constantine himself. According to the strictness of ecclesiastical language, the first of the Christian emperors was unworthy of that name, till the moment of his death; since it was only during his last illness that he received, as a catechumen, the imposition of hands, and was afterwards admitted, by the initiatory rites of baptism, into the number of the faithful. The Christianity of Constantine must be allowed in a much more vague and qualified sense; and the nicest accuracy is required in tracing the slow and almost imperceptible gradations by which the monarch declared himself the protector, and at length the proselyte, of the church. It was an arduous task to eradicate the habits and prejudices of his education, to acknowledge the divine power of Christ, and to understand that the truth of his revelation was incompatible with the worship of the gods. The obstacles which he had probably experienced in his own mind, instructed him to proceed with caution in the momentous change of a national religion; and he insensibly discovered his new opinions, as far as he could enforce them with safety and with effect. During the whole course of his reign, the stream of Christianity flowed with a gentle, though accelerated, motion: but its general direction was sometimes checked, and sometimes diverted, by the accidental circumstances of the times, and by the prudence, or possibly by the caprice, of the monarch.

. . .

While this important revolution yet remained in suspense, the Christians and the Pagans watched the conduct of their sovereign with the same anxiety, but with very opposite sentiments. The former were prompted by every motive of zeal, as well as vanity, to exaggerate the marks of his favor, and the evidences of his faith. The latter, till their just apprehensions were changed into despair and resentment, attempted to conceal from the world, and from themselves, that the gods of Rome could no longer reckon the emperor in the number of their votaries. The same passions and prejudices have engaged the partial writers of the times to connect the public profession of Christianity with the most glorious or the most ignominious era of the reign of Constantine.

Whatever symptoms of Christian piety might transpire in the discourses or actions of Constantine, he persevered till he was near forty years of age in the practice of the established religion.

. . .

The piety of Constantine was admitted as an unexceptionable proof of the justice of his arms; and his use of victory confirmed the opinion of the Christians, that their hero was inspired, and conducted, by the Lord of Hosts. The conquest of Italy produced a general edict of toleration; and as soon as the defeat of Licinius had invested Constantine with the sole dominion of the Roman world, he immediately, by circular letters, exhorted all his subjects to imitate, without delay, the example of their sovereign, and to embrace the divine truth of Christianity.

. . .

In all occasions of danger and distress, it was the practice of the primitive Christians to fortify their minds and bodies by the sign of the cross, which they used, in all their ecclesiastical rites, in all the daily occurrences of life, as an infallible preservative against every species of spiritual or temporal evil. The authority of the church might alone have had sufficient weight to justify the devotion of Constantine, who in the same prudent and gradual progress acknowledged the truth, and assumed the symbol, of Christianity. But the testimony of a contemporary writer, who in a formal treatise has avenged the cause of religion, bestows on the piety of the emperor a more awful and sublime character. He affirms, with the most perfect confidence, that in the night which preceded the last battle against Maxentius, Constantine was admonished in a dream to inscribe the shields of his soldiers with the celestial sign of God, the sacred monogram of the name of Christ; that he executed the commands of Heaven, and that his valor and obedience were rewarded by the decisive victory of the Milvian Bridge.

. . .

In one of the marches of Constantine, he is reported to have seen with his own eyes the luminous trophy of the cross, placed above the meridian sun and inscribed with the following words: By This Conquer. This amazing object in the sky astonished the whole army, as well as the emperor himself, who was yet undetermined in the choice of a religion: but his astonishment was converted into faith by the vision of the ensuing night. Christ appeared before his eyes; and displaying the same celestial sign of the cross, he directed Constantine to frame a similar standard, and to march, with an assurance of victory, against Maxentius and all his enemies.

. . .

But the Catholic church, both of the East and of the West, has adopted a prodigy which favors, or seems to favor, the popular worship of the cross. The vision of Constantine maintained an honorable place in the legend of superstition, till the bold and sagacious spirit of criticism presumed to depreciate the triumph, and to arraign the truth, of the first Christian emperor.

. . .

Personal interest is often the standard of our belief, as well as of our practice; and the same motives of temporal advantage which might influence the public conduct and professions of Constantine, would insensibly dispose his mind to embrace a religion so propitious to his fame and fortunes. His vanity was gratified by the flattering assurance, that he had been chosen by Heaven to reign over the earth; success had justified his divine title to the throne, and that title was founded on the truth of the Christian revelation. As real virtue is sometimes excited by undeserved applause, the specious piety of Constantine, if at first it was only specious, might gradually, by the influence of praise, of habit, and of example, be matured into serious faith and fervent devotion.

. . .

The sacrament of baptism was supposed to contain a full and absolute expiation of sin; and the soul was instantly restored to its original purity, and entitled to the promise of eternal salvation. Among the proselytes of Christianity, there are many who judged it imprudent to precipitate a salutary rite, which could not be repeated; to throw away an inestimable privilege, which could never be recovered. By the delay of their baptism, they could venture freely to indulge their passions in the enjoyments of this world, while they still retained in their own hands the means of a sure and easy absolution.

. . .

At the time of the death of Crispus, the emperor could no longer hesitate in the choice of a religion; he could no longer be ignorant that the church was possessed of an infallible remedy, though he chose to defer the application of it till the approach of death had removed the temptation and danger of a relapse. The bishops whom he summoned, in his last illness, to the palace of Nicomedia, were edified by the fervor with which he requested and received the sacrament of baptism, by the solemn protestation that the remainder of his life should be worthy of a disciple of Christ, and by his humble refusal to wear the Imperial purple after he had been clothed in the white garment of a neophyte. The example and reputation of Constantine seemed to countenance the delay of baptism. Future tyrants were encouraged to believe, that the innocent blood which they might shed in a long reign would instantly be washed away in the waters of regeneration; and the abuse of religion dangerously undermined the foundations of moral virtue.

. . .

The gratitude of the church has exalted the virtues and excused the failings of a generous patron, who seated Christianity on the throne of the Roman world; and the Greeks, who celebrate the festival of the Imperial saint, seldom mention the name of Constantine without adding the title of Equal to the Apostles. Such a comparison, if it allude to the character of those divine missionaries, must be imputed to the extravagance of impious flattery. But if the parallel be confined to the extent and number of their evangelic victories the success of Constantine might perhaps equal that of the Apostles themselves.

. . .

As the lower ranks of society are governed by imitation, the conversion of those who possessed any eminence of birth, of power, or of riches, was soon followed by dependent multitudes. The salvation of the common people was purchased at an easy rate, if it be true that, in one year, twelve thousand men were baptized at Rome, besides a proportionable number of women and children, and that a white garment, with twenty pieces of gold, had been promised by the emperor to every convert.

Source: Edward Gibbon, *Decline and Fall of the Roman Empire.* Vol. 2 (London: Strahan & Cadell, 1781), chapter 20. Available at http://www.sacred-texts.com/cla /gibbon/02/daf02026.htm.

What Really Happened

More recently, historians have tended to favor the idea that Constantine was a sincere convert to Christianity. First of all, delayed baptism proves nothing. Even famous church fathers did the same, such as the great St. Ambrose. Others, such as Basil the Great, Gregory of Nyssa, Gregory of Nazianzus, John Chrysostom, and Augustine all put off baptism until the end of their studies, presumably so they could have the abundance of their youthful sins washed away before they began their religious careers (Stark 2011, 170; Daughrity 2016, 115).

When Constantine finally did receive baptism, it was by no means a trivial matter. The year was 337 and Constantine suspected he was dying. He wanted to travel to Palestine in order to be baptized in the Jordan, like Jesus, but his health broke down in Nicomedia, not far from

Constantinople. Attended by bishops, Constantine expressed his desire for God's salvation, and "the bishops performed the sacred ceremonies in the usual manner." Afterward, the emperor removed the purple and put on vestments of brilliant white. He never wore purple again. Constantine had a sense that he was now a true Christian and was thus unable to perform the tasks of a temporal ruler. The man who so strongly associated his leadership with Christian principles knew good and well that fully accepting Christ meant he would be expected to forsake that which connected him to his past. Constantine was now a full-fledged member of the Christian church. He was cleansed of his many sins, and he knew that his new course of life would have to be very different from his past. His death, however, prevents us from knowing to what extent his heart was actually regenerated and his soul perfected. We never get to see Constantine's rule from a post-baptismal perspective.

In addition, Stark asks, why didn't Constantine simply appeal to another god? He certainly could have done so. But the winds of change were blowing in the direction of Christianity. "Christianity . . . was the faith of the majority of residents of Rome and many other major cities." Thousands of conversions were occurring, and the reality was that the various Roman gods were losing the heavenly battle against the God of the Jews . . . at least in the minds of the Roman peoples (Stark 2011, 179).

Another important issue has to do with Constantine's own mother, Helena. She exercised great influence over her son and was a devout Christian. There is no doubt that Constantine would have been acquainted with Christian teaching, since his mother often resided with him. Historian Timothy Barnes writes, "From the days of his youth Constantine had probably been sympathetic to Christianity, and in 312 he experienced a religious conversion which profoundly affected his conception of himself" (Barnes 1981, 275).

Historians are now persuaded that when Constantine entered Rome, he "came in triumph and as a Christian." Most of the inhabitants of the city were joyous at his coming, but the pagans of the city—which included members of the Senate—were appalled that he failed to perform the customary victory sacrifices to the sky-god Jupiter (in Greek, Zeus). Constantine's loyalties were obviously elsewhere. It was Christ, the God of the Chi-Rho, who empowered his astonishingly rapid defeat of Maxentius. In fact, Constantine had Christian bishops in his entourage as he marched upon Rome, and "he publicly declared himself a Christian before battle."

Barnes says it well: "In the ultimate reckoning . . . the precise details of Constantine's conversion matter little. After 28 October 312 the emperor consistently thought of himself as God's servant, entrusted with a divine mission to convert the Roman Empire to Christianity" (Barnes 1981, 43–44).

Coin evidence suggests that Constantine did, indeed, see something the night before the Battle of the Milvian Bridge, and that something changed his religious sensibilities. Prior to that battle, Constantine's coinage honored the pagan gods Sol (the sun god) and Apollo (Zeus's son). After the battle, Constantine's coinage begins to favor Christian symbols (Leithart 2010, 77).

Constantine was persuaded by his advisor Lactantius (c. 250–325) that the God of the Christians opposes those who oppose God's people. Likewise, God blesses those who defend the church, and this god would avenge the blood of the martyrs who had suffered and died while Constantine was alive to see it. By choosing to side with this god, Constantine felt he might be able to escape God's judgment and wrath. Leithart calls Lactantius's theology "betting on the winning horse" or, expressed another way, having a healthy fear of God. However, Constantine may have framed his conversion in his own mind, there can be no doubt that a conversion indeed took place. To the end of his life, Constantine thought of himself as the great protector of Christians, a ruler who showed great tenderness and favor to the church. As the apostle Paul warned in 1 Corinthians 3:17: "If any man defile the temple of God, him shall God destroy; for the temple of God is holy, which temple ye are" (KJV). This passage was key to understanding the mind of Lactantius—himself a convert to Christianity. Lactantius had experienced firsthand the terrors of persecution in the years before Constantine's rule and routinely emphasized to Constantine that those who opposed God would live to see the same destruction that Constantine's predecessors had experienced (Leithart 2010, 82).

From coin evidence to eyewitness documentation, there can be little doubt that Constantine became a Christian. He thought Christ led him to victory. He marched into Rome believing himself a Christian. He immediately declared Christianity legal. He personally favored Christianity. His mother was a Christian. His coins and other iconography had Christian themes. Finally, in his death, he submitted himself to God through baptism. What more is needed to show that Constantine was a Christian? Only God really knows!

PRIMARY DOCUMENTS

EDICT OF MILAN, AD 313, BY CO-EMPERORS CONSTANTINE AND LICINIUS

The Edict of Milan was written shortly after the defeat of Maxentius at the famous Battle of the Milvian Bridge in Rome in 312. At that battle, Maxentius drowned in the Tiber River. Constantine's men pulled Maxentius's body from the river and decapitated it, where it was paraded through the streets of Rome. Constantine was praised as victor and the Arch of Constantine was built in commemoration of the event. The Edict of Milan *represents a turning point in Christianity's history. Previously the Christian faith was illegal, but this document made it legal, even preferred. Licinius was never favorable to Christianity, so the edict is often associated solely with Constantine. Licinius remained a pagan to the end of his life while Constantine converted to Christianity. As they grew apart due to power, politics, and possibly due to their differing opinions on Christianity, they ultimately went to battle against each other. Constantine defeated Licinius in 324 and had him executed by hanging in 325—the year of the famous Council of Nicaea—when he learned that Licinius was plotting a resurgence. The edict is preserved by both Eusebius and Lactantius, two important historians at the time. While the document is essentially an edict of toleration of all faiths, there can be no mistaking the fact that Constantine's great affection for the Christian faith is present, as is his commitment to Christianity's protection. A major theme of the document is that all properties that had ever been confiscated from the Christians must be returned to them "without any procrastination."*

Part I

I, Constantine Augustus, and I, Licinius Augustus, at a propitious juncture meeting in Milan, and taking under consideration the whole range of public interest and safety, have come to the conclusion, that among all matters conducive to the public weal those ought to be settled in the very first place, by which the reverence due to the Deity is safeguarded (to wit) that we give to the Christians as well as to all (others) free permission to follow the religion which each one chooses, in order that whatever Deity there is on the heavenly throne may be propitiated and show itself favorable to ourselves and to all that are under our power.

Hence, listening to the demands of both public welfare and sound reason, we have thought it our duty to enact that leave shall be refused to no one whatever who has given his heart either to the teachings of the Christians or to that (other) kind of religion which he himself feels to be the most suitable to him; so that the Supreme Divinity, worshipped by us with full freedom, may be able to show to us in all things its wonted favor and benevolence.

The Lordship will therefore take notice of our pleasure that all the restrictions which are contained in former instructions concerning the Christians and which appear to be very ill advised and out of keeping with our clemency, are all and entirely cancelled; and that each and every one desirous to observe the religion of the Christians may do so without any fear, and without any disadvantage to himself. We thought it our duty to express this to thy Lordship in the plainest terms, so that thou knowest we give to the afore said Christians free and unlimited permission to practice their religion. Thy Lordship understands, that for the tranquility of our times the same freedom as to religion and observance is likewise expressly and liberally granted to others, so that everyone may enjoy the fullest permission to worship what he chooses. We take this step with the intention of preventing the appearance as if we meant to slight anything deserving of honor or religious veneration.

Part II

As to the Christians we deem it our duty to issue still another enactment, (namely) concerning the places (buildings) in which they formerly were accustomed to assemble, and about which a well-known rule was laid down in the communications sent heretofore to thy Fidelity. Those persons who appear to have bought these identical places either from our treasury or from anybody else shall restore the same to the Christians without money and without charging any price, setting aside all deception and delay. Likewise, those who have received them as presents shall immediately surrender them to the same Christians. If the present owners, however, whether they acquired them by purchase or by gift, shall wish to receive anything (as compensation) from our bounty, let them apply to our representative, so that provision may be made for them also by our clemency. It will be thy duty to see to it that all this property be returned to the community of the Christians without any procrastination.

And since the Christians, as is well known, possessed not only those places where they used to meet, but also others which belonged not to individuals but to them as corporation, that is to the churches, we comprise all these in the aforesaid ordinance (of restitution). And thou wilt cause them to be returned without hesitancy and without litigation, to the same Christians, that is, to their corporation and communities; observing, however, the above mentioned caution, (to wit) that those who faithful to our order restore them without charging any price may expect indemnity from our benevolence.

Conclusion

In all these affairs thou shalt be obliged to yield to the body of the Christians thy most efficacious assistance, to the end that our ordinance be carried out as speedily as possible, and that at the same time through our clemency care be taken of the maintenance of public order. In this way the divine favor towards us, which as expressed above we have experienced on the most momentous occasions, will forever prosper our future enterprises and the happiness of our people.

But in order that the tenor of this our gracious rescript may come to the knowledge of all, thou shalt have copies of it certified by thy signature, posted up everywhere, and shalt promulgate it broadcast; so that the firm determination of our clemency may not remain in obscurity.

Source: Francis S. Betten, "The Milan Decree of A.D. 313: Translation and Comment," *Catholic Historical Review* 8:2 (July 1922): 191–197. Available at https://www.jstor.org/stable/pdf/25011854.pdf.

EUSEBIUS, *LIFE OF CONSTANTINE*, BATTLE OF THE MILVIAN BRIDGE

Whether believed or not, Eusebius (c. 260–339) was convinced that Constantine was being truthful about this story, which happened just before the Battle of the Milvian Bridge. According to Eusebius, who was Constantine's official biographer, this vision was the point at which the emperor rushed headlong into the Christian faith, never to depart from it on an official level. In this reading, Constantine's famous vision of the cross occurs, with the words "by this, conquer." Eusebius claims the entire army saw the sight. We also read about Constantine's first usage of the Chi-Rho (first letters of "Christ") as his battle flag and insignia, which he had emblazoned on his helmet and on the shields of his troops.

Accordingly, he called on him with earnest prayer and supplications that he would reveal to him who he was, and stretch forth his right hand to help him in his present difficulties. And while he was thus praying with fervent entreaty, a most marvelous sign appeared to him from heaven, the account of which it might have been hard to believe had it been related by any other person. But since the victorious emperor himself long afterwards declared it to the writer of this history, when he was honored with his acquaintance and society, and confirmed his statement by an oath, who could hesitate to accredit the relation, especially since the testimony of after-time has established its truth? He said that about noon, when the day was already beginning to decline, he saw with his own eyes the trophy of a cross of light in the heavens, above the sun, and bearing the inscription, CONQUER BY THIS. At this sight he himself was struck with amazement, and his whole army also, which followed him on this expedition, and witnessed the miracle.

He said, moreover, that he doubted within himself what the import of this apparition could be. And while he continued to ponder and reason on its meaning, night suddenly came on; then in his sleep the Christ of God appeared to him with the same sign which he had seen in the heavens, and commanded him to make a likeness of that sign which he had seen in the heavens, and to use it as a safeguard in all engagements with his enemies.

At dawn of day he arose, and communicated the marvel to his friends: and then, calling together the workers in gold and precious stones, he sat in the midst of them, and described to them the figure of the sign he had seen, bidding them represent it in gold and precious stones. And this representation I myself have had an opportunity of seeing.

Now it was made in the following manner. A long spear, overlaid with gold, formed the figure of the cross by means of a transverse bar laid over it. On the top of the whole was fixed a wreath of gold and precious stones; and within this, the symbol of the Saviour's name, two letters indicating the name of Christ by means of its initial characters, the letter P being intersected by X in its centre: and these letters the emperor was in the habit of wearing on his helmet at a later period. From the cross-bar of the spear was suspended a cloth, a royal piece, covered with a profuse embroidery of most brilliant precious stones; and which, being also richly interlaced with gold, presented an indescribable degree of beauty to the beholder. This banner was of a square form, and the upright staff, whose lower section was of great length, bore a golden half-length portrait of the pious emperor and his children on its upper part, beneath the trophy of the cross, and immediately above the embroidered banner.

The emperor constantly made use of this sign of salvation as a safeguard against every adverse and hostile power, and commanded that others similar to it should be carried at the head of all his armies.

These things were done shortly afterwards. But at the time above specified, being struck with amazement at the extraordinary vision, and resolving to worship no other God save Him who had appeared to him, he sent for those who were acquainted with the mysteries of His doctrines, and enquired who that God was, and what was intended by the sign of the vision he had seen. They affirmed that He was God, the only begotten Son of the one and only God: that the sign which had appeared was the symbol of immortality, and the trophy of that victory over death which He had gained in time past when sojourning on earth. They taught him also the causes of His advent, and explained to him the true account of His incarnation. Thus he was instructed in these matters, and was impressed with wonder at the divine manifestation which had been presented to his sight. Comparing, therefore, the heavenly vision with the interpretation given, he found his judgment confirmed; and, in the persuasion that the knowledge of these things had been imparted to him by Divine teaching, he determined thenceforth to devote himself to the reading of the Inspired writings.

Moreover, he made the priests of God his counselors, and deemed it incumbent on him to honor the God who had appeared to him with all devotion. And after this, being fortified by well-grounded hopes in Him, he hastened to quench the threatening fire of tyranny.

Source: Eusebius, *Life of Constantine*, Battle of the Milvian Bridge, translated by Ernest Cushing Richardson, in *Nicene and Post-Nicene Fathers*, Second Series, Vol. 1, edited by Philip Schaff and Henry Wace (Buffalo, NY: Christian Literature Publishing Co., 1890), book 1, sections 28–32. Available at http://www.newadvent.org/fathers/25021.htm.

EUSEBIUS, *LIFE OF CONSTANTINE,* CONSTANTINE'S BAPTISM AND DEATH

Eusebius was clearly an ally of Constantine, as he served as one of Constantine's advisors. He sat at Constantine's right hand at the Council of Nicaea in 325 and even gave the opening address. He was the bishop of Caesarea and a prolific author. He sided with Arius during the great Christological controversy, and thus was never made a saint. In this reading, we see Eusebius's eyewitness account of Constantine's final days, baptism, and death. Eusebius's account is clearly hagiographical, but extremely valuable nonetheless.

Chapter 61: Constantine's Sickness at Helenopolis, and Prayers Respecting His Baptism

At first he experienced some slight bodily indisposition, which was soon followed by positive disease. In consequence of this he visited the hot baths of his own city; and thence proceeded to that which bore the name of his mother. Here he passed some time in the church of the martyrs, and offered up supplications and prayers to God. Being at length convinced that his life was drawing to a close, he felt the time had come at which he should seek purification from sins of his past career, firmly believing that whatever errors he had committed as a mortal man, his soul would be purified from them through the efficacy of the mystical words and the salutary waters of baptism. Impressed with these thoughts, he poured forth his supplications and confessions to God, kneeling on the pavement in the church itself, in which he also now for the first time received the imposition of hands with prayer. After this he proceeded as far as the suburbs of Nicomedia, and there, having summoned the bishops to meet him, addressed them in the following words.

Chapter 62: Constantine's Appeal to the Bishops, Requesting Them to Confer upon Him the Rite of Baptism

The time is arrived which I have long hoped for, with an earnest desire and prayer that I might obtain the salvation of God. The hour has come in which I too may have the blessing of that seal which confers immortality; the hour in which I may receive the seal of salvation. I had thought to do this in the waters of the river Jordan, wherein our Saviour, for our example, is recorded to have been baptized: but God, who knows what is expedient for us, is pleased that I should receive this blessing here. Be it so, then, without delay: for should it be his will who is Lord of life and death, that my existence here should be prolonged, and should I be destined henceforth to associate with the people of God, and unite with them in prayer as a member of his Church, I will prescribe to myself from this time such a course of life as befits his service. After he had thus spoken, the prelates performed the sacred ceremonies in the usual manner, and, having given him the necessary instructions, made him a partaker of the mystic ordinance. Thus was Constantine the first of all sovereigns who was regenerated and perfected in a church dedicated to the martyrs of Christ; thus gifted with the Divine seal of baptism, he rejoiced in spirit, was renewed, and filled with heavenly light: his soul was gladdened by reason of the fervency of his faith, and astonished at the manifestation of the power of God. At the conclusion of the ceremony he arrayed himself in shining imperial vestments, brilliant as the light, and reclined on a couch of the purest white, refusing to clothe himself with the purple any more.

Chapter 63: How after His Baptism He Rendered Thanks to God

He then lifted his voice and poured forth a strain of thanksgiving to God; after which he added these words. Now I know that I am truly blessed: now I feel assured that I am accounted worthy of immortality, and am made a partaker of Divine light. He further expressed his compassion for the unhappy condition of those who were strangers to such blessings as he enjoyed: and when the tribunes and generals of his army appeared in his presence with lamentations and tears at the prospect of their bereavement, and with prayers that his days might yet be prolonged, he assured them in reply that he was now in possession of true life; that none but himself could know the value of the blessings he had received; so that he was anxious rather to hasten than to defer his departure to God. He then proceeded to complete the needful arrangement of his affairs, bequeathing an annual donation to the Roman inhabitants of his imperial city; apportioning the inheritance of the empire, like a patrimonial estate, among his own children; in short, making every disposition according to his own pleasure.

Chapter 64: Constantine's Death at Noon on the Feast of Pentecost

All these events occurred during a most important festival, I mean the august and holy solemnity of Pentecost, which is distinguished by a period of seven weeks, and sealed with that one day on which the holy Scriptures attest, the ascension of our common Saviour into heaven, and the descent of the Holy Spirit among men. In the course of this feast the emperor received the privileges I have described; and on the last day of all, which one might justly call the feast of feasts, he was removed about mid-day to the presence of his God, leaving his mortal remains to his fellow mortals, and carrying into fellowship with God that part of his being which was capable of understanding and loving him. Such was the close of Constantine's mortal life. Let us now attend to the circumstances which followed this event.

Source: Eusebius, *Life of Constantine,* Constantine's Baptism and Death, translated by Ernest Cushing Richardson, in *Nicene and Post-Nicene Fathers,* Second Series. Vol. 1, edited by Philip Schaff and Henry Wace (Buffalo, NY: Christian Literature Publishing Co., 1890), book 4, sections 61–64. Available at http://www.newadvent.org/fathers /25024.htm.

Further Reading

Barnes, Timothy D. 1981. *Constantine and Eusebius.* Cambridge, MA: Harvard University Press.

Baynes, Norman H. (1930) 1972. *Constantine the Great and the Christian Church.* 2nd ed. London: Oxford University Press.

Bradbury, Scott. 1994. "Constantine and the Problem of Anti-Pagan Legislation in the Fourth Century." *Classical Philology* 89:2 (April): 120–139.

Brown, Peter. 1995. *Authority and the Sacred: Aspects of the Christianization of the Roman World.* Cambridge: Cambridge University Press.

Burckhardt, Jacob. (1880) 1949. *The Age of Constantine the Great.* New York: Pantheon Books.

Casiday, Augustine, and Frederick Norris, eds. 2007. *The Cambridge History of Christianity.* Vol. 2. Cambridge: Cambridge University Press.

Daughrity, Dyron B. 2016. *Roots: Uncovering Why We Do What We Do in Church.* Abilene, TX: Leafwood.

Digeser, Elizabeth DePalma. 1999. *The Making of a Christian Empire: Lactantius and Rome.* Ithaca, NY: Cornell University Press.

Drake, H. A. 1996. "Lambs into Lions: Explaining Early Christian Intolerance." *Past and Present* 153:1: 3–36.

Drake, H. A. 2000. *Constantine and the Bishops: The Politics of Intolerance.* Baltimore: Johns Hopkins University Press.

Duffy, Eamon. 1997. *Saints and Sinners: A History of Popes.* New Haven, CT: Yale University Press.

Elliott, T. G. 1996. *The Christianity of Constantine the Great.* Scranton, PA: University of Scranton Press.

Esler, Philip E. 2000. *The Early Christian World.* Vol. 2. London: Routledge.

Geffcken, Johannes. (1920) 1978. *The Last Days of Greco-Roman Paganism.* Amsterdam: North-Holland.

Goffart, Walter. 1971. "Zosimus, the First Historian of Rome's Fall." *American Historical Review* 76:2 (April): 412–441.

Grant, Robert M. (1970) 1990. *Augustus to Constantine: The Rise and Triumph of Christianity in the Roman World*. San Francisco: Harper San Francisco.

Jordan, David. 1969. "Gibbon's 'Age of Constantine' and the Fall of Rome." *History and Theory* 8:1: 71–96.

Leithart, Peter J. 2010. *Defending Constantine*. Downers Grove, IL: IVP Academic.

Moffett, Samuel Hugh. *A History of Christianity in Asia*. Vol. 1, *Beginnings to 1500*. Maryknoll, NY: Orbis, 1998.

Myers, Eric M., and Mark A. Chancey. 2012. *Alexander to Constantine: Archaeology of the Land of the Bible*. New Haven, CT: Yale University Press.

Odahl, Charles M. 2004. *Constantine and the Christian Empire*. London: Routledge.

Pohlsander, Hans A. 1996. *The Emperor Constantine*. 2nd ed. London: Routledge.

Potter, David. 2013. *Constantine the Emperor*. New York: Oxford University Press.

Stark, Rodney. 2011. *The Triumph of Christianity*. New York: HarperOne.

Stephenson, Paul. 2009. *Constantine: Roman Emperor, Christian Victor*. New York: Overlook Press.

5

Medieval Europe Was a Profoundly Christian Society

What People Think Happened

Before entering more deeply into their studies of history, most of the students I teach have some fairly standard preconceptions about medieval Christianity, the period that dates roughly from AD 500 to 1500. This era lasted from the time of the supposed "fall" of Rome (although it did not actually fall, it just started being ruled by various Germanic tribes) to Luther's revolution in the sixteenth century.

My students tend to think of Western civilization in the medieval era as an extremely religious place, intensely devoted to Christianity. Unless they have been taught better, they will think of this period as the "Dark Ages"—a time when innovation and the creation of knowledge virtually ceased. The magnificence of the Greco-Roman era faded as Vandals, Saxons, and Franks invaded and ransacked the Roman Empire, ending that golden era in human civilization—what academicians call "classical antiquity."

Just the naming of these eras is fraught with bias. For example, the Greco-Roman era is called "classical antiquity," while the so-called barbarian invasions—essentially people from what we call Germany today—ruined the former glory of that beautifully sophisticated society. After Rome "fell" in 476 to groups of Germanic people, there existed a long period of darkness. For a very long time, textbooks called this era the "Dark Ages." What they meant by this label was that virtually all innovation and progress ceased. Art entered a particularly unfortunate period of decline and debasement. The medieval era was known for its darkness; it was a world ruled by religion. American historian William Manchester titled his textbook on medieval history as *A World Lit Only by Fire*. The light of knowledge—knowledge that came from Greece and Rome—was snuffed out, and Western civilization didn't awaken from its slumber until the "Enlightenment." Yes, indeed, the lights came on once again. With Spinoza, Voltaire, Diderot, Hume, and other atheist or secularist thinkers, the world began to throw off the chains of religion and reach out for a new age—an "Enlightened" age. The clear implication of this metaphor is that the world would be better off with the lights on and the darkness of religion demoted to its rightful place alongside goblins, trolls, and dragons.

Unfortunately for those who created it, this line of reasoning is full of holes to the point that it sinks—and sink it should because it is awfully biased and is patently misguided. First off, the greatest thinkers of the Enlightenment were not anti-religious at all. Some of them were clergy (more on that in chapter 7). Another myth implicated here is that medieval Europe was all about religion. Again, false, it wasn't. The United States today is in many aspects far more religious than Western Europe was between 500 and 1500. The medieval era was an extremely fertile time in human ingenuity, in philosophy, in ideas of government, and in materialistic endeavors such as mapmaking and shipbuilding. Religion was there, but it was by no means the only show in town. This chapter unpacks the myth of soaring religiosity in the medieval era.

According to commentators who wrote during the medieval era, Europe was a rather debased place. Crime rates were high. Corruption was rampant. Immorality was common. Churches struggled to fill the pews, and when the pews did have people in them, they were often sleeping. The basics of the Christian faith were virtually unknown to most people. Only the privileged had access to literacy. Monks and nuns learned to read, so they studied the Christian faith and therefore understood how to live a godly life. But even they had iniquities of their own.

The common people were occupied with making a living, trying to remain healthy, and caring for large families. They couldn't make it to church services most of the time. Once they got there, they often didn't understand what they were witnessing. They relied on stained-glass windows to tell them some basic Bible stories, but that was a far cry from a thoughtful and reasoned understanding of the faith. The only segment of society that truly understood the Christian faith was the upper class because they knew how to read and had access to texts.

How the Story Became Popular

The concept of a "Dark Age" was pioneered by the Italian poet and scholar Petrarch, who lived in the fourteenth century. Petrarch had a very high view of classical Roman culture, which he understood to be a period of light, as opposed to the fall of Rome in 476 that ushered in a period of darkness. Petrarch drew often from this light and dark metaphor, which was common at the time, but he turned the concept on its head. Before Petrarch, the general understanding was that the time before Christ was a period of darkness, but when Christ came, people became enlightened to the truth. It was a strategy employed to critique paganism and the religions of Rome. Petrarch turned it around, however, with a very different way of thinking. He began to refer to the rise of northern Europe and its conquest of Italy as the beginning of the Dark Age, essentially showing his Italian bias.

Petrarch spent his youth near Florence and then later at Avignon—which was at that time the home of the Roman Catholic papacy (1309–1376). He was highly learned, and he believed strongly that a revival of Greco-Roman culture was good for Western Europe. He touched off a renaissance of learning by traveling widely in Europe and collecting old Latin manuscripts. Petrarch believed that a revival of the Latin poets and writers—such as Cicero—would lead Europe out of its (what he perceived) profound darkness.

In the seventeenth and eighteenth centuries, however, the term "Dark Ages" began to take on a new meaning with the rise of the *philosophes*, a school of French intellectuals who were antagonistic toward Christianity and pressed hard for what they perceived to be "progress" and "reason." They were profoundly distrustful of organized religion, and many of them were atheists. They sowed their ideas into the fabric of French academia and the intellectual elite, leaving a fertile ground for radical opposition to the church. That radical opposition reached its zenith in the French Revolution (began in 1789), where its "Reign of Terror" (1793–1794) abolished the church, killed thousands of people, and unleashed a particularly brutal persecution of the Roman Catholic clergy. In the early years of the French Revolution, Christianity was merely an ideological fiction that stifled progress. By 1793, however, anti-religious ideas had radicalized to the point that priests were singled out as being a source of the problem and were often executed publicly.

While the history is complex, in many ways it was the French wing of the Enlightenment that handed historians the notion that the medieval era was profoundly religious. They painted a very ugly picture of medieval religion, and the "Enlightenment" was a welcomed era in history that would usher humans out of the intellectual straitjacket brought to them by the Roman Catholic Church. Therefore, the church gets demonized in this way of thinking. Christianity gets associated with backward ideas, with superstition, with an anti-scientific posture (more on this in chapter 7), and a general disregard for the common people in favor of padding its relationship with the nobility. In the minds of the *philosophes*, Christianity was more concerned with preserving power—and therefore the old ways of doing things—than with progress and human development. By placing the blame on the church and the aristocracy, these so-called Enlightened thinkers were able to destroy the credibility of the church in France and essentially de-Christianize the nation, which indeed happened. Clergy were hunted and executed, while some found refuge in the homes of private citizens willing to risk their own necks to protect a priest.

This is the general context in which this line of thinking was popularized. The Roman Catholic Church—specifically the Pope and his long tentacles of power all throughout Europe—was a convenient target for the most radical wing of the Enlightenment. The French *philosophes* were brilliant men whose ideas trickled down throughout the end of the eighteenth century and into the nineteenth. And while few historians outside of France had such a disdain for the church, the legacy of this anti-Catholicism persisted. And thus the medieval era—chock full of an ignorance that was perpetuated for centuries by the church—has never fully shaken its reputation as being one of backwardness, churchliness, superstition, and tyrannical puritanism.

Even in recent times this notion of a profoundly religious medieval era continues. The era of St. Francis and Thomas Aquinas are two images that we hold fast to. Francis forsook his great inheritance and gave it all away in order to start a monastery and minister to the poor and sick. Aquinas was the quintessential medieval philosopher who ostensibly posed absurd questions such as "How many angels can dance on the head of a pin?"

The reason these images survive is because the vast majority of people living in Western Europe during the medieval era were illiterate. The people who did know how to read tended to be clergy and monastics. Thus, when literacy rates began to soar in the aftermath of the Protestant

Reformation, the only writings that people had available to them was religious writing: sermons, biographies of saints, catechisms, liturgical texts, folk religious writing, and scripture. As the field of history began to develop during the late seventeenth and early eighteenth century, the texts most available to that early era of historians were religious texts. The medieval era thus lives on in our minds as an era devoted to the Christian religion: the construction of cathedrals, the ubiquitous monasteries, the conversion of the Western world to Christianity through missions, and the dominance of the Roman Catholic Church. When we think of the medieval era, we most likely think of Christianity as a monolithic "Christendom" with a vast network of religious institutions.

The problem is, on the whole, medieval Europeans were not that religious.

PRIMARY DOCUMENTS

THE LITTLE FLOWERS OF ST. FRANCIS

St. Francis of Assisi (1181–1225) is perhaps the most notable medieval Christian, famous for his Christ-like life lived in renunciation of his father's wealth and his commitment to the order he founded: the Franciscans. Together with his female devotee, St. Clare, he revolutionized monastic life in Western Europe. A huge following rose up during Francis's life, and he has become one of Catholicism's most beloved saints. He was known to preach to animals and evangelize Muslims. He is the person who introduced the celebration of the nativity during Christmas, and he is purported to have received the stigmata—the wounds of Christ. In these readings from The Little Flowers—*a collection of stories about him composed a century or more after his death—is one of the most delightful works of the medieval era. It shows the profoundly religious worldview of medieval people and how St. Francis was already perceived as being uniquely connected to God even during his life.*

Chapter VII

How St Francis Passed the Time of Lent in an Island, on the Lake of Perugia, Where He Fasted Forty Days and Forty Nights, Eating No More Than Half of One Loaf

The true servant of Christ, St Francis, was in certain things like unto a second Christ given to the world for the salvation of souls. Wherefore God the Father willed that in many points he should be conformed to his Son, Jesus Christ, as we have already explained in the calling of his twelve companions, as also in the mystery of the holy stigmata, and in a fast of forty days which he made in the manner following:

St Francis, one day of the Carnival, was near the Lake of Perugia, in the house of one of his devout children, with whom he had spent the night, when he was inspired by God to go and pass the time of Lent in an island on the lake. Wherefore St Francis begged his friend, for the love of God, to convey him in his boat to an island uninhabited by man: the which he should do during the night of Ash-Wednesday, so that none might know where he was; and the friend, because of the great devotion he bore to St Francis, agreed to his request, and conveyed him to the said island, St Francis taking with him naught but two small loaves.

When they had reached the island, his friend left him and returned home; the saint earnestly entreating him to reveal to no one where he was, and not to come and fetch him before Holy Thursday; to which he consented. St Francis being left alone, and there being no dwelling in the island in which he could take shelter, entered into a thick part of the wood all overgrown with brambles and other creeping plants, and forming as it were a kind of hut, there he began to pray and enter into the contemplation of divine things. And there he passed the whole of Lent without drinking or eating save half of one of the small loaves he had taken with him, as we learned from his friend who, going to fetch him on Holy Thursday, found one of the loaves untouched and the other only half consumed.

It is believed that St Francis ate this half out of reverence for our Blessed Lord, who fasted forty days and forty nights without taking any material food; for by eating this bit of bread he put aside the temptation to vain-glory, and yet fasted forty days and forty nights in imitation of the Savior.

In later times God worked many miracles, through the merits of the saint, on the spot where St Francis had fasted so wonderfully, on which account people began to build houses and dwell there, and little by little a town rose up, with a convent called the Convent of the Isle; and to this day the inhabitants of that town hold in great respect and great devotion the spot in which St Francis passed the time of Lent.

Chapter XIV

How the Lord Appeared to St Francis and to His Brethren as He Was Speaking with Them

In the beginning of the Order, St Francis, having assembled his companions to speak to them of Christ, in a moment of great fervor of spirit commanded one of them, in the name of God, to open his mouth and speak as the Holy Spirit should inspire him. The brother, doing as he was ordered, spoke most wonderfully of God. Then St Francis bade him to be silent, and ordered another brother to speak in the same way, which having done with much penetration, St Francis ordered him likewise to be silent, and commanded a third brother to do the same. This one began to speak so deeply of the things of God, that St Francis was convinced that both he and his companion had spoken through the Holy Spirit. Of which also he received a manifest proof; for whilst they were thus speaking together, our Blessed Lord appeared in the midst of them, under the form of a beautiful young man, and blessed them all. And they, being ravished out of themselves, fell to the ground as if they had been dead, and were all unconscious of things external.

And when they recovered from their trance, St Francis said to them: "My beloved brothers, let us thank God, who has deigned to reveal to the world, through his humble servants, the treasures of divine wisdom. For the Lord it is who openeth the mouth of the dumb, and maketh the tongues of the simple to speak wisdom."

Chapter XVII

How a Little Child Who Had Entered the Order Saw St Francis in Prayer One Night, and Saw Also the Saviour, the Virgin Mary, and Many Other Saints Talk with Him

A certain pure and innocent child was received into the Order during the lifetime of St Francis, and the convent in which he lived was so small that the monks were obliged to sleep on mats.

It chanced that St Francis came one day to that convent, and in the evening, after Compline, he went to rest, so as to rise up early to pray, as was his custom, when all the other friars were still asleep. The said little child had made up his mind carefully to watch St Francis, to learn something of his sanctity, and find out more especially what he did in the night when he got up; and in order that he might not be overtaken by sleep, he laid him down by St Francis, tying the end of the cord he wore round his waist to the one which the saint wore, so that he was sure of being awakened when the latter got up in the night; and this he did so gently, that St Francis was not aware of his contrivance.

When all the other friars were fast asleep, St Francis rose from sleep, and finding the child's cord tied to his own, he carefully untied it so as not to awake him and went alone into the wood which was near the convent.

Entering into a little cell which was there, he began to pray. Shortly after, the child awoke, and finding St Francis gone, and the cord untied, he rose up quickly and went to seek him. Perceiving the door open which led to the wood, he thought St Francis had gone that way; and entering into the wood, and hurrying on to the little cell, he heard the sound of many voices.

Approaching near to hear and see whence they came, he saw a great and wonderful light all around the saint, and in the light was Jesus Christ, with the Virgin Mary, St John the Baptist, St John the Evangelist, and a great multitude of angels, all talking with St Francis.

On seeing this the child fell to the ground as if he had been dead. The miracle of this holy vision being ended, St Francis rose to return to the convent, and stumbling in the way against the child, who appeared to be dead, with great compassion he took him up in his arms and carried him in his bosom, as the good shepherd is wont to carry his lambs. Having learned from him how he had seen the vision, he forbade him to tell any man thereof so long as he, St Francis, lived.

The little child grew up in the grace of God, and had a great devotion to St Francis. He became one of the most distinguished men of the Order. After the death of St Francis, he related the vision to the brethren.

Source: *The Little Flowers of St. Francis*, Part 1, first English translation, revised and emended by Dom Roger Hudleston, Part One, chapters 7, 14, 17. Courtesy of Eternal Word Television Network. Available at https://www.ewtn.com/library/mary/flowers1.htm.

ST. THOMAS AQUINAS, *SUMMA THEOLOGIAE*

St. Thomas Aquinas (1225–1274) was the chief Roman Catholic philosopher of the medieval era. Identified within the larger school of scholasticism, he was an extremely careful thinker, and his approach to knowledge is today known as Thomism. Aquinas used Aristotle extensively, knowing him simply as "the Philosopher." His teaching is still considered authoritative within the Roman Catholic Church, and clergy are still required to become acquainted with his system of thought. Outside of the biblical witness, no other Catholic thinker has impacted the church as much as Aquinas, save the possible exception of St. Augustine. In this reading, we see Aquinas's profoundly systematic and inductive way of thinking on full display when he considers whether angels occupy space and time. It was lines of questions such as this that some Protestant and Enlightenment thinkers mocked for its absurdity and irrelevance to real life issues both in the church and in society.

Question 52. The Angels in Relation to Place

1. Is the angel in a place?
2. Can he be in several places at once?
3. Can several angels be in the same place?

Article 1. Whether an angel is in a place?

Objection 1. It would seem that an angel is not in a place. For Boethius says (De Hebdom.): "The common opinion of the learned is that things incorporeal are not in a place." And again, Aristotle observes (Phys. iv, text 48,57) that "it is not everything existing which is in a place, but only a movable body." But an angel is not a body, as was shown above (Article 50). Therefore, an angel is not in a place.

Objection 2. Further, place is a "quantity having position." But everything which is in a place has some position. Now to have a position cannot benefit an angel, since his substance is devoid of quantity, the proper difference of which is to have a position. Therefore, an angel is not in a place.

Objection 3. Further, to be in a place is to be measured and to be contained by such place, as is evident from the Philosopher (Phys. iv, text 14,119). But an angel can neither be measured nor contained by a place, because the container is more formal than the contained; as air with regard to water (Phys. iv, text 35,49). Therefore, an angel is not in a place.

On the contrary, It is said in the Collect [Prayer at Compline, Dominican Breviary]: "Let Thy holy angels who dwell herein, keep us in peace."

I answer that, It is befitting an angel to be in a place; yet an angel and a body are said to be in a place in quite a different sense. A body is said to be in a place in such a way that it is applied to such place according to the contact of dimensive quantity; but there is no such quantity in the angels, for theirs is a virtual one. Consequently, an angel is said to be in a corporeal place by application of the angelic power in any manner whatever to any place.

Accordingly, there is no need for saying that an angel can be deemed commensurate with a place, or that he occupies a space in the continuous; for this is proper to a located body which is endowed with dimensive quantity. In similar fashion it is not necessary on this account for the angel to be contained by a place; because an incorporeal substance virtually contains the thing with which it comes into contact, and is not contained by it: for the soul is in the body as containing it, not as contained by it. In the same way an angel is said to be in a place which is corporeal, not as the thing contained, but as somehow containing it.

And hereby we have the answers to the objections.

Article 2. Whether an angel can be in several places at once?

Objection 1. It would seem that an angel can be in several places at once. For an angel is not less endowed with power than the soul. But the soul is in several places at once, for it is entirely in every part of the body, as Augustine says (De Trin. vi). Therefore, an angel can be in several places at once.

Objection 2. Further, an angel is in the body which he assumes; and, since the body which he assumes is continuous, it would appear that he is in every part thereof. But according to the various parts there are various places. Therefore, the angel is at one time in various places.

Objection 3. Further, Damascene says (De Fide Orth. ii) that "where the angel operates, there he is." But occasionally he operates in several places at one time, as is evident from the angel destroying Sodom (Genesis 19:25). Therefore, an angel can be in several places at the one time.

On the contrary, Damascene says (De Fide Orth. ii) that "while the angels are in heaven, they are not on earth."

I answer that, An angel's power and nature are finite, whereas the Divine power and essence, which is the universal cause of all things, is infinite: consequently, God through His power touches all things, and is not merely present in some places, but is everywhere. Now since the angel's power is finite, it does not extend to all things, but to one determined thing. For whatever is compared with one power must be compared therewith as one determined thing. Consequently, since all being is compared as one thing to God's universal power, so is one particular being compared as one with the angelic power. Hence, since the angel is in a place by the application of his power to the place, it follows that he is not everywhere, nor in several places, but in only one place.

Some, however, have been deceived in this matter. For some who were unable to go beyond the reach of their imaginations supposed the indivisibility of the angel to be like that of a point; consequently, they thought that an angel could be only in a place which is a point. But they were manifestly deceived, because a point is something indivisible, yet having its situation; whereas the angel is indivisible, and beyond the genus of quantity and situation. Consequently, there is no occasion for determining in his regard one indivisible place as to situation: any place which is either divisible or indivisible, great or small suffices, according as to his own free-will he applies his power to a great or to a small body. So the entire body to which he is applied by his power, corresponds as one place to him.

Neither, if any angel moves the heavens, is it necessary for him to be everywhere. First of all, because his power is applied only to what is first moved by him. Now there is one part of the heavens in which there is movement first of all, namely, the part to the east: hence the Philosopher (Phys. vii, text 84) attributes the power of the heavenly mover to the part which is in the east. Secondly, because philosophers do not hold that one separate substance moves all the spheres immediately. Hence it need not be everywhere.

So, then, it is evident that to be in a place appertains quite differently to a body, to an angel, and to God. For a body is in a place in a circumscribed fashion, since it is measured by the place. An angel, however, is not there in a circumscribed fashion, since he is not measured by the place, but definitively, because he is in a place in such a manner that he is not in another. But God is neither circumscriptively nor definitively there, because He is everywhere.

From this we can easily gather an answer to the objections: because the entire subject to which the angelic power is immediately applied, is reputed as one place, even though it be continuous.

Article 3. Whether several angels can be at the same time in the same place?

Objection 1. It would seem that several angels can be at the same time in the same place. For several bodies cannot be at the same time in the same place, because they fill the place. But the angels do not fill a place, because only a body fills a place, so that it be not empty, as appears from the Philosopher (Phys. iv, text 52,58). Therefore, several angels can be in the one place.

Objection 2. Further, there is a greater difference between an angel and a body than there is between two angels. But an angel and a body are at the one time in the one place: because there is no place which is not filled with a sensible body, as we find proved in Phys. iv, text. 58. Much more, then, can two angels be in the same place.

Objection 3. Further, the soul is in every part of the body, according to Augustine (De Trin. vi). But demons, although they do not obsess souls, do obsess bodies occasionally; and thus the soul and the demon are at the one time in the same place; and consequently for the same reason all other spiritual substances.

On the contrary, there are not two souls in the same body. Therefore, for a like reason there are not two angels in the same place.

I answer that, there are not two angels in the same place. The reason of this is because it is impossible for two complete causes to be the causes immediately of one and the same thing. This is evident in every class of causes: for there is one proximate form of one thing, and there is one proximate mover, although there may be several remote movers. Nor can it be objected that several individuals may row a boat, since no one of them is a perfect mover, because no one man's strength is sufficient for moving the boat; while all together are as one mover, in so far as their united strengths all combine in producing the one movement. Hence, since the angel is said to be in one place by the fact that his power touches the place immediately by way of a perfect container, as was said (Article 1), there can be but one angel in one place.

Reply to Objection 1. Several angels are not hindered from being in the same place because of their filling the place; but for another reason, as has been said.

Reply to Objection 2. An angel and a body are not in a place in the same way; hence the conclusion does not follow.

Reply to Objection 3. Not even a demon and a soul are compared to a body according to the same relation of causality; since the soul is its form, while the demon is not. Hence the inference does not follow.

Source: *The Summa Theologiae of St. Thomas Aquinas*, 2nd and revised ed., 1920, First Part, Question 52. Literally translated by the Fathers of the English Dominican Province. *Nihil Obstat*. F. Innocentius Apap, O.P., S.T.M., Censor. Theol. Imprimatur: Edus. Canonicus Surmont, Vicarius Generalis. Westmonasterii. Available at http://www.newadvent.org/summa/1052.htm#article1.

What Really Happened

The medieval era, famously labeled "The Age of Faith" by philosopher Will Durant, was not so faithful after all. In fact, there was a fair bit of paganism going on. Despite Emperor Theodosius's legislation in 395 that made paganism illegal, it persisted. In the 430s, the Christian empire introduced the death penalty for those who made "sacrifice to demons." Paganism continued in Italy, under the nose of various popes, well into the sixth century. Even governors and nobility succumbed to the pull of the old Roman religions. Relapses were common, illustrating the tenuous hold of Christianity (Geffcken 1978, 224).

In Spain, some clergy—even bishops—were still consulting magicians into the seventh century. A missionary sermon from 572 shows the people still celebrating pagan feast days and festivals. Christian women were given in marriage to pagan priests, and Christians commonly lapsed back to the religions of old. In France, the old deities of Luna, Diana, Sol, Hercules, and Neptune continued on well into the sixth century. In Turkey, during the year 532, we find "many thousands" of pagans being converted to Christianity from their "cult of demons and the worship of idols." A church synod in 692 addressed the problem of people celebrating Dionysius—the Greek god of fertility. The Greek historian Zosimus, one of our most important sources for the early sixth century, was staunchly opposed to the Christianization of society, as he blamed Christianity for the decline of Rome. Zosimus himself was a pagan. Northern Europeans—in northern Germany and Scandinavia—tended not to become Christian until the tenth or eleventh centuries because they found Christ to be a weak figure, and they found the torment on the cross to be "unintelligible." Christianity seemed like an effeminate religion to them. Those who did convert usually did so at the end of life, and "conversion often did not at all affect the real inner life of either individuals or a community" (Geffcken 1978, 230–234, 308).

It is difficult for twenty-first century people to understand the social context of the medieval world. Philip Schaff explains it well with typical concision: "'Every man did that which was right in his own eyes.' It was a time of civil and political commotions and upheavings, of domestic wars and foreign invasions. Society was in a chaotic state and bordering on the brink of anarchy. Might was right." Developed understandings of social morality could hardly stabilize in a context so unpredictable. Rulers were extremely corrupt—whether in the church or in secular government. Seemingly endless cycles of murder, adultery, and incest fill the annals of medieval Christendom. There was a "frightful amount of immorality" among the common peasantry (Schaff 1910, 327).

One would expect the clergy at least to shine as sterling examples, but even they were prone to wander. They struggled with drunkenness and sexual temptations. One bishop named Cautinus became so inebriated he had to be carried away from the table by four men. Ample written evidence shows clergy were routinely punished for all manner of "sins and vices." Fornication was a common problem, especially when celibacy became mandatory for clergy in the twelfth century. Many clergymen proved themselves, then as now, unable to keep this extreme vow of chastity, as our reading on Heloise and Abelard will illustrate. Avarice—extreme greed—ran rampant in the ecclesial ranks as clergy often became rich. Theater attendance was supposed to be forbidden for priests, but they couldn't resist (Schaff 1910, 331).

Pope Gregory X declared in 1274 that the clergy was "the ruin of Christendom." By no means did ordination ensure godliness. Indeed, "the nearer we approach Rome, the more numerous the scandals are," one historian wrote. The very term "Romans" became synonymous with "unscrupulous greed" (Schaff 1907, 891).

Sermons from thirteenth-century Italy repeatedly emphasize a trio of sins: lust, pride, and avarice. "Userers" are often singled out for their laser focus on making a profit off others. The problem with usury is that it is rarely outgrown. Many sins, such as adultery and fornication, tend to go away as a person grows in the faith. "Not the userer. Healthy or sick, young or old, he persists in his wickedness. . . . Money becomes the aim of all he does" (Murray 1972, 89–90).

Church attendance in the medieval era was often poor. "Substantial sections of thirteenth-century society hardly attended church at all." Even members of the clergy "never went." Poor people were the least likely to go to church, and as a result they had very little knowledge of the Christian faith. Sermons from the era show that people would go "ten or twenty years" without making a confession to a priest. The "neglect of sacraments" was rife. Gluttony and lust were regular sermon fare. Some members of medieval society didn't even believe in Christ's resurrection, some denied the afterlife, while others doubted the idea of transubstantiation. Skepticism was as common then as now (Murray 1972, 92–94).

Sermons from thirteenth-century Italy acknowledge "a general prevalence of sin" and a correspondingly low level of religious observance. Some of the blame in the late medieval era could be placed on the disastrous crusades. The men were often gone, and families suffered as a result.

But the crusading era also represents a time when some people in society were moving upward and experiencing economic success. War often boosts economies, and economic advancement can be enticing. But the end result during that abysmal era was that Christian conviction suffered, as the average person questioned how Islam could prove so resilient to Christian crusaders if God was on the side of the Christians. More on that in the next chapter (Murray 1972, 103–106).

By the end of the medieval era, coinciding with the time of Martin Luther in the later fifteenth and early sixteenth centuries, church life in Western Europe was bleak indeed. Pastors complained that parishioners were far more inclined to go fishing than to attend church. Parents refused to send their children to catechism because of the fees. "Blasphemy, fornication, adultery, drunkenness and gambling abounded" writes one scholar of the era. "Churches are half empty while taverns are full." Pastors complained that on many occasions not one soul showed up to hear their sermon. Children failed their catechism exams when they took them and were accused of being raised "like the dumb beasts of the field, without an inkling of the word of God." Oddly, men are reported as getting drunk on brandy and singing indecent songs just outside the church building during services, and some of them were wife-beaters. Parishioners involved themselves in sorcery. One sixteenth-century pastor wrote that his people could not cite one scripture in the Bible, and "few of them can pray." Then, to drive home the point, he argued that this is not limited to a few . . . "many of them are like this!" (Strauss 1975, 49–51)

Historian Keith Thomas provides an equally dreadful picture of English Christianity in the early sixteenth century. During services, people "hawked and spit," while many of them knitted, told jokes, and even accidentally shot their guns that they brought into the church with them. Many just slept. Church attendees would sometimes holler back to the priest during a sermon with ridiculous questions. One preacher mentioned that Adam and Eve made themselves garments of fig leaves. One loud-mouthed parishioner shouted, "Where did they get the thread to sew them together?" During a service in Cambridge in 1589, a man continued to fart so loathsomely that he was charged with indecent behavior. In Gloucestershire, after catechism class, a gang of boys got drunk and wrote a bawdy, sacrilegious catechism of their own. Indeed, the late medieval age was "an unregenerate world." The godly were in "a tiny minority." And virtually everyone around them seemed to have no interest in religion whatsoever (Thomas 1971, 161–162).

PRIMARY DOCUMENTS

HELOISE TO ABELARD, *LETTER 4*

The love story of Heloise and Abelard is one of the most entertaining yet conflicting stories of the medieval era. They lived in twelfth-century France. Abelard was one of the most important and esteemed academicians of his age. He is still studied in theological programs. Heloise was his brilliant student whom he fell madly in love with. Their illicit affair produced a child, and that's where things began to go badly for the both of them. Heloise's uncle found out about their relationship and with a group of men castrated Abelard as an act of revenge. Their story illustrates so many aspects of the medieval world, and their letters of confession—of their sin—are fraught with ambivalence. They treasured the pleasures they shared, but as public religious figures, they were both deeply conflicted about it. Upon learning of Heloise's pregnancy, Abelard did the responsible thing and they married privately in Paris, but after the brutal castration they lived separate lives and corresponded only through letters. This letter illustrates the impressive intellectual capabilities of Heloise, but also shows her deep ambivalence about the entire ordeal, which, she felt, was almost too painful to have to bear for the rest of her life.

Dear *Abelard*, pity my despair! Was ever anything so miserable! The higher you raised me above other women who envied me your love, the more sensible am I now of the loss of your heart. I was exalted to the top of happiness, only that I might have a more terrible fall. Nothing could formerly be compared to my pleasures, and nothing now can equal my misery. My glory once raised the envy of my rivals; my present wretchedness moves the compassion of all that see me. My fortune has been always in extremes, she has heaped on me her most delightful favors, that she might load me with the greatest of her afflictions. Ingenious in tormenting me, she has made the memory of the joys I have lost, an inexhaustible spring of my tears. Love, which possessed was her greatest gift, being taken away, occasions all my sorrow. In short, her malice has entirely succeeded, and I find my present afflictions proportionately bitter as the transports which charmed me were sweet.

But what aggravates my sufferings yet more, is, that we began to be miserable at a time when we seemed the least to deserve it. While we gave ourselves up to the enjoyment of a criminal love, nothing opposed our vicious pleasures. But scarce had we retrenched what was unlawful in our passion, and taken refuge in marriage against that remorse which might have pursued us, but the whole wrath of heaven fell on us in all its weight. But how barbarous was your punishment? The very remembrance makes me shake with horror. Could an outrageous husband make a villain suffer more that had dishonored his bed? Ah! What right had a cruel uncle over us? We were joined to each other even before the altar, which should have protected you from the rage of your enemies. Must a wife draw on you that punishment which ought not to fall on any but an adulterous lover?

Besides, we were separated; you were busy in your exercises, and instructed a learned auditory in mysteries which the greatest geniuses before you were not able to penetrate; and I, in obedience to you, retired to a cloister. I there spent whole days in thinking of you, and sometimes meditating on holy lessons, to which I endeavored to apply myself. In this very juncture you became the victim of the most unhappy love. You alone expiated the crime common to us both: You only were punished, though both of us were guilty. You, who were least so, was the object of the whole vengeance of a barbarous man. But why should I rave at your assassins? I, wretched I, have ruined you, I have been the original of all your misfortunes! Good Heaven! Why was I born to be the occasion of so tragical an accident? How dangerous is it for a great man to suffer himself to be moved by our sex!. . .

If I have committed a crime in having loved you with constancy, I shall never be able to repent of that crime. Indeed, I gave myself up too much to the captivity of those soft errors into which my rising passion seduced me. I have endeavored to please you even at the expense of my virtue, and therefore deserve those pains I feel. My guilty transports could not but have a tragical end. As soon as I was persuaded of your love, alas! I scarce delayed a moment, resigning myself to all your protestations. To be beloved by *Abelard* was, in my esteem, too much glory, and I too impatiently desired it not to believe it immediately. I endeavored at nothing but convincing you of my utmost passion. I made no use of those defenses of disdain and honor; those enemies of pleasure which tyrannize over our sex, made in me but a weak and unprofitable resistance. I sacrificed all to my love, and I forced my duty to give place to the ambition of making happy the most gallant and learned person of the age. If any consideration had been able to stop me, it would have been without doubt the interest of my love. I feared, lest having nothing further for you to desire, your passion might become languid, and you might seek for new pleasures in some new conquest. But it was easy for you to cure me of a suspicion so opposite to my own inclination. I ought to have foreseen other more certain evils, and to have considered, that the idea of lost enjoyments would be the trouble of my whole life.

How happy should I be could I wash out with my tears the memory of those pleasures which yet I think of with delight? At least I will exert some generous endeavor, and, by smothering in my heart those desires to which the frailty of my nature may give birth, I will exercise torments upon myself, like those the rage of your enemies has made you suffer. I will endeavor by that means to satisfy you at least, if I cannot appease an angry God. For, to show you what a deplorable condition I am in, and how far my repentance is from being available, I dare even accuse Heaven every moment of cruelty for delivering you into those snares which were prepared for you. . . .

During the still night, when my heart ought to be in quiet in the midst of sleep, which suspends the greatest disturbances, I cannot avoid those illusions my heart entertains. I think I am still with my dear *Abelard*. I see him, I speak to him, and hear him answer. Charmed with each other, we quit our philosophic studies to entertain ourselves with our passion. Sometimes, too, I seem to be a witness of the bloody enterprise of your enemies; I oppose their fury; I fill our apartment with fearful cries, and in a moment I wake in tears. Even in holy places before the altar I carry with me the memory of our guilty loves. They are my whole business, and, far from lamenting for having been seduced, I sigh for having lost them.

I remember (for nothing is forgot by lovers) the time and place in which you first declared your love to me, and swore you would love me till death. Your words, your oaths, are all deeply graven in my heart. The disorder of my discourse discovers to everyone the trouble of my mind. My sighs betray me; and your name is continually in my mouth. When I am in this condition, why dost not thou, O Lord, pity my weakness, and strengthen me by thy grace?

You are happy, *Abelard*; this grace has prevented you; and your misfortune has been the occasion of your finding rest. The punishment of your body has cured the deadly wounds of your soul. The tempest has driven you into the haven. God who seemed to lay his hand heavily upon you, fought only to help you: he is a father chastising, and not an enemy revenging; a wife physician, putting you to some pain in order to preserve your life. I am a thousand times more to be lamented than you; I have a thousand passions to combat with. I must resist those fires which Jove kindles in a young heart. Our sex is nothing but weakness, and I have the greater difficulty to defend myself, because the enemy that attacks me pleases. I dote on the danger which threatens me, how then can I avoid falling?. . .

Happy enough, if I can escape shipwreck, and at last gain the port. Heaven commands me to renounce that fatal passion which unites me to you; but oh! my heart will never be able to consent to it. Adieu.

Source: Heloise, *Letters of Abelard and Heloise* (London: for W. Osborne, and T. Griffin, 1782). Available at https://www.gutenberg.org/files/35977/35977-h/35977-h.htm.

MARTIN LUTHER'S PREFACE TO THE *SMALL CATECHISM* (1529)

Martin Luther (1483–1546) revolutionized the Christian faith perhaps more than anyone in history. His reforms directly led to the Protestant Reformation which is usually given the date of 1517 as its origins—when Luther nailed the 95 Theses to the Castle Church door in Wittenberg, Germany. This reading is the preface to Luther's famous Small Catechism. *It explains why Luther felt he needed a catechism—which is essentially a summary of the Christian faith used for new converts or people intending to start their faith journey. What spawned the writing of this catechism was Luther's tour of parishes in Germany, which he found to be woefully lacking in Christian principle and in knowledge of the faith. Luther was actually surprised as to how "deplorable" and "wretched" was the state of Christianity in his homeland. In Luther's deliciously lively writing style, he explains in vivid terms that the people "live like dumb brutes and irrational hogs." He criticizes the bishops for "shameful neglect" and then lays out precisely what he felt people needed to be taught in order to come to a real knowledge of the religion of Jesus Christ. Luther exalts in the fact that "the tyranny of the Pope has been abolished," but he realizes that for some people this meant they no longer had to practice their faith. Luther's* Small Catechism *is meant to be a corrective.*

Martin Luther to All Faithful and Godly Pastors and Preachers:

Grace, Mercy, and Peace in Jesus Christ, our Lord.

The deplorable, miserable condition which I discovered lately when I, too, was a visitor, has forced and urged me to prepare [publish] this Catechism, or Christian doctrine, in this small, plain, simple form. Mercy! Good God! what manifold misery I beheld! The common people, especially in the villages, have no knowledge whatever of Christian doctrine, and, alas!

many pastors are altogether incapable and incompetent to teach [so much so, that one is ashamed to speak of it]. Nevertheless, all maintain that they are Christians, have been baptized and receive the [common] holy Sacraments. Yet they [*do not* understand and] cannot [*even*] recite either the Lord's Prayer, or the Creed, or the Ten Commandments; they live like dumb brutes and irrational hogs; and yet, now that the Gospel has come, they have nicely learned to abuse all liberty like experts.

O ye bishops! [to whom this charge has been committed by God,] what will ye ever answer to Christ for having so shamefully neglected the people and never for a moment discharged your office? [You are the persons to whom alone this ruin of the Christian religion is due. You have permitted men to err so shamefully; yours is the guilt; for you have ever done anything rather than what your office required you to do.] May all misfortune flee you! [I do not wish at this place to invoke evil on your heads.] You command the Sacrament in one form [but is not this the highest ungodliness coupled with the greatest impudence that you are insisting on the administration of the Sacrament in one form only, and on your traditions] and insist on your human laws, and yet at the same time you do not care in the least [while you are utterly without scruple and concern] whether the people know the Lord's Prayer, the Creed, the Ten Commandments, or any part of the Word of God. Woe, woe, unto you forever!

Therefore, I entreat [and adjure] you all for God's sake, my dear sirs and brethren, who are pastors or preachers, to devote yourselves heartily to your office, to have pity on the people who are entrusted to you, and to help us inculcate the Catechism upon the people, and especially upon the young. And let those of you who cannot do better [If any of you are so unskilled that you have absolutely no knowledge of these matters, let them not be ashamed to] take these tables and forms and impress them, word for word, on the people, as follows:

In the first place, let the preacher above all be careful to avoid many kinds of or various texts and forms of the Ten Commandments, the Lord's Prayer, the Creed, the Sacraments, etc., but choose one form to which he adheres, and which he inculcates all the time, year after year. For [I give this advice, however, because I know that] young and simple people must be taught by uniform, settled texts and forms, otherwise they easily become confused when the teacher to-day teaches them thus, and in a year some other way, as if he wished to make improvements, and thus all effort and labor [which has been expended in teaching] is lost.

Also our blessed fathers understood this well; for they all used the same form of the Lord's Prayer, the Creed, and the Ten Commandments.

Therefore, we, too, should [imitate their diligence and be at pains to] teach the young and simple people these parts in such a way as not to change a syllable, or set them forth and repeat them one year differently than in another [no matter how often we teach the Catechism].

Hence, choose whatever form you please, and adhere to it forever. But when you preach in the presence of learned and intelligent men, you may exhibit your skill, and may present these parts in as varied and intricate ways and give them as masterly turns as you are able. But with the young people stick to one fixed, permanent form and manner, and teach them, first of all, these parts, namely, the Ten Commandments, the Creed, the Lord's Prayer, etc., according to the text, word for word, so that they, too, can repeat it in the same manner after you and commit it to memory.

But those who are unwilling to learn it should be told that they deny Christ and are no Christians, neither should they be admitted to the Sacrament, accepted as sponsors at baptism, nor exercise any part of Christian liberty, but should simply be turned back to the Pope and his officials, yea, to the devil himself. Moreover, their parents and employers should refuse them food and drink, and [they would also do well if they were to] notify them that the prince will drive such rude people from the country, etc.

For although we cannot and should not force any one to believe, yet we should insist and urge the people that they know what is right and wrong with those among whom they dwell and wish to make their living. For whoever desires to reside in a town must know and observe the town laws, the protection of which he wishes to enjoy, no matter whether he is a believer or at heart and in private a rogue or knave.

In the second place, after they have well learned the text, then teach them the sense also, so that they know what it means, and again choose the form of these tables, or some other brief uniform method, whichever you like, and adhere to it, and do not change a single syllable, as was just said regarding the text; and take your time to it. For it is not necessary that you take up all the parts at once, but one after the other. After they understand the First Commandment well, then take up the Second, and so on, otherwise they will be overwhelmed, so as not to be able to retain any well.

In the third place, after you have thus taught them this Short Catechism, then take up the Large Catechism, and give them also a richer and fuller knowledge. Here explain at large every commandment, [article,] petition, and part with its various works, uses, benefits, dangers, and injuries, as you find these abundantly stated in many books written about these matters. And particularly, urge that commandment or part most which suffers the greatest neglect among your people. For instance, the

Seventh Commandment, concerning stealing, must be strenuously urged among mechanics and merchants, and even farmers and servants, for among these people many kinds of dishonesty and thieving prevail. So, too, you must urge well the Fourth Commandment among the children and the common people, that they may be quiet and faithful, obedient and peaceable, and you must always adduce many examples from the Scriptures to show how God has punished or blessed such persons.

Especially should you here urge magistrates and parents to rule well and to send their children to school, showing them why it is their duty to do this, and what a damnable sin they are committing if they do not do it. For by such neglect they overthrow and destroy both the kingdom of God and that of the world, acting as the worst enemies both of God and of men. And make it very plain to them what an awful harm they are doing if they will not help to train children to be pastors, preachers, clerks [also for other offices, with which we cannot dispense in this life], etc., and that God will punish them terribly for it. For such preaching is needed. [Verily, I do not know of any other topic that deserves to be treated as much as this.] Parents and magistrates are now sinning unspeakably in this respect. The devil, too, aims at something cruel because of these things [that he may hurl Germany into the greatest distress].

Lastly, since the tyranny of the Pope has been abolished, people are no longer willing to go to the Sacrament and despise it [as something useless and unnecessary]. Here again urging is necessary, however, with this understanding: We are to force no one to believe, or to receive the Sacrament, nor fix any law, nor time, nor place for it, but are to preach in such a manner that of their own accord, without our law, they will urge themselves and, as it were, compel us pastors to administer the Sacrament. This is done by telling them: Whoever does not seek or desire the Sacrament at least some four times a year, it is to be feared that he despises the Sacrament and is no Christian, just as he is no Christian who does not believe or hear the Gospel; for Christ did not say, This omit, or, This despise, but, *This do ye, as oft as ye drink it*, etc. Verily, He wants it done, and not entirely neglected and despised. *This do* ye, He says.

Now, whoever does not highly value the Sacrament thereby shows that he has no sin, no flesh, no devil, no world, no death, no danger, no hell; that is, he does not believe any such things, although he is in them over head and ears and is doubly the devil's own. On the other hand, he needs no grace, life, Paradise, heaven, Christ, God, nor anything good. For if he believed that he had so much that is evil, and needed so much that is good, he would not thus neglect the Sacrament, by which such evil is remedied and so much good is bestowed. Neither will it be necessary to force him to the Sacrament by any law, but he will come running and racing of his own accord, will force himself and urge you that you must give him the Sacrament.

Hence, you must not make any law in this matter, as the Pope does. Only set forth clearly the benefit and harm, the need and use, the danger and the blessing, connected with this Sacrament, and the people will come of themselves without your compulsion. But if they do not come, let them go and tell them that such belong to the devil as do not regard nor feel their great need and the gracious help of God. But if you do not urge this, or make a law or a bane of it, it is your fault if they despise the Sacrament. How could they be otherwise than slothful if you sleep and are silent? Therefore, look to it, ye pastors and preachers. Our office is now become a different thing from what it was under the Pope; it is now become serious and salutary. Accordingly, it now involves much more trouble and labor, danger and trials, and, in addition thereto, little reward and gratitude in the world. But Christ Himself will be our reward if we labor faithfully. To this end may the Father of all grace help us, to whom be praise and thanks forever through Christ, our Lord! Amen.

Source: Martin Luther, *The Small Catechism*, originally published in 1529. This is the 1921 Triglotta version, published at St. Louis: Concordia Publishing House, 1921. Available at http://bookofconcord.org/smallcatechism.php.

Further Reading

Adair, James R. 2008. *Introducing Christianity*. New York: Routledge.

Barnum, Priscilla Heath. 2004. *Dives and Pauper*. Vols. 1–2. Oxford: Oxford University Press.

Bornstein, Daniel E. 2009. *Medieval Christianity*. Minneapolis, MN: Fortress.

Brown, Peter. 1996. *The Rise of Western Christendom: Triumph and Diversity, A.D. 200–1000*. Chichester, UK: John Wiley.

Cantor, Norman F. 1993. *The Civilization of the Middle Ages*. New York: HarperPerennial.

Christian, William A., Jr. 1981. *Apparitions in Late Medieval and Renaissance Spain*. Princeton, NJ: Princeton University Press.

Coulton, C. G. 1938. *Medieval Panorama*. New York: Macmillan.

Daughrity, Dyron B. 2012. *Church History: Five Approaches to a Global Discipline*. New York: Peter Lang.

Deanesley, Margaret. 1925. *A History of the Medieval Church, 590–1500*. London: Routledge.

Durant, Will. 1950. *The Age of Faith*. Vol. 4 of *The Story of Civilization*. New York: Simon and Schuster.

Fletcher, Richard. 1997. *The Barbarian Conversion: From Paganism to Christianity*. New York: Henry Holt.

Freemantle, Anne. 1954. *The Age of Belief*. New York: Mentor.

Fuhrmann, Horst. 1986. *Germany in the High Middle Ages, c. 1050–1200*. Cambridge: Cambridge University Press.

Geffcken, Johannes. 1978. *The Last Days of Greco-Roman Paganism*. Translated by Sabine MacCormack. New York: North-Holland.

Halverson, James L., ed. 2008. *Contesting Christendom: Readings in Medieval Religion and Culture*. New York: Rowman & Littlefield.

Jordan, William Chester. 2009. *A Tale of Two Monasteries: Westminster and Saint-Denis in the Thirteenth Century*. Princeton, NJ: Princeton University Press.

Latourette, Kenneth Scott. 1997. *A History of Christianity*. Vol. 1, *To A.D. 1500*. Peabody, MA: Prince Press. First edition 1953.

Lea, Henry C. 1902. "The Eve of the Reformation." In *The Cambridge Modern History*, edited by Lord Acton, Stanley Mordaunt Leathes, Sir Adolphus William Ward, and G. W. Prothero, 1:653–692. Cambridge: Cambridge University Press.

Levack, Brian P. 2016. *The Witch-Hunt in Early Modern Europe*. 4th ed. London: Routledge.

Logan, F. Donald. 2013. *A History of the Church in the Middle Ages*. 2nd ed. London: Routledge.

Madigan, Kevin. 2015. *Medieval Christianity: A New History*. New Haven, CT: Yale University Press.

Manchester, William. 1992. *A World Lit Only by Fire*. New York: Little, Brown.

McClure, Judith, and Roger Collins, eds. 1994. *Bede: The Ecclesiastical History of the English People, The Greater Chronicle, Bede's Letter to Egbert*. Oxford: Oxford University Press.

McManners, John. 1990. *The Oxford Illustrated History of Christianity*. Oxford: Oxford University Press.

Mommsen, Theodore E. 1942. "Petrarch's Conception of the 'Dark Ages.'" *Speculum* 17:2 (April): 226–242.

Murray, Alexander. 1972. "Piety and Impiety in Thirteenth-Century Italy." *Studies in Church History* 8: 83–106.

Nichols, Francis Morgan. 1904. *The Epistles of Erasmus*. Vols. 1–2. New York: Longmans, Green.

Ozment, Steven. 1980. *The, Age of Reform, 1250–1550*. New Haven, CT: Yale University Press.

Parker, Geoffrey. 1992. "Success and Failure during the First Century of the Reformation." *Past and Present* 136: 43–82.

Pastor, Ludwig. 1898. *The History of the Popes*. Vol. 5. St. Louis: B. Herder.

Rubin, Miri. 2014. *The Middle Ages: A Very Short Introduction*. Oxford: Oxford University Press.

Schaff, Philip. (1907) 1984. *History of the Christian Church*. Vol. 5, *The Middle Ages*. Grand Rapids, MI: Eerdmans.

Schaff, Philip. 1910. *History of the Christian Church*. Vol. 4, *Mediaeval Christianity*. Grand Rapids: Eerdmans.

Southern, R. W. 1970. *Western Society and the Church in the Middle Ages*. Harmondsworth, UK: Penguin.

Stark, Rodney. 2011. *The Triumph of Christianity*. New York: HarperCollins.

Strauss, Gerald. 1975. "Success and Failure in the German Reformation." *Past and Present* 67: 30–63.

Strauss, Gerald. 1978. *Luther's House of Learning: Indoctrination of the Young in the German Reformation*. Baltimore: Johns Hopkins University Press.

Strauss, Gerald. 1988. "The Reformation and Its Public in an Age of Orthodoxy." In *The German People and the Reformation*, edited by R. Po-Chia Hsia, 194–214. Ithaca, NY: Cornell University Press.

Swanson, R. N. 1995. *Religion and Devotion in Europe, c. 1215–c. 1515*. Cambridge: Cambridge University Press.

Thomas, Keith. 1971. *Religion and the Decline of Magic*. New York: Scribner.

Walzer, Michael. 1965. *The Revolution of the Saints*. Cambridge, MA: Harvard University Press.

6

The Crusades Were a Series of Brutal, Unprovoked Attacks

What People Think Happened

It is common to hear people speak of the crusades—which took place between 1099 and 1204—as one of the worst tragedies in the history of Christianity. For many it represents the very worst that the Christian faith has to offer, up there with the Inquisition, the period of Western slavery, and even genocide.

The crusades have been thoroughly renounced today, and the renunciation continues unabated on a popular level. Their legacy is often cited as the nadir of medieval Christendom, a useful event to illustrate just how awful and corrupt Christianity became in the medieval era. For example, *New York Times* op-ed columnist Maureen Dowd once wrote, "History teaches that when religion is injected into politics—the Crusades, Henry VIII, Salem, Father Coughlin, Hitler, Kosovo—disaster follows."

Routine and trenchant criticism of the crusades is even a cause célèbre for many committed Christians in recent times. In the late 1990s, an interdenominational "Reconciliation Walk" was organized that paraded through many Western European and Middle Eastern nations. Participants openly condemned the damage caused by the crusades all along the way. Events were designed by Christians as a "serious effort to repair this damage" stemming from the crusades. From 1996 to 1999, around 2,500 Christian walkers, often wearing T-shirts and caps with the words

"I apologize" written in Arabic or Hebrew, made their away into cities and towns with a message of reconciliation (Robinson [1996] 2005).

The walk culminated in Jerusalem in July 1999, in memory of the 900th anniversary of the Christian defeat of Muslim armies in that city. However, this was no triumphal celebration. It was undoubtedly a somber occasion, a moment of profound regret. The statement of apology read: "Nine hundred years ago, our forefathers carried the name of Jesus Christ in battle across the Middle East. Fueled by fear, greed and hatred, they betrayed the name of Christ by conducting themselves in a manner contrary to His wishes and character. The Crusaders lifted the banner of the Cross above your people. By this act they corrupted its true meaning of reconciliation, forgiveness and selfless love" (Robinson [1996] 2005).

Former president Bill Clinton weighed in on the crusades in the aftermath of the events of September 11, 2001, while giving a speech at Georgetown University. He offered these comments to the students: "Those of us who come from various European lineages are not blameless. Indeed, in the First Crusade, when the Christian soldiers took Jerusalem, they first burned a synagogue with three hundred Jews in it, and proceeded to kill every woman and child who was Muslim on the Temple Mount . . . with blood running up to their knees. . . . I can tell you that that story is still being told today in the Middle East, and we are still paying for it" (Madden 2009, 1).

Another former president, Barack Obama, offered similar sentiments about the crusades during the 2015 National Prayer Breakfast. While addressing the threat of the Islamic State, he argued that "humanity has been grappling with" tensions among religions for centuries. And then he said something that immediately had media outlets spinning, "And lest we get on our high horse and think this [religious violence] is unique to some other place, remember that during the Crusades and the Inquisition, people committed terrible deeds in the name of Christ" (Jaffe 2015).

The crusades are misunderstood for a variety of reasons: they occurred a thousand years ago, few professors today are specialists in medieval Christianity, and they represent a time when Christianity was understood so differently than it is today. Nevertheless, the misunderstanding of this particular era in the Christian faith is conspicuous and pronounced, largely because it is built on assumptions that have been shaped in a context that abhors the idea of Christians voluntarily killing others in the context of holy war. People in the Western world today, in a postcolonial context, have little appetite for a kind of Christianity that was inextricably tied to the state. In the medieval era, there was hardly a war that was not a holy war on some level, due to the ubiquity of religion throughout the society and, therefore, its political institutions. That kind of Christianity is repulsive to many.

Thus, today, the crusades are associated with overzealousness, with a worldview in which there was no separation between church and state, and with violence. And while all three of these charges are true in some respects, they fail to include the broader context.

How the Story Became Popular

The historiography of the crusades is actually quite well-researched among those few scholars who specialize in this area, and what emerges is a fascinating story of how civilization can dramatically change its perspective on a person or event in history. During the era of the crusades, Western Europeans tended to write about them in a "triumphalistic" way. However, by the end of the eighteenth century, that interpretation had completely changed to one of "skepticism and sharp criticism" (Peters 2004, 6).

Muslim historians did not pay much attention to the crusades while they were happening. They occurred in "a politically and economically marginal area" that attracted little attention. At the time, Muslims regarded the crusaders as "primitive, unlearned, impoverished, and non-Muslim people." Muslim scholars "knew and cared little" for these Western warriors. Their view of the crusaders could be summarized with one word: indifference. Indeed, Arab chroniclers had no word for "crusades" until the mid-nineteenth century, when they began using the expression "wars of the cross" (*al-hurub al-salibiyya*) (Peters 2004, 6–7).

The Ottoman Turks did write some on the crusades, but by far the dominant concern of their historians during the thirteenth century was the Mongol conquests. Interest in the crusades did not resurface in any significant way in the Muslim world until the mid-nineteenth century, when French histories of the crusades began to be translated into Arabic and Turkish by Europeans. This period "marks the beginning of European revisionist historiography on the Crusades." In the eighteenth and nineteenth centuries, some of Europe's most prolific historians turned their attention to the crusades. In the eighteenth century, Voltaire, Hume, Diderot, and Gibbon dominated European historiography and tended to characterize the crusades as a papist concern to invigorate the finances of the Roman Catholic Church (Peters 2004, 7). Safe to say, their understanding of the crusades was openly critical and terribly biased—against the church.

These so-called Enlightenment historians were deeply impacted by Protestant antipathy toward the Catholic Church, as well as French thinkers who would lead the way toward overthrowing the power of Rome in the French nation. Thus, they painted a picture of Roman Catholic corruption and greed as being the chief motivators for the crusades. In their view, the crusades were all about expanding territory and gaining wealth, and had little to do with religious motives.

Between 1812 and 1817, French historian Joseph François Michaud (1767–1839) published his monumental, three-volume *Histoire des croisades* which was revised and expanded to six volumes in 1841. It was the standard history of the crusades throughout the duration of the nineteenth century. Considered a titanic achievement, the author maintained a balanced approach that neither defamed Muslims nor heralded Christians. Michaud's work was a masterpiece and set the stage for several decades of scientific research on the crusading era. His publications and collected materials were vital for preserving sources in various languages such as Armenian, Greek, and Arabic. In Germany, Friedrich Wilken's seven-volume history of the crusades appeared between 1807 and 1832. In England, it was Charles Mills who published two volumes on the crusades in 1820. Both Wilken and Mills did much to popularize crusader history in their own languages, but it was the Frenchman Michaud who set the bar and touched off a renewed interest in the crusading era in Christian history (Peters 2004, 8–9).

Another of the fundamental reasons that there was a resurgence in crusader history goes back to the year 1453—the Fall of Constantinople to the Ottoman Turks. When Muslim armies took the great city of Christendom, the Western empire became flooded with Christians who had moved west to escape Islamic rule. That influx of people brought knowledge, awareness, and resources that had not been available in the Latin world before. This migration from east to west also led to a renewed emphasis on sources, as scholars were excited to compare Western texts with their Eastern counterparts.

One prominent scholar during this era who turned his considerable gifts toward understanding the crusades was the famous English intellectual Francis Bacon (1561–1626). He investigated the crusades carefully and came to the perhaps predictable conclusion—being a devout Anglican in an era of extreme Protestant-Catholic strife—that the popes who launched the crusades were blinded by "lust for terrestrial power." They were full of greed, deceiving the "honest and pious crusaders" by making them think their cause was holy (Theron and Oliver 2018, 4).

In the seventeenth century, historians were able to detach their history from the impending threat of Islam, as the Ottoman Empire has ceased to expand into Europe. This created a climate of more academic distance and measured judgment. The chief historians of the crusades in that century were Jacques Bongars and Thomas Fuller. Bongars took a balanced approach that reasoned the crusades brought national unity but were a moral failure. His book impacted Edward Gibbon's views deeply. Fuller concluded that Islam was "a senseless religion" and the crusades were "a wasteful enterprise." Fuller blamed the papacy for being arrogant during the crusading era, and the popes were guilty for "spilling blood unnecessarily" (Theron and Oliver 2018, 4).

The eighteenth century saw a turning of the tables, as the Christian West was rising to global dominance, and the Ottoman Empire was visibly weakening. It was during this era that the crusades were roundly criticized in virtually every way. The leading intellectual figures of the day were Voltaire and Edward Gibbon. It probably doesn't need to be pointed out that neither of these towering individuals had any regard for religion or for the medieval era in general. For them, the classical world of Greece and Rome had unfortunately given way to the "ignorance, superstition, and fanaticism" of Christendom. It was an extremely lamentable and dark era when Christianity rose to such prominence in the former, illustrious, Roman Empire. Gibbon considered the crusades to be the prime example of the "grossest barbarism." Voltaire, too, considered the crusades to be completely "wasteful and pointless." The thousands of men who went on crusade were nothing but "a band of corrupt and ignorant criminals" who had been deceived into thinking that they would go to heaven if they died while on their mission (Theron and Oliver 2018, 5).

Other notable figures of the eighteenth century took very similar interpretations of the crusades. David Hume believed the crusades to be "the most signal and most durable monument of human folly that has yet appeared in any age or nation." Denis Diderot regarded the crusades a completely worthless cause for a completely worthless place, meaning Jerusalem. And while Jean-Jacques Rousseau was probably a Christian, he was a constant critic of the church in his day, regarding the crusades as thoroughly pagan, since "the Gospel sets up no national religion, a holy war is impossible among Christians" (Theron and Oliver 2018, 5).

Interestingly, during the nineteenth century, there was a sea-change in European perspectives on the crusades. These new views were tied to European conquests, as soldiers traveled to the Holy Land, to Asia, Oceania, and Africa in order to colonize, Christianize, and civilize the peoples of those lands. Thus, for a time, crusading "became popularly admired," as soldiers were fighting for a noble cause. Several writers during the nineteenth century, such as Joseph François Michaud, Friedrich Wilken, Charles Mills, and the novelist Sir Walter Scott considered the crusading era to be a heroic one and the crusaders to be archetypal colonialists. Thus, as their countries expanded into new regions of the world, focused on civilizing them, a great wave of empathy toward the crusaders rose up, even in the best scholarship of the day (Tyerman 1998, 117).

Twentieth-century historiography on the crusades was dominated by the English historian Sir Steven Runciman. His three-volume history of the crusades, published in the 1950s, has yet to be surpassed and still receives the greatest admiration from crusader historians. Tyerman called Runciman's history "the last chronicle of the crusades." He praised Runciman's style and lasting influence with these words: "Runciman's three volumes represent the most astonishing literary phenomenon in crusade historiography since Michaud. Almost sixty years after the publication of the first volume, in educated circles in Britain, if anyone talks about the crusades 'Runciman' is almost certain to be invoked. Across the Anglophone world he continues as a base reference for popular attitudes, evident in print, film, television and on the internet" (Tyerman 2011, 196, 192–193).

Runciman considered the crusades a huge mistake, not so much because of its impact on Islam but because of its egregious and unjustified conquering of Constantinople—the capital of the Byzantine (Christian) Empire—in 1204, the year of the Fourth Crusade. Runciman wrote, "There was never a greater crime against humanity than the Fourth Crusade." His argument was that instead of helping the Byzantines win the war with Islam by taking Constantinople, the Latin crusaders crippled New Rome forever. It signaled the rise of Moscow—the Third Rome—to take its prestigious place on the stage of Eastern Christendom. Perhaps most unfortunate of all, the Latin destruction of Constantinople gave strength to the Turks. That ill-advised crusade was, all in all, "wholly disastrous." For centuries the Byzantine Empire had been "the guardian of Europe against the infidel East and the barbarian North," but with the conquest of Constantinople by the Roman Catholics that defense was forever punctured. Not only did the Turks take advantage of the situation and slowly turn Byzantium into the Ottoman Empire but also there was a theological problem that unfolded and left the Christian world in a state of fracture. Indeed, after the crusaders conquered Constantinople in 1204, the schism between the Latin West and the Greek East was now "complete, irremediable, and final" (Runciman 1966, 130–131).

PRIMARY DOCUMENTS

DAVID HUME ON THE CRUSADES

David Hume (1711–1776) was a Scottish intellectual who exerted profound influence over the English world in the eighteenth century. He is known today mainly as a philosopher, but during his era he was also considered an authoritative historian. In this reading, from Hume's History of England, *he betrays a snide view toward the crusades and indeed toward religion in general. He believed the crusaders were fanatical, immoral men (as well as some women who disguised themselves in order to accompany the men for improper reasons). Hume's interpretation of the crusades was that these unfortunate soldiers were pawns for the pope's ambition, and the massive flow of people to Jerusalem was a grand and deplorable mistake.*

But the noise of these petty wars and commotions was quite sunk in the tumult of the Crusades, which now engrossed the attention of Europe, and have ever since engaged the curiosity of mankind, as the most signal and most durable monument of human folly, that has yet appeared in any age or nation. After Mahomet had, by means of his pretended revelations, united the dispersed Arabians under one head, they issued forth from their deserts in great multitudes; and being animated with zeal for their new religion, and supported by the vigor of their new government, they made deep impression on the eastern empire, which was far in the decline, with regard both to military discipline and to civil policy. Jerusalem, by its situation, became one of their most early conquests; and the Christians had the mortification to see the holy sepulcher, and the other places, consecrated by the presence of their religious founder, fallen into the possession of infidels.

But the Arabians or Saracens were so employed in military enterprises, by which they spread their empire, in a few years, from the banks of the Ganges, to the Straits of Gibraltar, that they had no leisure for theological controversy: And though the *Quran*, the original monument of their faith, seems to contain some violent precepts, they were much less infected with the spirit of bigotry and persecution than the indolent and speculative Greeks, who were continually refining on the several articles of their religious system. They gave little disturbance to those zealous pilgrims, who daily flocked to Jerusalem; and they allowed every man, after paying a moderate tribute, to visit the holy sepulcher, to perform his religious duties, and to return in peace.

But the Turks, a tribe of Tartars, who had embraced Mahomedanism [Islam], having wrested Syria from the Saracens [Muslims], and having in the year 1065 made themselves masters of Jerusalem, rendered the pilgrimage much more difficult and dangerous to the Christians. The barbarity of their manners, and the confusions attending their unsettled government, exposed the pilgrims to many insults, robberies, and extortions; and these zealots, returning from their meritorious fatigues and sufferings, filled all Christendom with indignation against the infidels, who profaned the holy city by their presence, and derided the sacred mysteries in the very place of their completion. Gregory VII, among the other vast ideas which he entertained, had formed the design of uniting all the western Christians against the Mahometans [Muslims]; but the egregious and violent invasions of that pontiff on the civil power of princes, had created him so many enemies, and had rendered his schemes so suspicious, that he was not able to make great progress in this undertaking. . . .

Men of all ranks flew to arms with the utmost ardor; and an exterior symbol too, a circumstance of chief moment, was here chosen by the devoted combatants. The sign of the cross, which had been hitherto so much revered among Christians, and which, the more it was an object of reproach among the pagan world, was the more passionately cherished by them, became the badge of union, and was affixed to their right shoulder, by all who enlisted themselves in this sacred warfare.

Europe was at this time sunk into profound ignorance and superstition. The ecclesiastics had acquired the greatest ascendant over the human mind. The people, who, being little restrained by honor, and less by law, abandoned themselves to the worst crimes and disorders, knew of no other expiation than the observances imposed on them by their spiritual pastors. And it was easy to represent the holy war as an equivalent for all penances, and an atonement for every violation of justice and humanity. But amidst the abject superstition, which now prevailed, the military spirit also had universally diffused itself; and though not supported by art or discipline, was become the general passion of the nations, governed by the feudal law. All the great lords possessed the right of peace and war: They were engaged in perpetual hostilities with each other. The open country was become a scene of outrage and disorder. The cities, still mean and poor, were neither guarded by walls, nor protected by privileges, and were exposed to every insult. Individuals were obliged to depend for safety on their own force, or their private alliances. And valor was the only excellence, which was held in esteem, or gave one man the preeminence above another. When all the particular superstitions, therefore, were here united in one great object, the ardor for military enterprises took the same direction; and Europe, impelled by its two ruling passions, was loosened, as it were, from its foundations, and seemed to precipitate itself in one united body upon the east.

All orders of men, deeming the crusades the only road to heaven, enlisted themselves under these sacred banners, and were impatient to open the way with their sword to the holy city. Nobles, artisans, peasants, even priests enrolled their names; and to decline this meritorious service was branded with the reproach of impiety, or what perhaps was esteemed still more disgraceful, of cowardice and pusillanimity. The infirm and aged contributed to the expedition by presents and money; and many of them, not satisfied with the merit of this atonement, attended it in person, and were determined, if possible, to breathe their last, in sight of that city where their Savior had died for them.

Women themselves, concealing their sex under the disguise of armor, attended the camp; and commonly forgot still more the duty of their sex, by prostituting themselves, without reserve, to the army. The greatest criminals went forward in a service, which they regarded as a propitiation for all crimes; and the most enormous disorders were, during the course of those expeditions, committed by men, inured to wickedness, encouraged by example, and impelled by necessity.

The multitude of the adventurers soon became so great, that their more sagacious leaders, Hugh count of Vermandois, brother to the French king, Raymond count of Toulouse, Godfrey of Boüillon, prince of Brabant, and Stephen count of Blois, became apprehensive lest the greatness itself of the armament should disappoint its purpose. And they permitted an undisciplined multitude, computed at 300,000 men, to go before them, under the command of Peter the Hermit, and Walter the Moneyless. These men took the road toward Constantinople through Hungary and Bulgaria; and trusting, that Heaven, by supernatural assistance, would supply all their necessities, they made no provision for subsistence on their march. They soon found themselves obliged to obtain by plunder what they had vainly expected from miracles; and the enraged inhabitants of the countries through which they passed, gathering together in arms, attacked the disorderly multitude, and put them to slaughter without resistance. The more disciplined armies followed after; and passing the straits at Constantinople, they were mustered in the plains of Asia, and amounted in the whole to the number of 700,000 combatants.

Amidst this universal frenzy, which spread itself by contagion throughout Europe, especially in France and Germany, men were not entirely forgetful of their present interest; and both those who went on this expedition, and those who stayed behind, entertained schemes of gratifying, by its means, their avarice or their ambition. The nobles who enlisted themselves were moved, from the romantic spirit of the age, to hope for opulent establishments in the east, the chief seat of arts and commerce during those ages; and in pursuit of these chimerical projects, they sold at the lowest price their ancient castles and inheritances, which had now lost all value in their eyes.

The greater princes, who remained at home, besides establishing peace in their dominions by giving occupation abroad to the inquietude and martial disposition of their subjects, took the opportunity of annexing to their crown many considerable fiefs, either by purchase or by the extinction of heirs. The pope frequently turned the zeal of the crusaders from the infidels against his own enemies, whom he represented as equally criminal with the enemies of Christ. The convents and other religious societies bought the possessions of the adventurers; and as the contributions of the faithful were commonly entrusted to their management, they often diverted to this purpose what was intended to be employed against the infidels. But no one was a more immediate gainer by this epidemic fury than the king of England, who kept aloof from all connections with those fanatical and romantic warriors.

Source: David Hume, *The History of England.* Vol. 1 (London: T. Cadell, 1778), 234–240.

VOLTAIRE'S VIEWS ON THE CRUSADES

Voltaire (1694–1778) was one of the most prolific authors of the so-called French "Enlightenment"—although that term is disputed today. He was a trenchant critic of Christianity and the Roman Catholic Church. His view of Christianity was that it was fanatical and ridiculous. Voltaire's view that Christianity was probably what led to the fall of the Roman Empire was an interpretation that the English historian Edward Gibbon embraced with gusto. In this passage, Voltaire's interpretation of the crusaders is clearly biased. In his view the Christians were full of debauchery, they had a "passion for plunder," and they massacred innocent people wherever they went. Voltaire's

*interpretation of Saladin was highly sanitized, and he was one of the Euro-
pean thinkers who had the effect of turning Saladin into something of a chiv-
alrous knight.*

Alexius Comnenus, the Grecian emperor, and father of that princess
who wrote the history of her times, sent ambassadors to this council, to
demand some assistance against the Mussulmen [Muslims]. . . . Another
council was therefore held at Clermont, in Auvergne, where the pope
made a speech in the market place. The Italians had wept over the calam-
ities of the Christians in Asia, but the French took up arms. This country
was peopled by a great number of new lords, who were restless, independent, fond of a life of war and dissipation, for the most part plunged in
crimes that are the natural attendants of debauchery, and in an ignorance
equal to their guilt: but the Pope proposed to grant them the remission
of all their sins, and to open to them the gates of heaven, only imposing
on them as a penance, the gratification of their predominant passion for
plunder. They therefore took up the cross with a spirit of emulation; and
then the churches and cloisters bought at a low rate many of the estates
of their lords, who imagined that a little money and their arms were sufficient to enable them to conquer kingdoms in Asia. . . . Religion, avarice,
and inquietude, equally encouraged these migrations. They enlisted an
infinite number of infantry, and horsemen under a thousand different
banners. This crowd of crusaders appointed their rendezvous at Constantinople: monks, women, merchants, mechanics, all set out, imagining
that they should find none on the road but Christians, who would gain
indulgences by furnishing them with subsistence. Above eighty thousand
of these vagabonds arranged themselves under the standard of . . . Peter
the Hermit, who walked at the head of the army with sandals on his feet,
and a rope tied round his waist. A new species of vanity!
    The first exploit of this hermetic general was his besieging a Christian
city in Hungary called Malavilla, because its inhabitants had refused to furnish with provisions the soldiers of Jesus Christ, who notwithstanding the
sanctity of their enterprise behaved like a band of highway robbers. This
city was taken by storm, given up to be pillaged, and the inhabitants murdered. The hermit was then no longer master of his crusaders, who were
intoxicated with the thirst of plunder. One of Peter's lieutenants, called
Gautier sans Argent, who commanded half his forces, behaved in the same
manner in Bulgaria; but the country uniting to oppose these bandits, the
greatest part of them were cut off, and the hermit at length appeared before
Constantinople with twenty thousand persons dying with hunger.

Another swarm of these adventurers, composed of about two hundred thousand persons, women, priests, scholars, and peasants, imagining that they were going to defend Jesus Christ, thought that they ought to exterminate all the Jews wherever they found them. There were great numbers of these on the frontiers of France, and the trade of the kingdom was all in their hands; these Christians therefore, in order to execute the vengeance of heaven, put all those unhappy persons to the sword: never was there since the time of Adrian, so great a massacre of the people of that nation, who were exterminated at Verdun, Spires, Worms, Cologne, and Mentz; and many killed themselves after having ripped open the bellies of their wives, to prevent their falling into the hands of those barbarians. Hungary, however, was the grave of this third army of crusaders. . . .

It is certain however, that after a siege of five weeks Jerusalem was taken by storm, and that all who were not Christians were massacred. The hermit Peter, who from being a general was become a chaplain, was present both at the taking of the city, and at the slaughter of its inhabitants. Some Christians, whom the Mussulmen [Muslims] had suffered to live in that place, led the conquerors into the most private caves, in which the mothers had hid themselves with their children, and none of them were suffered to escape. All historians agree, that after this butchery the Christians, glutted with human blood, went in procession to the spot which they were told was the sepulcher of Christ, and there burst into tears. It is very probable that they might there show some signs of religion; but this tenderness, expressed by tears, is scarcely possible to such giddy, furious, debauched, and cruel minds. The same men indeed may be furious and tender, but not at one and the same time. Jerusalem was taken by the crusaders the fifth of July 1099. Alexius Comnenus being then emperor of the East, Henry IV of the West, and Urban II supreme head of the church of Rome. This pope died, before he heard of this triumph of the crusade, of which he had been the author. . . .

But what perhaps further proves the extreme weakness of the principality of Jerusalem, is the establishment of those religious soldiers, called the Templars and Hospitallers; for it is certain that these monks, whose institution at first was to serve the sick, were not in safety, since they took up arms. Besides, when the community in general is well governed, private associations are seldom made.

The religious, consecrated to the service of the wounded, having made a vow to take up arms in the year 1118, there was suddenly formed a militia of the same kind, under the name of Templars; a title which they assumed from their living near a church, which was said to have been formerly Solomon's temple. These establishments were founded by the French, or at least by the natives of a country since annexed to France. Raymond Dupuy, first grand-master and founder of the militia of hospitallers, was born in Dauphine. Scarcely were these two orders established by the pope's bulls, when they grew rich and turned rivals; they then fought as often against each other, as against the Mussulmen. Soon after a new order was instituted in favor of the poor Germans, who had been abandoned in Palestine, there were the Teutonic monks, who afterwards in Europe became a militia of conquerors.

At length the situation of the Christians was so precarious, that Baldwin, the first king of Jerusalem, who reigned after the death of Godfrey his brother, was taken almost at the gates of the city by a Turkish prince.

The strength of the Christians in these conquered countries decreased every day. The first conquerors were now dead, and their successors were sunk into effeminacy. Edessa was retaken by the Turks in the year 1140, and Jerusalem was threatened. The Greek emperors finding their neighbors, the princes of Antioch, were only new usurpers, made war upon them, and not without reason; and thus the Christians of Asia, ready to be overpowered on every side, solicited Europe for a new crusade. . . .

In the midst of all these troubles arose the great Saladin. He was of Persian extraction, from the little province of the Curdes (Kurds), who have been always a warlike and independent nation. He was one of those captains who seized on the dominions of the caliphs; but none of them were equal to him in power. In a short time he subdued Egypt, Syria, Arabia, Persia, and Mesopotamia. Having made himself master of all these countries, he soon formed the design of conquering the kingdom of Jerusalem, when the violent factions, which tore in pieces this little state, hastened its ruin. Guy of Lufignan who had been crowned king, but whose title had been disputed, reassembled in Galilee all the divided Christians whom the common danger had united, and marched against Saladin; the bishop of Ptolemais wearing a cope [cloak] over his armor, and holding in his arms a cross, which he persuaded the Christians was the same on which Christ died. However, all the Christians were either killed or taken prisoners; when the captive king, who expected nothing but death, was astonished at being treated by Saladin as prisoners of war are now treated by generals of the greatest humanity.

Saladin with his own hand presented Lufignan a cup of liquor cooled with snow, when the king, after having drank, offered the cup to one of his captains, whose name was Rainaud de Chatillon. It was an inviolable custom established among the Mussulmen, and is still preserved among some of the Arabians, never to put those prisoners to death to whom they had given meat or drink. This ancient law of hospitality was regarded as sacred by Saladin, who would not suffer Rainaud de Chatillon to drink after the king; for the captain had frequently violated his promise, and the conqueror had sworn to punish him. To show therefore that he knew how to punish as well as to show mercy, he struck off the head of the perfidious wretch with one blow of his sabre. Being arrived at the gates of Jerusalem, which the inhabitants were now incapable of defending, he granted the queen, Lufignan's wife, a capitulation, which she could not hope to obtain; and permitted her to retire wheresoever she pleased, without demanding any ransom from the Greeks who lived in the city. On his making his entry into Jerusalem, many women came and threw themselves at his [Saladin's] feet; some begging that he would restore to them their husbands, and others their children or their fathers, who were his prisoners. And he granted their requests with a generosity, of which that part of the world had yet afforded no example. Saladin caused the mosque, which had been converted into a church, to be washed with rose-water by the Christians themselves, and placed in it a magnificent chair, which Noradin, sultan of Aleppo, had made with his own hands. He also caused to be carved on the door these words: SALADIN THE KING, SERVANT OF GOD, SET UP THIS INSCRIPTION, AFTER GOD HAD TAKEN JERUSALEM BY HIS HANDS. He [Saladin] established Mahometan schools; but notwithstanding his attachment to his religion, he restored to the Oriental Christians the church of the holy sepulcher. It must also be added, that within the compass of a year he granted Guy of Lufignan his liberty, on swearing never to take up arms against his deliverer; but Lufignan paid no regard to his oath. . . .

Thus in the twelfth and thirteenth centuries there was an uninterrupted series of devastations throughout our whole hemisphere. Nations fell back upon one another by prodigious emigrations, which laid the foundation of vast empires. For while the crusaders poured in great swarms upon Syria, the Turks were undermining the Arabs; and at length started up the Tartars, who fell upon the Turks, the Arabs, the Indians, and the Chinese. These Tartars, under the command of Jenghiz-chan [Genghis Khan] and his sons, changed the whole face of the greater Asia, while Asia Minor and Syria were the grave of the Saracens and Franks.

Source: *An Essay on Universal History, the Manners, and Spirit of Nations, from the reign of Charlemagne to the age of Lewis XIV*, written in French by M. de Voltaire, translated into English, with additional notes and chronological tables, by Mr. Nugent (London: J. Nourse, 1759), 348–401.

What Really Happened

While the crusaders are often portrayed as bloody, merciless, crazed zealots who set out to wreak havoc on anyone and everyone who got in their way on their quest to retake Jerusalem, there is so much more to the story than that.

The bottom line, however, is that the Christian crusades were defensive wars. Islam had been conquering Christian lands since the time of Muhammad (AD 570–632). Muslims took the Christian city Damascus in 635. They took the Holy Land—including Jerusalem, the Holy City—in 638. Christian Egypt—including the city of Alexandria, one of the original four Christian patriarchates—was conquered in 642. The North African Coast, known as a strongly Christian land, so closely associated with the life of Saint Augustine, was taken in the 670s. Most of Spain fell to Islam 714. Even much of France had been taken by 732, when Charles Martel—de facto ruler of the Franks—barely managed to stop their advance into Paris and toward the English Channel. Sicily fell to Islamic forces in 831. Even Rome was sacked by the Arabs in 846.

Much more was in store. In the eleventh century, Muslim Seljuk Turks began harassing Christian pilgrims as they came south to visit the Holy City of Jerusalem. The church of the Holy Sepulcher in Jerusalem was completely destroyed in 1009. Christians were required to pay heavy tolls to visit the Holy Land. Some pilgrims were captured and marketed for the slave trade. Pilgrims were mocked and even tortured, and many returned to Europe with horrifying tales to tell. Anger and anxiety was growing (Stark 2011, 218).

Indeed, that anxiety was well-justified, as Islam continued to expand in dramatic fashion, defeating much of the Christian world between the 630s and the Siege of Vienna in 1683. That year marks the end of Ottoman advances into Europe and represents a major turning point in world history. For over a thousand years, Islam made repeated, and successful, invasions into Europe, even sacking Rome and completely conquering Constantinople—the greatest Christian city in the history of Christendom. With the fall of Constantinople in 1453, the city became the new center of the Muslim world. New rounds of invasions into Europe began afresh once Constantinople was captured for Islam.

The crusades were birthed out of this context. They were a response to a continual assault that had seen two-thirds of the Christian world fall into Islamic hands. Christianity was on the cusp of vanishing altogether, becoming much like those lands that were conquered by Islam during that era: North Africa, the Middle East, Turkey, Pakistan, Afghanistan, and on we could go (Madden 2011, 3).

The Christian world knew there was only one solution—to fight back. Pope Urban II called upon Christians in the West to make a personal sacrifice and go and try to win back the Holy City of Jerusalem. Thousands agreed to go, with the understanding that they were taking a stand for the Christian world, for the continuation of Christian pilgrimage to the land of Jesus, and to help the Byzantine Christians who were under continual assault by Muslim empires.

Sometimes it is asserted that crusaders were trying to convert Muslims but this is not true. The goal was not to convert them but to defeat them in battle. When the Christians took Jerusalem and established a crusader kingdom there, Muslims were allowed to practice their faith freely, keep their property, and continue their normal livelihood. Eventually some Franciscans attempted to evangelize Muslims in the Holy Land, but the project was abandoned due to complete lack of success. Muslims far outnumbered Christians in the crusader kingdoms, a fact that goes ignored in the scholarship (Madden 2011, 5).

The battles and wars that rose out of the crusades were brutal. Islam was not about to give up these lands they had taken from Christians. It was a titanic confrontation of two civilizations. The Christians had lost two-thirds of their territories, and the Muslims were intent on gaining even more. Christians simply wanted all of this to stop. And organizing an army for the purpose of fighting Islam is precisely what the crusades were all about. Yes, there was violence. Yes, there were times when innocent victims were caught in the crossfire. Yes, there were tragedies and immoral acts and crimes during this period of about a century—from 1095 to 1204. But war is war. And atrocities, from both sides, were a regular part of that. Usually atrocities are an accompaniment to war. For example, early on in the crusades there were atrocities committed against Jews as the crusaders made their way south, but these attacks were strongly condemned, albeit after they had happened. Let us not miss the point: attacks against Jews were considered wrong and misguided by leaders of the age, including the pope. The goals of the crusades were to regain the Holy City of Jerusalem and assist the Christians of the East (Madden 2011, 6).

The early crusades were successful. The Latin Christians had indeed come to the aid of the Byzantine Christians. Antioch and Jerusalem were back in Christian hands. Pilgrimages could resume, and Europe had been delivered from the rapid expansion of Islam into its territory. The goals of the crusades were working.

However, slowly, the tide began to turn. "The colossus of the medieval world was Islam, not Christendom." And the Christian success was very short lived. As Western Europe sent as many people as it could to the front lines in a gargantuan struggle against Islam, it proved to be almost futile. The twelfth century was an abysmal experiment in how not to conduct warfare. The Christians were outmaneuvered at every turn. The great warrior Saladin rose up in the 1180s and by 1187—at the Battle of Hattin—had completely wrested control of the Holy Land back into Muslim possession. "Defenseless, the Christian cities began surrendering one by one, culminating in the surrender of Jerusalem on October 2 [1187]. Only a tiny handful of ports held out (Madden 2011, 7).

A series of weaker, less unified crusades lingered on until 1291—when Muslims essentially eradicated Western Europe's attempts at crusading in the Levant. The crusaders were defeated, and most of them were killed, except the few who managed to escape back to the West with their tails between their legs. On the more positive side, Saladin announced that Christians could continue their pilgrimages to Jerusalem. The land that the crusaders had worked so hard to gain, however, was firmly in the hands of Islam. For two centuries, crusaders had marched on the Islamic world in hopes of winning back some of that land that Muslim armies had taken from them. But it was to no avail. They profited nothing. It was a complete loss.

Once the crusading era ended, Islamic forces once again turned their sights toward the Christian world. And they won battle after battle. In 1453, the capital of the Christian world—Constantinople—was conquered and the greatest church in the history of Christianity was turned into a mosque. The Hagia Sophia was now a mosque! Christians couldn't believe it. But Muslim armies pressed on. In 1480, Sultan Mehmed II began his invasion of Italy; the city of Rome was evacuated. But the sultan died, disrupting the event. Muslim armies nearly conquered Vienna on a number of occasions, but always came up a bit short. The failed Siege of Vienna in 1683 marked the end of Muslim incursions into Europe. But it is probably as good a date as any to mark the beginning of the vast and global European expansion we often refer to as the period of European colonialism. Islam finally met its match. And Europe's rise would prevent any real threat from the Muslim world until the early twenty-first century—September 11, 2001—when a new battle began. Although this time the enemy was not an entire civilization. This time it was lone wolves out to cause disproportionate terror.

The crusades were a huge loss for Christianity. Some scholars argue that they caused enough damage to stop the Muslim advance into Europe.

That is debatable, since so much of the Christian world—including Constantinople—fell centuries after the crusades. Either way, what is obvious is that the crusades are usually taught the wrong way. The Christians tried to win back their land, and they lost. Islam ran the table. Most crusaders were put to the sword. It did not end well for them.

PRIMARY DOCUMENTS

POPE URBAN II'S SPEECH AT THE COUNCIL OF CLERMONT (1095) WHICH LAUNCHED THE FIRST CRUSADE

Around 1094, Pope Urban received a letter from the Byzantine Emperor, Alexios I Komnenos (Latinized Alexius I Comnenus). In that letter, Komnenos asked the pope for aid from the West to help him defend his realm from the Seljuk Turks, who had taken nearly all of Asia Minor from him. Pope Urban responded swiftly and asked everyone who could to go and help the Christians of the East. Those who went would be granted a plenary indulgence, meaning they would not have to pass through purgatory prior to acceptance into heaven. They would have "immediate remission of sins." This reading includes only the second half of the speech, as the first half basically pointed out to the huge crowd present that their society had fallen into grave sin, and they each needed to repent and do penance. The first half of the speech opened the door for Urban's plea to rescue the Byzantines.

Most beloved brethren: Urged by necessity, I, Urban, by the permission of God chief bishop and prelate over the whole world, have come into these parts as an ambassador with a divine admonition to you, the servants of God.

Although, O sons of God, you have promised more firmly than ever to keep the peace among yourselves and to preserve the rights of the church, there remains still an important work for you to do. Freshly quickened by the divine correction, you must apply the strength of your righteousness to another matter which concerns you as well as God. For your brethren who live in the east are in urgent need of your help, and you must hasten to give them the aid which has often been promised them. For, as the most of you have heard, the Turks and Arabs have attacked them and have conquered the territory of Romania [the Greek empire] as far west as the shore of the Mediterranean and the Hellespont, which is called the Arm of St. George. They have occupied more and more of the lands of those

Christians, and have overcome them in seven battles. They have killed and captured many, and have destroyed the churches and devastated the empire. If you permit them to continue thus for a while with impunity, the faithful of God will be much more widely attacked by them. On this account I, or rather the Lord, beseech you as Christ's heralds to publish this everywhere and to persuade all people of whatever rank, foot-soldiers and knights, poor and rich, to carry aid promptly to those Christians and to destroy that vile race from the lands of our friends. I say this to those who are present, it meant also for those who are absent. Moreover, Christ commands it.

"All who die by the way, whether by land or by sea, or in battle against the pagans, shall have immediate remission of sins. This I grant them through the power of God with which I am invested. O what a disgrace if such a despised and base race, which worships demons, should conquer a people which has the faith of omnipotent God and is made glorious with the name of Christ! With what reproaches will the Lord overwhelm us if you do not aid those who, with us, profess the Christian religion! Let those who have been accustomed unjustly to wage private warfare against the faithful now go against the infidels and end with victory this war which should have been begun long ago. Let those who for a long time, have been robbers, now become knights. Let those who have been fighting against their brothers and relatives now fight in a proper way against the barbarians. Let those who have been serving as mercenaries for small pay now obtain the eternal reward. Let those who have been wearing themselves out in both body and soul now work for a double honor. Behold! on this side will be the sorrowful and poor, on that, the rich; on this side, the enemies of the Lord, on that, his friends. Let those who go not put off the journey, but rent their lands and collect money for their expenses; and as soon as winter is over and spring comes, let them eagerly set out on the way with God as their guide."

Source: Bongars, *Gesta Dei per Francos*, pp. 382 f., in *A Source Book for Medieval History*, translated and edited by Oliver J. Thatcher and Edgar Holmes McNeal (New York: Scribners, 1905), 513–517. There are four versions of Urban's speech extant; this version is by the chronicler Fulcher of Chartres.

GESTA FRANCORUM (THE DEEDS OF THE FRANKS)

The Gesta Francorum *(The Deeds of the Franks) is a valuable chronicle written by an anonymous author, probably a simple soldier, who wrote in Latin around the year 1100. It is an eyewitness account of the journeys and battles of the First Crusade from 1095 to 1099. It narrates the trip from France to Jerusalem, with careful notes taken on the methods used to attain victory in battle. The reading here shows a strong religious motive was involved in the First Crusade. It also makes clear that this was not an unwarranted massacre. This was war. And the crusaders felt they were obligated to regain some of their lost cities, but most especially the Holy City of Jerusalem.*

Urban II: Speech at Clermont

When now that time was at hand which the Lord Jesus daily points out to His faithful, especially in the Gospel, saying, "If any man would come after me, let him deny himself and take up his cross and follow me," a mighty agitation was carried on throughout all the region of Gaul. (Its tenor was) that if anyone desired to follow the Lord zealously, with a pure heart and mind, and wished faithfully to bear the cross after Him, he would no longer hesitate to take up the way to the Holy Sepulchre.

And so Urban, Pope of the Roman see, with his archbishops, bishops, abbots, and priests, set out as quickly as possible beyond the mountains and began to deliver sermons and to preach eloquently, saying: "Whoever wishes to save his soul should not hesitate humbly to take up the way of the Lord, and if he lacks sufficient money, divine mercy will give him enough." Then the apostolic lord continued, "Brethren, we ought to endure much suffering for the name of Christ—misery, poverty, nakedness, persecution, want, illness, hunger, thirst, and other (ills) of this kind, just as the Lord saith to His disciples: 'Ye must suffer much in My name,' and 'Be not ashamed to confess Me before the faces of men; verily I will give you mouth and wisdom,' and finally, 'Great is your reward in Heaven.'" And when this speech had already begun to be noised abroad, little by little, through all the regions and countries of Gaul, the Franks, upon hearing such reports, forthwith caused crosses to be sewed on their right shoulders, saying that they followed with one accord the footsteps of Christ, by which they had been redeemed from the hand of hell.

Source: August C. Krey, *The First Crusade: The Accounts of Eyewitnesses and Participants* (Princeton, NJ: Princeton University Press, 1921), 28–30.

The Franks' Victory at Nicaea

The Turks, moreover, seeing that they could have no further aid from their armies, sent a message to the Emperor that they would willingly surrender the city, if he would permit them to go entirely away with their wives and children and all their substance. Then the Emperor, full of vain and evil thinking, ordered them to depart unpunished, without any fear, and to be brought to him at Constantinople with great assurance (of safety). These he cared for zealously, so that he had them prepared against any damage or hindrance from the Franks. We were engaged in that siege for seven weeks and three days. Many of our men there received martyrdom, and, glad and rejoicing, gave back their happy souls to God. Many of the very poor died of hunger for the name of Christ, and these bore triumphantly to heaven their robes of martyrdom crying with one voice, "Avenge, Lord, our blood which has been shed for Thee, who are blessed and praiseworthy forever and ever. Amen." In the meanwhile, after the city had been surrendered and the Turks had been conducted to Constantinople, the Emperor, more and more rejoiced because the city had been surrendered to his power, ordered the greatest alms to be distributed to our poor.

Source: August C. Krey, *The First Crusade: The Accounts of Eyewitnesses and Participants* (Princeton, NJ: Princeton University Press, 1921), 101–103.

The Battle of Dorylaeum

On the third day, the Turks made a violent assault on Bohemund and his companions. The Turks began unceasingly to shout, babble, and cry in a loud voice, making some devilish sound, I know not how, in their own tongue. When the wise Bohemund saw from afar the innumerable Turks shouting and crying a diabolical sound, be straightway ordered all the knights to dismount and pitch the tents immediately. Before the tents had been erected, be spoke to all the soldiers: "My lords and strongest of Christ's soldiers! A difficult battle is now building up around us. Let everyone advance against them courageously and let the infantry put up the tents carefully and quickly."

By the time all this had been done, the Turks had already surrounded us on all sides. They attacked us, slashing, hurling, and shooting arrows far and wide, in a manner strange to behold. Although we could scarcely bold them back or even bear up under the weight of such a host, nevertheless we all managed to hold our ranks. Our women were a great blessing to us that day, for they carried drinking water zip to our fighting men and comforted the fighters and defenders. The wise Bohemund at once commanded the others, namely the Count of St-Gilles, Duke Godfrey, Hugh of France, the Bishop of Le Puy, and all the rest of Christ's soldiers to make speed and to march quickly to the battle scene. He said: "If they wish to fight today, let them come on with full force." The strong and courageous Duke Godfrey and Hugh of France both came on ahead with their forces. The Bishop of Le Puy followed with his troops, and the Count of St-Gilles with a large force came after him.

Our people were very curious about where such a multitude of Turks, Arabs, Saracens, and others whom I cannot name, had come from. Indeed, this excommunicated race filled all the mountains, hills, valleys, and plains on all sides, both inside and outside of the battlefield. We had a secret parley among ourselves and, after praising God and taking counsel, we said: "Let us all unite in Christ's faith and the victory of the Holy Cross, for, God willing, today we shall all be made rich."

As soon as our knights arrived, the Turks, Arabs, Saracens, Angulans, and all the barbarian tribes speedily took flight through the byways of the mountains and plains. The Turks, Persians, Paulicians, Saracens, Angulans, and other pagans numbered 360,000, besides the Arabs, whose numbers are known only to God. With extraordinary speed they fled to their tents but were unable to remain there for long. Again they took flight and we followed, killing them as we went, for a whole day. We took many spoils: gold, silver, horses, donkeys, camels, sheep, cattle, and many other things of which we know not. Had the Lord not been with us in the battle and had he not suddenly sent us the other force, none of our men would have escaped, for the battle lasted from the third to the ninth hour. But Almighty God is merciful and kind. He did not allow his troops to perish, nor did he deliver them into the hands of the enemy; rather he sent help to us quickly. Two of our honored knights were killed, namely Godfrey of Monte-Scaglioso and William the son of the Marquis and the brother of Tancred. Some other knights and infantrymen whose names I do not know were also killed.

Who will ever be wise or learned enough to dare to describe the prudence, prowess, and valor of the Turks? They believed they could terrify the Frankish race by threatening them with their arrows, as they had terrified the Arabs, Saracens, Armenians, Syrians, and Greeks. But, please God, they will never be as powerful as our men. Indeed, the Turks say that they are related to the Franks and that no man ought by nature to be a knight save the Franks and themselves. I speak the truth, which no one can deny. That if they had always been steadfast in Christ's faith and in Christianity, if they had wished to confess one triune Lord, and if they had honestly believed in good faith that the Son of God was born of the Virgin, that he suffered and rose from the dead and ascended into heaven in the presence of his disciples, that he has sent the perfect comfort of the Holy Spirit, and that he reigns in heaven and on earth; if they had believed all this, it would have been impossible to find a people more powerful, more courageous, or more skilled in the art of war. By the grace of God, however, we defeated them. The battle took place on the first of July.

Source: Translated by James Brundage, *The Crusades: A Documentary History* (Milwaukee, WI: Marquette University Press, 1962), 49–51.

The Defeat of Kerbogha

From that hour we took counsel of battle among ourselves. Forthwith, all our leaders decided upon the plan of sending a messenger to the Turks, enemies of Christ, to ask them with assured address: "Wherefore have you most haughtily entered the land of the Christians, and why have you encamped, and why do you kill and assail servants of Christ?" When their speech was already ended, they found certain men, Peter the Hermit and Herlwin, and they told them as follows: "Go to the accursed army of the Turks and carefully tell them all this, asking them why they have boldly and haughtily entered the land of the Christians and our own?"

At these words, the messengers left and went to the profane assemblage, saying everything to *Curbara* and the others as follows: "Our leaders and nobles wonder wherefore you have rashly and most haughtily entered their land, the land of the Christians? We think, forsooth, and believe that you have thus come hither because you wish to become Christians fully; or have you come hither for the purpose of harassing the Christians in every way? All our leaders together ask you, therefore, quickly to leave the land of God and the Christians, which the blessed apostle, Peter by his preaching converted long ago to the worship of Christ. But they grant, in addition, that you may take away all your belongings, horses, mules, asses, camels, sheep, and cattle; all other belongings they permit you to carry with you, wherever you may wish."

Then *Curbara*, chief of the army of the Sultan of Persia, with all the others full of haughtiness, answered in fierce language "Your God and your Christianity we neither seek nor desire, and we spurn you and them absolutely. We have now come even hither because we marveled greatly why the princes and nobles who you mention call this land theirs, the land we took from an effeminate people. Now, do you want to know what we are saying to you? Go back quickly, therefore, and tell your leaders that if they desire to become Turks in everything, and wish to deny the God whom you worship with bowed heads, and to spurn your laws, we will give them this and enough more of lands, castles, and cities. In addition, moreover, (we will grant) that none of you will longer remain a foot soldier, but will all be knights, just as we are; and we will ever bold you in the highest friendship. But if not, let them know that they will all undergo capital sentence, or will be led in chains to Chorosan, to serve us and our children in perpetual captivity forever."

Our messengers speedily came back, reporting all this most cruel race had replied. Herlwin is said to have known both tongues, and to have been the interpreter for Peter the Hermit, Meanwhile, our army, frightened on both sides, did not know what to do; for on one side excruciating famine harassed them, on the other fear of the Turks constrained them. . . .

Thereupon, we invoked the Living and True God and charged against them, and in the name of Jesus Christ and of the Holy Sepulcher we began the battle, and, God helping, we overcame them. But the terrified Turks took to flight, and our men followed them to the tents. Thereupon, the knights of Christ chose rather to pursue them than to seek any spoils, and they pursued them even to the Iron Bridge, and then up to the fortress of Tancred. The enemy, indeed, left their pavilions there, gold, silver, and many ornaments, also sheep, cattle, horses, mules, camels, asses, grain, wine, butter, and many other things which we needed. When the Armenians and Syrians who dwelt in those regions heard that we had overcome the Turks, they ran to the mountain to meet them and killed as many of them as they could catch. We, however, returned to the city with great joy and praised and blessed God, who gave the victory to His people.

This battle was fought on the fourth day before the Kalends of July, on the vigil of the apostles Peter and Paul, in the reign of our Lord Jesus Christ, who has honor and glory forever and ever. Amen. And after our enemies had now been completely conquered, we gave fitting thanks to God, Three and One, and the Highest. Some of the enemy, exhausted, others, wounded in their flight hither and thither, succumbed to death in valley, forest, fields, and roads. But the people of Christ, that is, the victorious pilgrims, returned to the city, rejoicing in the happy triumph over their defeated foes.

Source: August C. Krey, *The First Crusade: The Accounts of Eyewitnesses and Participants* (Princeton, NJ: Princeton University Press, 1921), 182–185.

The Fall of Jerusalem

At length, our leaders decided to beleaguer the city with siege machines, so that we might enter and worship the Savior at the Holy Sepulcher. They constructed wooden towers and many other siege machines. Duke Godfrey made a wooden tower and other siege devices, and Count Raymond did the same, although it was necessary to bring wood from a considerable distance. However, when the Saracens saw our men engaged in this work, they greatly strengthened the fortifications of the city and increased the height of the turrets at night. On a certain Sabbath night, the leaders, after having decided which parts of the wall were weakest, dragged the tower and the machines to the eastern side of the city. Moreover, we set up the tower at earliest dawn and equipped and covered it on the first, second, and third days of the week. The Count of St. Gilles erected his tower on the plain to the south of the city.

While all this was going on, our water supply was so limited that no one could buy enough water for one *denarius* to satisfy or quench his thirst. Both day and night, on the fourth and fifth days of the week, we made a determined attack on the city from all sides. However, before we made this assault on the city, the bishops and priests persuaded all, by exhorting and preaching, to honor the Lord by marching around Jerusalem in a great procession, and to prepare for battle by prayer, fasting, and almsgiving. Early on the sixth day of the week we again attacked the city on all sides, but as the assault was unsuccessful, we were all astounded and fearful. However, when the hour approached on which our Lord Jesus Christ deigned to suffer on the Cross for us, our knights began to fight bravely in one of the towers—namely, the party with Duke Godfrey and his brother, Count Eustace. One of our knights, named Lethold, clambered up the wall of the city, and no sooner had he ascended than the defenders fled from the walls and through the city. Our men followed, killing and slaying even to the Temple of Solomon, where the slaughter was so great that our men waded in blood up to their ankles. . . . Count Raymond brought his army and his tower up near the wall from the south, but between the tower and the wall there was a very deep ditch. Then our men took counsel how they might fill it, and had it proclaimed by heralds that anyone who carried three stones to the ditch would receive one *denarius*. The work of filling it required three days and three nights, and when at length the ditch was filled, they moved the tower up to the wall, but the men defending this portion of the wall fought desperately with stones and fire. When the Count heard that the Franks were already in the city, he said to his men, "Why do you loiter? Lo, the Franks are even now within the city." The Emir who commanded the Tower of St. David surrendered to the Count and opened that gate at which the pilgrims had always been accustomed to pay tribute. But this time the pilgrims entered the city, pursuing and killing the Saracens up to the Temple of Solomon, where the enemy gathered in force. The battle raged throughout the day, so that the Temple was covered with their blood. When the pagans had been overcome, our men seized great numbers, both men and women, either killing them or keeping them captive, as they wished. On the roof of the Temple a great number of pagans of both sexes had assembled, and these were taken under the protection of Tancred and Gaston of *Beert*. Afterward, the army scattered throughout the city and took possession of the gold and silver, the horses and mules, and the houses filled with goods of all kinds.

Source: August C. Krey, *The First Crusade: The Accounts of Eyewitnesses and Participants* (Princeton, NJ: Princeton University Press, 1921), 256–257.

The Vision of Peace

Then our leaders in council decided that each one should offer alms with prayers, that the Lord might choose for Himself whom He wanted to reign over the others and rule the city. They also ordered all the Saracen dead to be cast outside because of the great stench, since the whole city was filled with their corpses; and so the living Saracens dragged the dead before the exits of the gates and arranged them in heaps, as if they were houses. No one ever saw or heard of such slaughter of pagan people, for funeral pyres were formed from them like pyramids, and no one knows their number except God alone.

But Raymond caused the Emir and the others who were with him to be conducted to Ascalon, whole and unhurt. However, on the eighth day after the city was captured, they chose Godfrey as head of the city to fight the pagans and guard the Christians. On the day of St. Peter ad Vincula they likewise chose as Patriarch a certain very wise and honorable man, Arnulf by name. This city was captured by God's Christians on the fifteenth day of July, the sixth day of the week.

Source: August C. Krey, *The First Crusade: The Accounts of Eyewitnesses and Participants* (Princeton, NJ: Princeton University Press, 1921), 262.

Further Reading

Armstrong, Karen. (1991) 2001. *Holy War: The Crusades and Their Impact on Today's World*. 2nd ed. New York: Random House.

Dixon, Tomas. 1999. "Jerusalem: Reconciliation Walk Reaches Pinnacle." *Christianity Today*, September 6. Available at https://www.christianitytoday.com/ct/1999/september6/9ta024.html.

Dowd, Maureen. 1999. "Liberties; The God Squad." *New York Times*, June 20. Available at https://www.nytimes.com/1999/06/20/opinion/liberties-the-god-squad.html.

Edbury, Peter. 1999. "Warfare in the Latin East." In *Medieval Warfare: A History*, edited by Maurice Keen, 89–112. Oxford: Oxford University Press.

Hillenbrand, Carole. 1999. *The Crusades: Islamic Perspectives*. Edinburgh: Edinburgh University Press.

Irwin, Robert. 2006. *Dangerous Knowledge: Orientalism and Its Discontents*. New York: Overlook Press.

Jaffe, Alexandra. 2015. "Obama Takes Fire for Crusades Comparison." *CNN*, February 7. Available at https://www.cnn.com/2015/02/06/politics/obama-isis-crusades-comparison/index.html.

Kedar, Benjamin Z. 1974. "The General Tax of 1183 in the Crusading Kingdom of Jerusalem: Innovation or Adaptation?" *English Historical Review* 89:351: 339–345.

Kedar, Benjamin Z. 2003. *Crusades*. Vol. 2. Aldershot, UK: Ashgate.

Knobler, Adam. 2006. "Holy Wars, Empires, and the Portability of the Past: The Modern Uses of Medieval Crusades." *Comparative Studies in Society and History* 48:2 (April): 293–325.

Madden, Thomas. 1999. *A Concise History of the Crusades*. Lanham, MD: Rowman & Littlefield.

Madden, Thomas. 2001. "Crusade Propaganda." *National Review*, online edition, November 2.

Madden, Thomas. 2002a. "Crusade Myths." *Catholic Dossier*, online edition, January/February. Available at http://www.ignatiusinsight.com/features2005/tmadden_crusademyths_feb05.asp.

Madden, Thomas, ed. 2002b. *The Crusades: The Essential Readings*. Oxford: Blackwell.

Madden, Thomas. 2009. "Inventing the Crusades." *First Things*, June.

Madden, Thomas. 2011. "The Real History of the Crusades." *Crisis Magazine*, online edition, April 1. Available at https://www.crisismagazine.com/2011/the-real-history-of-the-crusades.

Mayer, Hans Eberhard. 1972. *The Crusades*. Oxford: Oxford University Press.

Michaud, Joseph. 1999. *The History of the Crusades*. Vol. 3. Cambridge: Cambridge University Press.

Payne, Robert. 1984. *The Dream and the Tomb: A History of the Crusades*. New York: Stein & Day.

Peters, Edward. 2004. "The Firanj are Coming—Again." *Orbis* 48:1: 3–17.

Phillips, Jonathan. 1995. "The Latin East 1098–1291." In *The Oxford Illustrated History of the Crusades*, edited by Jonathan Riley-Smith, 112–140. Oxford: Oxford University Press.

Prawer, Joshua. 1972. *The Crusaders' Kingdom: European Colonialism in the Middle Ages*. New York: Praeger.

Richard, Jean. 1999. *The Crusades, c. 1071–c. 1291*. Cambridge: Cambridge University Press.

Riley-Smith, Jonathan. 1998. *The First Crusaders, 1095–1131*. Cambridge: Cambridge University Press.

Riley-Smith, Jonathan. 2005. *The Crusades: A History*. 2nd ed. London: Continuum.

Riley-Smith, Jonathan. 2011. *The Crusades, Christianity, and Islam*. New York: Columbia University Press.

Robinson, B. A. (1996) 2005 (updated). "Christian Apology for the Crusades: The Reconciliation Walk." *Religious Tolerance*, November 4. Available at http://www.religioustolerance.org/chr_cru1.htm.

Runciman, Sir Steven. 1951. *A History of the Crusades*. 3 vols. Cambridge: Cambridge University Press.

Runciman, Sir Steven. 1966. *A History of the Crusades*. Vol. 3. Cambridge: Cambridge University Press.

Sivan, Emmanuel. 1973. *Modern Arab Historiography of the Crusades*. Tel Aviv: Tel Aviv University, Shiloah Center for Middle Eastern and African Studies.

Stark, Rodney. 2009. *God's Battalions: The Case for the Crusades*. San Francisco: HarperOne.

Stark, Rodney. 2011. *The Triumph of Christianity*. New York: HarperCollins.

Theron, Jacques, and Erna Oliver. 2018. "Changing Perspectives on the Crusades." *HTS Teologiese Studies/Theological Studies* 74:1: a4691.

Tyerman, Christopher. 1998. *The Invention of the Crusades*. London: Palgrave.

Tyerman, Christopher. 2006. *God's War: A New History of the Crusades*. Cambridge, MA: Belknap.

Tyerman, Christopher. 2011. *The Debate on the Crusades, 1099–2010*. Manchester: Manchester University Press.

7

Christianity Is Anti-Science

What People Think Happened

The United States has a long history of pitting science and religion against each other. It is often characterized as a battle. The reason for this is that many Americans—unlike virtually any other Christian-majority country—have bought into this idea that you have to choose one or the other. If science is right, then there must be no God. If God exists, then science must be a malevolent force.

In the United States, this conversation is set up as a standoff between two titanic powers. But it is a mistake to think like this. This chapter counters the widespread myth that science and religion are enemies. They're not. That's thoroughly fictional. In U.S. history, some have argued that Christianity impedes progress. The claim is that without Christianity, and especially those utterly vacuous "Dark Ages," then we probably would have advanced a lot faster than we did. Finally, the argument goes, religion is now receding, and science is taking its rightful place. This chapter argues that virtually all of the stories used to bolster this narrative are bogus.

Story number one: It is often said that before Columbus, people thought that sea voyagers would sail over the side of a flat earth. Supposedly, the church taught this idea, and it took brave Columbus to make a mockery of all of the religious zealots by proving them wrong.

Story number two: Galileo discovered that the sun is at the center of our cosmic reality, and the earth goes around it. But the church condemned him because he disrupted ancient—and factually incorrect—church teaching. So the church put him in prison for the rest of his life. Poor Galileo, all he did was prove the truth, and the church just wanted to cover it up.

Finally, there are those stubborn Christian Creationists. You can put all the evidence in the world in front of them, and they still believe in a God who created the world and everything in it over a period of six days. They need to accept the fact that scientists no longer need the God hypothesis to account for why the world is here, as well as everything in it. Science has proved itself victorious repeatedly, most notably at the Scopes Trial of 1925, when religious believers were utterly humiliated and atheists were justified during the "trial of the century," otherwise known as the "monkey trial."

Indeed, the narrative continues, religious people believe in all sorts of strange phenomena: angels, the healing power of relics, prayers that can actually change events in the physical world, a God who intervenes in the world, and resurrection from the dead. It's time to move on from these obsolete fictions.

These examples are discussed often. The problem, however, is that these stories are largely fictional, biased, and overly dramatized. This chapter will discuss how the fictions came to be, and then we'll look into the facts.

How the Story Became Popular

Textbooks today still teach the myth that after the fall of classical antiquity—by which they mean ancient Rome—the Western world entered a long, cold winter called the "Dark Ages." In the Dark Ages, people discovered nothing, invented nothing, and created virtually nothing. It was a world utterly devoted to religion. Religion's tyranny and control over the people kept their intellects in chains. The church feared innovation and intelligence, so the idea goes. And the Dark Ages became a debased period, devoid of progress. Only in the Renaissance did humans start emerging from their barbarity. And when the so-called Enlightenment came along, the lights came on, showing us just how senseless and ludicrous people really were between about 476—the fall of the last Italian emperor—and the "rebirth" of European society during the Italian renaissance in the fourteenth century. Nobody notices the Italian bias there, of course.

This fiction began with the writings of the (predictably) Italian poet Petrarch (1304–1374). It got reinforced by, you guessed it, Voltaire and Gibbon in the 1700s. They organized history into three periods: (1) classical

CHRISTIANITY IS ANTI-SCIENCE

antiquity; (2) the Dark Ages; (3) the Renaissance and glorious Enlightenment—which was, of course, their own era. Today, we supposedly have a fourth era: the modern era. But I must agree with Rodney Stark who has written that this fourfold typology of history is inappropriate on a number of levels. First off, "there *never were any Dark Ages!* . . . In fact, it was during the 'Dark Ages' that Europe took the great technological and intellectual leap forward that put it ahead of the rest of the world" (Stark 2011, 239–240).

The medieval era (let's drop "Dark Ages" from our vocabulary forevermore) was full of innovation. Half of Rome's population was enslaved. That hideous institution disappeared from Europe in the medieval era. Advances in naval techniques allowed the Christian civilizations to finally stop the seemingly unstoppable encroachment of Islam into Christendom. Revolutions in agriculture, weaponry, and education put Europe on a path that laid the groundwork for what became a highly advanced civilization.

Progress in technology was rampant in medieval Europe. Without slaves, they needed power. So they found ways to use the water, wind, animals, and innovation to get the power formerly supplied by slaves. In 1086, England had nearly 6,000 water mills working full-time, mechanizing the textile industry. Dams were built all over Europe, sometimes 1,300 feet across. Bridges—even 500 feet across—were constructed in the 800s. Windmills were everywhere, thousands of them, all across Europe. In agriculture, they invented the three-field system to allow one field to lay fallow and re-fertilize so its productivity would soar. Inventions such as the horse collar, eyeglasses, chimneys, high-back saddles, and stirrups allowed the Western Europeans to defeat the nearly indomitable Muslim armies after they conquered Spain and most of France. After that battle, at Tours, in 732, the Muslims realized they would not take France, and withdrew south into Spain, where they eventually had to leave again in the fifteenth century when European war tactics began to gain the upper hand (Stark 2011, 242–243).

Thus, it is a fiction that the medieval era was intellectually backward, or at least stagnant. These people were doing science. They were creating and innovating, through falsification and observation. How else could they have built a 1,300-foot dam or have pioneered a fallow theory that would significantly improve the fecundity of their fields? The Dark Age theory persists in spite of the historical evidence.

Many other stories that are oft-repeated are almost entirely fictional. Columbus was supposed to sail off the edge of the flat earth. Everyone knows that story. However, the famous Harvard paleontologist, Stephen Jay Gould (1941–2002) wrote that this is the "silliest and most flagrantly false of all tales within the venerable genre of 'moral lessons for kiddies.'" He argued that this story "provides the best example I know for exposing the harm done by the false model of warfare between science and religion." Gould demonstrated that this widely believed lie actually dates to two books published in the late 1800s. The first was written by John William Draper and published in 1874 with the title *History of the Conflict between Religion and Science*. That book was extremely popular and gave birth to a genre of writing that hopped on the bandwagon of condemning religion as an impediment to science. Scholars now call this the "conflict thesis." In other words, religion and science are at odds with each other in a perpetual state of conflict (Gould 1999, 99–103).

The second book Gould mentions was written by Andrew Dickson White, a scientist and first president of Cornell University. In 1896, he published, in two volumes, *A History of the Warfare of Science with Theology in Christendom*. White began his book with a complex analogy that effectively said religion had dammed up science for hundreds of years, and we are now witnessing the dam being breached by science and human progress. White launched himself into the myth of Columbus fighting against flat-earth clergymen in his book with great prose, causing generations of people to believe that Columbus's heroic defeat of the clergy is really what allowed him to set sail and discover the New World. Had the clergy won, there would be no discovery of America.

Even authors of children's books got in on the action of claiming the church is precisely what held back science all these years. Washington Irving, author of *The Legend of Sleepy Hollow*, "gave the flat-earth story a good boost in his largely fictional history of Columbus, published in 1828." Both Draper and White capitalized on this children's myth to create a widespread visual that has been very hard to shake: science is at war with religion (Gould 1999, 117).

So the stories that started with the anti-Christian intellectuals of the eighteenth century, chiefly Voltaire and Gibbon, continued on through the decades with the works of other atheist writers such as Ludwig Feuerbach, Karl Marx, Sigmund Freud, Bertrand Russell, and, more recently, the so-called New Atheist movement led by the unholy trinity of Sam Harris, Richard Dawkins, and (now deceased) Christopher Hitchens.

A more recent event in "religion versus science" history was the infamous Scopes Trial of 1925, in the small town of Dayton, Tennessee. That's when the American Civil Liberties Union (ACLU) recruited a substitute high school biology teacher, John Scopes, to break the laws of Tennessee by teaching the theory of evolution in his class. After a week of feverish debate and exhilarating American courtroom entertainment, the case was decided. John Scopes had, in fact, taught evolution in class. He was found guilty. The ACLU offered to pay his $100 fine, but the verdict was overturned due to a strange technicality. The end result was that conservative Bible-believing Christians were mocked as being out of touch with modern scientific theories, and liberals—both Christian and non-Christian—came to be seen as the adversaries of conservatives. The Scopes Trial played a major role in the liberal-conservative divide that still racks the social fabric of the United States of America today.

PRIMARY DOCUMENTS

JOHN WILLIAM DRAPER'S *HISTORY OF THE CONFLICT BETWEEN RELIGION AND SCIENCE* (1874)

John William Draper (1811–1882) was a British-American scholar active in many fields of knowledge. He gained fame as a chemist and went on to co-found the New York University School of Medicine. His book History of the Conflict between Religion and Science *was the first book to popularize what is known today as the "conflict thesis"—meaning religion and science are at war with one another, and science will (or certainly should according to him) prevail. This book was extremely popular and was translated into several languages. In this reading, we see Draper's adversarial view of religion, specifically of the Roman Catholic Church—an institution he clearly detests. He actually has positive things to say here about the Greek Orthodox and Protestant Christians, since they seem to be much more accommodating to science. Evident throughout this reading is Draper's anti-Catholic bias, such as when he says of the Roman Catholic clergy in light of the Inquisition: "The hands that are now raised in appeals to the Most Merciful are crimsoned. They have been steeped in blood!"*

Whoever has had an opportunity of becoming acquainted with the mental condition of the intelligent classes in Europe and America, must have perceived that there is a great and rapidly-increasing departure from the public religious faith, and that, while among the more frank this divergence is not concealed, there is a far more extensive and far more dangerous secession, private and unacknowledged.

So wide-spread and so powerful is this secession, that it can neither be treated with contempt nor with punishment. It cannot be extinguished by derision, by vituperation, or by force. The time is rapidly approaching when it will give rise to serious political results.

Ecclesiastical spirit no longer inspires the policy of the world. Military fervor in behalf of faith has disappeared. Its only souvenirs are the marble effigies of crusading knights, reposing in the silent crypts of churches on their tombs.

That a crisis is impending is shown by the attitude of the great powers toward the papacy. The papacy represents the ideas and aspirations of two-thirds of the population of Europe. It insists on a political supremacy in accordance with its claims to a divine origin and mission, and a restoration of the mediaeval order of things, loudly declaring that it will accept no reconciliation with modern civilization.

The antagonism we thus witness between Religion and Science is the continuation of a struggle that commenced when Christianity began to attain political power.

Can we exaggerate the importance of a contention in which every thoughtful person must take part whether he will or not? In a matter so solemn as that of religion, all men, whose temporal interests are not involved in existing institutions, earnestly desire to find the truth. They seek information as to the subjects in dispute, and as to the conduct of the disputants.

The history of Science is not a mere record of isolated discoveries; it is a narrative of the conflict of two contending powers, the expansive force of the human intellect on one side, and the compression arising from traditionary faith and human interests on the other.

No one has hitherto treated the subject from this point of view. Yet from this point it presents itself to us as a living issue—in fact, as the most important of all living issues.

A few years ago, it was the politic and therefore the proper course to abstain from all allusion to this controversy, and to keep it as far as possible in the background. The tranquility of society depends so much on the stability of its religious convictions, that no one can be justified in wantonly disturbing them. But faith is in its nature unchangeable, stationary; Science is in its nature progressive; and eventually a divergence between them, impossible to conceal, must take place. It then becomes the duty of those whose lives have made them familiar with both modes of thought, to present modestly, but firmly, their views; to compare the antagonistic pretensions calmly, impartially, philosophically. History shows that, if this be not done, social misfortunes, disastrous and enduring, will ensue. When the old mythological religion of Europe broke down under the weight of its own inconsistencies, neither the Roman emperors nor the philosophers of those times did anything adequate for the guidance of public opinion. They left religious affairs to take their chance, and accordingly those affairs fell into the hands of ignorant and infuriated ecclesiastics, parasites, eunuchs, and slaves.

The intellectual night which settled on Europe, in consequence of that great neglect of duty, is passing away; we live in the daybreak of better things. Society is anxiously expecting light, to see in what direction it is drifting. It plainly discerns that the track along which the voyage of civilization has thus far been made, has been left; and that a new departure, on all unknown sea, has been taken.

For this reason, I have had little to say respecting the two great Christian confessions, the Protestant and Greek Churches. As to the latter, it has never, since the restoration of science, arrayed itself in opposition to the advancement of knowledge. On the contrary, it has always met it with welcome. It has observed a reverential attitude to truth, from whatever quarter it might come. Recognizing the apparent discrepancies between its interpretations of revealed truth and the discoveries of science, it has always expected that satisfactory explanations and reconciliations would ensue, and in this it has not been disappointed. It would have been well for modern civilization if the Roman Church had done the same.

In speaking of Christianity, reference is generally made to the Roman Church, partly because its adherents compose the majority of Christendom, partly because its demands are the most pretentious, and partly because it has commonly sought to enforce those demands by the civil power. None of the Protestant Churches has ever occupied a position so imperious—none has ever had such wide-spread political influence. For the most part they have been averse to constraint, and except in very few instances their opposition has not passed beyond the exciting of theological odium.

As to Science, she has never sought to ally herself to civil power. She has never attempted to throw odium or inflict social ruin on any human being. She has never subjected any one to mental torment, physical torture, least of all to death, for the purpose of upholding or promoting her ideas. She presents herself unstained by cruelties and crimes. But in the Vatican—we have only to recall the Inquisition—the hands that are now raised in appeals to the Most Merciful are crimsoned. They have been steeped in blood!

Meantime, through the cultivation of astronomy, geography, and other sciences, correct views had been gained as to the position and relations of the earth, and as to the structure of the world; and since Religion, resting itself on what was assumed to be the proper interpretation of the Scriptures, insisted that the earth is the central and most important part of the universe, a third conflict broke out. In this Galileo led the way on the part of Science. Its issue was the overthrow of the Church on the question in dispute. Subsequently a subordinate controversy arose respecting the age of the world, the Church insisting that it is only about six thousand years old. In this she was again overthrown. The light of history and of science had been gradually spreading over Europe. In the sixteenth century the prestige of Roman Christianity was greatly diminished by the intellectual reverses it had experienced, and also by its political and moral condition. It was clearly seen by many pious men that Religion was not accountable for the false position in which she was found, but that the misfortune was directly traceable to the alliance she had of old contracted with Roman paganism. The obvious remedy, therefore, was a return to primitive purity. Thus arose the fourth conflict, known to us as the Reformation—the second or Northern Reformation. The special form it assumed was a contest respecting the standard or criterion of truth, whether it is to be found in the Church or in the Bible. The determination of this involved a settlement of the rights of reason, or intellectual freedom. Luther, who is the conspicuous man of the epoch, carried into effect his intention with no inconsiderable success; and at the close of the struggle it was found that Northern Europe was lost to Roman Christianity.

We are now in the midst of a controversy respecting the mode of government of the world, whether it be by incessant divine intervention, or by the operation of primordial and unchangeable law. The intellectual movement of Christendom has reached that point which Arabism had attained to in the tenth and eleventh centuries; and doctrines which were then discussed are presenting themselves again for review; such are those of Evolution, Creation, Development.

Source: John William Draper, *History of the Conflict between Religion and Science* (New York: Appleton, 1874), from the preface.

ANDREW DICKSON WHITE'S *HISTORY OF THE WARFARE OF SCIENCE WITH THEOLOGY IN CHRISTENDOM* (1896)

Andrew Dickson White (1832–1918) was an American historian. He was one of the founders of Cornell University and served as its first president from

1866 to 1885. He also served the government in a variety of capacities, as Ambassador to Germany and to Russia, and as a state senator in New York. Over the course of many years, White wrote his book History of the Warfare of Science with Theology in Christendom. *This book was extremely influential for generations and had the effect of cementing a "science versus religion" theme to describe the relationship of these two realms. This reading comes from the introduction to that two-volume work. In it, one can see his desire to see religion recede and science rise. Near the end of the reading, White gleefully expresses the changes he has witnessed in the great universities of Britain: "At my first visit to Oxford and Cambridge, forty years ago, they were entirely under ecclesiastical control. Now, all this is changed."*

It is something over a quarter of a century since I labored with Ezra Cornell in founding the university which bears his honored name.

Our purpose was to establish in the State of New York an institution for advanced instruction and research, in which science, pure and applied, should have an equal place with literature; in which the study of literature, ancient and modern, should be emancipated as much as possible from pedantry; and which should be free from various useless trammels and vicious methods which at that period hampered many, if not most, of the American universities and colleges.

We had especially determined that the institution should be under the control of no political party and of no single religious sect, and with Mr. Cornell's approval I embodied stringent provisions to this effect in the charter.

It had certainly never entered into the mind of either of us that in all this we were doing anything irreligious or unchristian. Mr. Cornell was reared a member of the Society of Friends; he had from his fortune liberally aided every form of Christian effort which he found going on about him, and among the permanent trustees of the public library which he had already founded, he had named all the clergymen of the town—Catholic and Protestant. As for myself, I had been bred a churchman, had recently been elected a trustee of one church college, and a professor in another; those nearest and dearest to me were devoutly religious; and, if I may be allowed to speak of a matter so personal to myself, my most cherished friendships were among deeply religious men and women, and my greatest sources of enjoyment were ecclesiastical architecture, religious music, and the more devout forms of poetry. So, far from wishing to injure Christianity, we both hoped to promote it; but we did not confound religion with sectarianism, and we saw in the sectarian character of American colleges and universities as a whole, a reason for the poverty of the advanced instruction then given in so many of them.

The reasons for the new foundation seemed to us, then, so cogent that we expected the co-operation of all good citizens, and anticipated no opposition from any source.

As I look back across the intervening years, I know not whether to be more astonished or amused at our simplicity.

Opposition began at once. In the State Legislature it confronted us at every turn, and it was soon in full blaze throughout the State—from the good Protestant bishop who proclaimed that all professors should be in holy orders, since to the Church alone was given the command, "Go, teach all nations," to the zealous priest who published a charge that Goldwin Smith—a profoundly Christian scholar—had come to Cornell in order to inculcate the "infidelity of the Westminster Review"; and from the eminent divine who went from city to city, denouncing the "atheistic and pantheistic tendencies" of the proposed education, to the perfervid minister who informed a denominational synod that Agassiz, the last great opponent of Darwin, and a devout theist, was "preaching Darwinism and atheism" in the new institution.

As the struggle deepened, as hostile resolutions were introduced into various ecclesiastical bodies, as honored clergymen solemnly warned their flocks first against the "atheism," then against the "infidelity," and finally against the "indifferentism" of the university, as devoted pastors endeavored to dissuade young men from matriculation, I took the defensive, and, in answer to various attacks from pulpits and religious newspapers, attempted to allay the fears of the public. "Sweet reasonableness" was fully tried. There was established and endowed in the university perhaps the most effective Christian pulpit, and one of the most vigorous branches of the Christian Association, then in the United States; but all this did nothing to ward off the attack. The clause in the charter of the university forbidding it to give predominance to the doctrines of any sect, and above all the fact that much prominence was given to instruction in various branches of science, seemed to prevent all compromise, and it soon became clear that to stand on the defensive only made matters worse. Then it was that there was borne in upon me a sense of the real difficulty—the antagonism between the theological and scientific view of the universe and of education in relation to it; therefore, it was that, having been invited to deliver a lecture in the great hall of the Cooper Institute at New York, I took as my subject The Battlefields of Science, maintaining this thesis which follows:In all modern history, interference with science in the supposed interest of religion, no matter how conscientious such interference may have been, has resulted in the direst evils both to religion and science, and invariably; and, on the other hand, all untrammeled scientific investigation, no matter how dangerous to religion some of its stages may have seemed for the time to be, has invariably resulted in the highest good both of religion and science.

The lecture was next day published in the *New York Tribune* at the request of Horace Greeley, its editor, who was also one of the Cornell University trustees. As a result of this widespread publication and of sundry attacks which it elicited, I was asked to maintain my thesis before various university associations and literary clubs; and I shall always remember with gratitude that among those who stood by me and presented me on the lecture platform with words of approval and cheer was my revered instructor, the Rev. Dr. Theodore Dwight Woolsey, at that time President of Yale College.

My lecture grew—first into a couple of magazine articles, and then into a little book called The Warfare of Science, for which, when republished in England, Prof. John Tyndall wrote a preface.

Sundry translations of this little book were published, but the most curious thing in its history is the fact that a very friendly introduction to the Swedish translation was written by a Lutheran bishop.

Meanwhile Prof. John W. Draper published his book on *The Conflict between Science and Religion*, a work of great ability, which, as I then thought, ended the matter, so far as my giving it further attention was concerned.

But two things led me to keep on developing my own work in this field: First, I had become deeply interested in it, and could not refrain from directing my observation and study to it; secondly, much as I admired Draper's treatment of the questions involved, his point of view and mode of looking at history were different from mine.

He regarded the struggle as one between Science and Religion. I believed then, and am convinced now, that it was a struggle between Science and Dogmatic Theology.

More and more I saw that it was the conflict between two epochs in the evolution of human thought—the theological and the scientific.

This book is presented as a sort of Festschrift—a tribute to Cornell University as it enters the second quarter-century of its existence, and probably my last tribute.

The ideas for which so bitter a struggle was made at its foundation have triumphed. Its faculty, numbering over one hundred and, fifty; its students, numbering but little short of two thousand; its noble buildings and equipment; the munificent gifts, now amounting to millions of dollars, which it has received from public-spirited men and women; the evidences of public confidence on all sides; and, above all, the adoption of its cardinal principles and main features by various institutions of learning in other States, show this abundantly. But there has been a triumph far greater and wider. Everywhere among the leading modern nations the same general tendency is seen. During the quarter-century just past the control of public instruction, not only in America but in the leading nations of Europe, has passed more and more from the clergy to the laity. Not only are the presidents of the larger universities in the United States, with but one or two exceptions, laymen, but the same thing is seen in the old European strongholds of metaphysical theology. At my first visit to Oxford and Cambridge, forty years ago, they were entirely under ecclesiastical control. Now, all this is changed. An eminent member of the present British Government has recently said, "A candidate for high university position is handicapped by holy orders." I refer to this with not the slightest feeling of hostility toward the clergy, for I have none; among them are many of my dearest friends; no one honors their proper work more than I; but the above fact is simply noted as proving the continuance of that evolution which I have endeavored to describe in this series of monographs—an evolution, indeed, in which the warfare of Theology against Science has been one of the most active and powerful agents. My belief is that in the field left to them—their proper field—the clergy will more and more, as they cease to struggle against scientific methods and conclusions, do work even nobler and more beautiful than anything they have heretofore done. And this is saying much. My conviction is that Science, though it has evidently conquered Dogmatic Theology based on biblical texts and ancient modes of thought, will go hand in hand with Religion; and that, although theological control will continue to diminish, Religion, as seen in the recognition of "a Power in the universe, not ourselves, which makes for righteousness," and in the love of God and of our neighbor, will steadily grow stronger and stronger, not only in the American institutions of learning but in the world at large. Thus may the declaration of Micah as to the requirements of Jehovah, the definition by St. James of "pure religion and undefiled," and, above all, the precepts and ideals of the blessed Founder of Christianity himself, be brought to bear more and more effectively on mankind.

Source: Andrew Dickson White, *A History of the Warfare of Science with Theology in Christendom* (New York: D. Appleton, 1896), from the introduction.

What Really Happened

From a historical perspective, it is very difficult to argue that Christianity stifled human progress and scientific study during the so-called Dark Ages. First, a "golden era" or a "classical" period of history never existed; these are terms created by people in more recent times. Science developed over the course of millennia and is still developing. Yes, painted and sculpted art was more lifelike in classical Greco-Roman culture than in the medieval era. But one look at the mammoth churches built during the middle ages shows that art and science didn't *cease*—they just flourished in other forms.

Similarly, human ingenuity and innovation didn't end during the "darkness" of medieval Europe. Rather, some anti-religious scholars had an ax to grind with religion, thus arguing that the Dark Ages were devoid of intellectual discovery. Some of the Enlightenment thinkers were atheists, to be sure. But many others were committed to their religion.

Take England as an example of the contrast here. Edward Gibbon was hostile to religion, but John Locke and Isaac Newton were devout Christians. In France, many of the *philosophes* were strident atheists, but many other French intellectuals were Christians, such as Rousseau. Blaise Pascal, one of the brightest intellects in France in the seventeenth century, had a born-again experience (thanks to "Pascal's wager") and wrote Christian theology to complement his brilliant treatises on mathematics. René Descartes, another devoutly Christian French thinker, is known today as the father of modern Western philosophy. His arguments for the existence of God are classics in the field of philosophy and theology.

The list of Christian intellectuals who contributed to the so-called scientific revolution and to the so-called Enlightenment is very long indeed. Francis Bacon—the father of the "scientific method"—was a devout Anglican. John Locke wrote of the "reasonableness of Christianity." Isaac Newton wrote several commentaries on the Bible. Copernicus was a committed Roman Catholic, was ordained into ministry, and nearly became a bishop. Galileo remained devoutly religious to the end of his days, clearly revealed in the surviving correspondence between himself and others.

But perhaps a bigger, more important point here is that scientific thinking was developing during the medieval world. People were thinking, innovating, creating, and discovering. A tremendously sophisticated university system developed during the medieval era, educating thousands of students. Europe was home to some of the greatest thinking in the world at the time, with superb universities in Bologna, Siena, Padua, Paris, Lisbon, Salamanca, Oxford, Cambridge, Florence, Pisa, Leipzig, Erfurt, Vienna, and Heidelberg. Some of them originated in the eleventh century. And while it could be argued that these universities emphasized theology as the "queen of the sciences," it could also be claimed that Christian theology created the conditions that gave rise to science. Christians believed that the world was discoverable. God made laws in nature, and humans could actually discover those laws if they thought long and hard enough. This was in total contrast to Eastern thinking, which held that there was no beginning or ending to the universe, and that the universe was an unfathomable mystery (Stark 2003, 123).

The stories that depict Christianity as stifling the scientific revolution are half-truths at best, and often they are flat-out fictions. These fictions get passed down, often without being called into question. The Columbus myth is a good example. The truth is that "no period of 'flat earth darkness' ever occurred among scholars." Even the ancient Greeks believed in the sphericity of the planets. And certainly no one in Columbus's day believed in a flat earth. When Columbus set sail in 1492, "no one questioned the earth's roundness." Indeed, Christian scholars throughout the centuries, like the ancient Greeks, knew the earth was round. The Venerable Bede (672–735), historian of the English people, wrote about the earth being a sphere. Both the brilliant Franciscan philosopher Roger Bacon as well as Catholicism's great theologian St. Thomas Aquinas in the thirteenth century believed in a round earth (Gould 1999, 114–115). Indeed, the most popular medieval astronomy textbook—written in the 1200s and used for those training for the priesthood—was entitled *Sphere* (Stark 2011, 274). The flat-earth narrative is flat wrong. Very few people ever believed it.

Regarding the story of Galileo, even more myths abound. While he was condemned during a trial in 1633, he was not imprisoned. They asked him to simply stay at home in his immense villa, beautifully located in the hills outside Florence, with a magnificent view. Galileo remained there, mostly, for the rest of his life. Part of the problem was that he became blind during that period, so travel was nearly out of the question. But he still lived a most productive existence while under "house arrest," writing some of his most important works during that last decade of his life.

Galileo's "imprisonment" wasn't an imprisonment at all. It was actually a dream situation. The scientist was able to live his final years in the bucolic countryside of Tuscany, sipping fine wine, researching and writing some of his most important contributions to scientific knowledge with the help of friends and relatives since his sight was nearly gone. Famous people came to visit him during his "imprisonment," including the English poet John Milton. Unfortunately, this episode "immortalized Galileo's image as a symbol of the struggle between individual freedom and institutional authority." In reality, that entire situation did not become a cause célèbre in Western Europe and North America until the mid-nineteenth century (Numbers 2007, 115).

Regarding Creationism, we must point out that most Christians in the developed world had few problems with scientific theories about the age of the earth or about the complex origins of *homo sapiens*. The "warfare" between science and religion was a strangely American phenomenon with many moving pieces, but suffice it to say it all became politicized at the Scopes Trial in 1925. That trial featured two men who were famous for their entrenched positions, and they both were extremists.

Clarence Darrow (1857–1938) was the lawyer who represented the ACLU at the famous "trial of the century" in 1925. He was a well-known, brutal critic of the Bible and of Christianity. He was a very effective rhetorician and seemed to spend his entire professional life in controversy because he excelled when in debate. At the Scopes Trial, his debate partner was even more famous: William Jennings Bryan (1860–1925). Bryan was the leading Democrat presidential candidate of his day. He was the Democrats' presidential nominee in 1896, 1900, and 1908, yet he lost all three elections. He did, however, serve in the House of Representatives, and later served as the Secretary of State to President Woodrow Wilson. It is ironic, however, that today Bryan is best known for an event that happened during the last few days of his life: the 1925 Scopes Trial.

It is difficult to talk objectively about the Scopes Trial today because it is "largely filtered and distorted" through plays and films, most importantly *Inherit the Wind*, which was initially a play that was released in 1955. The film version, released in 1960, was nominated for numerous awards but failed miserably in its historical accuracy. It is wildly fictionalized and presents religion as the enemy of science. It created a wedge between science and religion that is completely unnecessary (Gould 1999, 134).

Unfortunately, the Scopes Trial made a huge impact on how we understand science and religion in America today. It confronted many people with an either-or proposition: you have to choose one over the other. The truth, however, is that educated, open-minded Christians have always appreciated the discoveries of science. "The great majority of professional clergy and religious scholars stand *on the same side* with the great majority of scientists." The eminent scientist Stephen Jay Gould has called for "respectful and supportive dialogue" between the two important domains of religion and science. Each of them has important work to do, and they should admire and learn from each other. As Albert Einstein put it, "science without religion is lame, and religion without science is blind." For scientists, "the enemy is not religion but dogmatism and intolerance, a tradition as old as humankind, and impossible to extinguish" (Gould 1999, 129, 148–149).

PRIMARY DOCUMENTS

SCOPES TRIAL, TRANSCRIPT OF DAY 7 (1925)

The Scopes Trial of 1925 was truly remarkable on a number of levels. It is often referred to as "the trial of the century," and its final day 7 has been described as "the most amazing courtroom scene in Anglo-Saxon history." Below is the transcript of day 7. It is a most enjoyable read, but there is obvious tension between Darrow, the defense attorney, and Bryan, who bizarrely served as both prosecutor and witness. This trial set the tone for one of the U.S.'s national debates: creationism versus evolution. It had the effect of pitting science versus religion for many Americans. This unfortunate outcome is finally starting to dissipate, but there are still many passionate extremists on both sides. In this reading, we witness the dramatic moments on day 7 of the trial when Darrow and Bryan got into a very heated, and very memorable, exchange that was read in print or heard on the radio by thousands of Americans.

> **Darrow**—Your honor, before you send for the jury, I think it my duty to make this motion. Off to the left of where the jury sits a little bit and about ten feet in front of them is a large sign about ten feet long reading. "Read Your Bible," and a hand pointing to it. The word "Bible" is in large letters, perhaps, a foot and a half long, and the printing—
> **The Court**—Hardly that long I think, general.
> **Darrow**—What is that?
> **The Court**—Hardly that long.
> **Darrow**—Why, we will call it a foot. . . .
> **Darrow**—I move that it be removed.
> **The Court**—Yes.
> **McKenzie**—If your honor please, why should it be removed?

It is their defense and stated before the court, that they do not deny the Bible, that they expected to introduce proof to make it harmonize. Why should we remove the sign cautioning the people to read the Word of God just to satisfy the others in the case? . . .

Darrow—Let me say something. Your honor, I just want to make this suggestion. Mr. Bryan says that the Bible and evolution conflict. Well, I do not know, I am for evolution, anyway. We might agree to get up a sign of equal size on the other side and in the same position reading, "Hunter's Biology," or "Read your evolution." This sign is not here for no purpose, and it can have no effect but to influence this case, and I read the Bible myself—more or less—and it is pretty good reading in places. But this case has been made a case where it is to be the Bible or evolution, and we have been informed by Mr. Bryan, who himself, a profound Bible student and has an essay every Sunday as to what it means. We have been informed that a Tennessee jury who are not especially educated are better judges of the Bible than all the scholars in the world, and when they see that sign, it means to them their construction of the Bible. It is pretty obvious, it is not fair, your honor, and we object to it. . . .

The Court—The issues in this case, as they have been finally determined by this court is whether or not it is unlawful to teach that man descended from a lower order of animals. I do not understand that issue involved the Bible. If the Bible is involved, I believe in it and am always on its side, but it is not for me to decide in this case. If the presence of the sign irritates anyone, or if anyone thinks it might influence the jury in any way, I have no purpose except to give both sides a fair trial in this case. Feeling that way about it, I will let the sign come down. Let the jury be brought around.

(The sign was thereupon removed from the courthouse wall.)

Darrow's Examination of Bryan

Hays—The defense desires to call Mr. Bryan as a witness, and, of course, the only question here is whether Mr. Scopes taught what these children said he taught, we recognize what Mr. Bryan says as a witness would not be very valuable. We think there are other questions involved, and we should want to take Mr. Bryan's testimony for the purpose of our record, even if your honor thinks it is not admissible in general, so we wish to call him now.

The Court—Do you think you have a right to his testimony or evidence like you did these others?

McKenzie—I don't think it is necessary to call him, calling a lawyer who represents a client.

The Court—If you ask him about any confidential matter, I will protect him, of course.

Darrow—On scientific matters, Col. Bryan can speak for himself.

Bryan—If your honor please, I insist that Mr. Darrow can be put on the stand, and Mr. Malone and Mr. Hays.

The Court—Call anybody you desire. Ask them any questions you wish.

Bryan—Then, we will call all three of them.

Darrow—Not at once?

Bryan—Where do you want me to sit?

The Court—Mr. Bryan, you are not objecting to going on the stand?

Bryan—Not at all.

The Court—Do you want Mr. Bryan sworn?

Darrow—No.

Bryan—I can make affirmation; I can say "So help me God, I will tell the truth."

Darrow—No, I take it you will tell the truth, Mr. Bryan.

Examination of W. J. Bryan by Clarence Darrow, of Counsel for the Defense

Q—You have given considerable study to the Bible, haven't you, Mr. Bryan?

A—Yes, sir, I have tried to.

Q—Then you have made a general study of it?

A—Yes, I have; I have studied the Bible for about fifty years, or sometime more than that, but, of course, I have studied it more as I have become older than when I was but a boy.

Q—You claim that everything in the Bible should be literally interpreted?

A—I believe everything in the Bible should be accepted as it is given there: some of the Bible is given illustratively. For instance: "Ye are the salt of the earth." I would not insist that man was actually salt, or that he had flesh of salt, but it is used in the sense of salt as saving God's people.

Q—But when you read that Jonah swallowed the whale—or that the whale swallowed Jonah— excuse me please—how do you literally interpret that?

A—When I read that a big fish swallowed Jonah—it does not say whale. . . . That is my recollection of it. A big fish, and I believe it, and I believe in a God who can make a whale and can make a man and make both what He pleases.

Q—Now, you say, the big fish swallowed Jonah, and he there remained how long—three days— and then he spewed him upon the land. You believe that the big fish was made to swallow Jonah?

A—I am not prepared to say that; the Bible merely says it was done.

Q—You don't know whether it was the ordinary run of fish, or made for that purpose?

A—You may guess; you evolutionists guess. . . .

Q—You are not prepared to say whether that fish was made especially to swallow a man or not?

A—The Bible doesn't say, so I am not prepared to say.

Q—But do you believe He made them—that He made such a fish and that it was big enough to swallow Jonah?

A—Yes, sir. Let me add: One miracle is just as easy to believe as another

Q—Just as hard?

A—It is hard to believe for you, but easy for me. A miracle is a thing performed beyond what man can perform. When you get within the realm of miracles; and it is just as easy to believe the miracle of Jonah as any other miracle in the Bible.

Q—Perfectly easy to believe that Jonah swallowed the whale?

A—If the Bible said so; the Bible doesn't make as extreme statements as evolutionists do. . . .

Q—The Bible says Joshua commanded the sun to stand still for the purpose of lengthening the day, doesn't it, and you believe it?

A—I do.

Q—Do you believe at that time the entire sun went around the earth?

A—No, I believe that the earth goes around the sun.

Q—Do you believe that the men who wrote it thought that the day could be lengthened or that the sun could be stopped?

A—I don't know what they thought.

Q—You don't know?

A—I think they wrote the fact without expressing their own thoughts.

Q—Have you an opinion as to whether or not the men who wrote that thought?

Gen. Stewart—I want to object, your honor; it has gone beyond the pale of any issue that could possibly be injected into this lawsuit, expect by imagination. I do not think the defendant has a right to conduct the examination any further and I ask your honor to exclude it.

The Witness—It seems to me it would be too exacting to confine the defense to the facts; if they are not allowed to get away from the facts, what have they to deal with?

The Court—Mr. Bryan is willing to be examined. Go ahead.

Mr. Darrow—I read that years ago. Can you answer my question directly? If the day was lengthened by stopping either the earth or the sun, it must have been the earth?

A—Well, I should say so.

Q— Now, Mr. Bryan, have you ever pondered what would have happened to the earth if it had stood still?

A—No.

Q—You have not?

A— No; the God I believe in could have taken care of that, Mr. Darrow.

Q— I see. Have you ever pondered what would naturally happen to the earth if it stood still suddenly?

A— No.

Q—Don't you know it would have been converted into molten mass of matter?

A—You testify to that when you get on the stand, I will give you a chance.

Q—Don't you believe it?

A—I would want to hear expert testimony on that.

Q—You have never investigated that subject?

A—I don't think I have ever had the question asked.

Q—Or ever thought of it?

A—I have been too busy on things that I thought were of more importance than that.

Q—You believe the story of the flood to be a literal interpretation?

A—Yes, sir.

Q—When was that Flood?

A—I would not attempt to fix the date. The date is fixed, as suggested this morning.

Q—About 4004 B.C.?

A—That has been the estimate of a man that is accepted today. I would not say it is accurate.

Q—That estimate is printed in the Bible?

A—Everybody knows, at least, I think most of the people know, that was the estimate given.

Q—But what do you think that the Bible, itself says? Don't you know how it was arrived at?

A—I never made a calculation.

Q—A calculation from what?

A—I could not say.

Q—From the generations of man?

A—I would not want to say that.

Q—What do you think?

A—I do not think about things I don't think about.

Q—Do you think about things you do think about?

A—Well, sometimes.

(Laughter in the courtyard.)

Policeman—Let us have order. . . .

Stewart—Your honor, he is perfectly able to take care of this, but we are attaining no evidence. This is not competent evidence.

Witness—These gentlemen have not had much chance—they did not come here to try this case. They came here to try revealed religion. I am here to defend it and they can ask me any question they please.

The Court—All right.

(Applause from the court yard.)

Darrow—Great applause from the bleachers.

Witness—From those whom you call "Yokels."

Darrow—I have never called them yokels.

Witness—That is the ignorance of Tennessee, the bigotry.

Darrow—You mean who are applauding you? (Applause.)

Witness—Those are the people whom you insult.

Darrow—You insult every man of science and learning in the world because he does not believe in your fool religion.

The Court—I will not stand for that.

Darrow—For what he is doing?

The Court—I am talking to both of you. . . .

Q—Wait until you get to me. Do you know anything about how many people there were in Egypt 3,500 years ago, or how many people there were in China 5,000 years ago?

A—No.

Q—Have you ever tried to find out?

A—No, sir. You are the first man I ever heard of who has been in interested in it. (Laughter.)

Q—Mr. Bryan, am I the first man you ever heard of who has been interested in the age of human societies and primitive man?

A—You are the first man I ever heard speak of the number of people at those different periods.

Q—Where have you lived all your life?

A—Not near you. (Laughter and applause.)

Q—Nor near anybody of learning?

A—Oh, don't assume you know it all.

Q—Do you know there are thousands of books in our libraries on all those subjects I have been asking you about?

A—I couldn't say, but I will take your word for it. . . .

Q—Have you any idea how old the earth is?

A—No.

Q—The Book you have introduced in evidence tells you, doesn't it?

A—I don't think it does, Mr. Darrow.

Q—Let's see whether it does; is this the one?

A—That is the one, I think.

Q—It says B.C. 4004?

A—That is Bishop Usher's calculation.

Q—That is printed in the Bible you introduced?

A—Yes, sir. . . .

Q—Would you say that the earth was only 4,000 years old?

A—Oh, no; I think it is much older than that.

Q—How much?

A—I couldn't say.

Q—Do you say whether the Bible itself says it is older than that?

A—I don't think it is older or not.

Q—Do you think the earth was made in six days?

A—Not six days of twenty-four hours.

Q—Doesn't it say so?

A—No, sir. . . .

The Court—Are you about through, Mr. Darrow?

Darrow—I want to ask a few more questions about the creation.

The Court—I know. We are going to adjourn when Mr. Bryan comes off the stand for the day. Be very brief, Mr. Darrow. Of course, I believe I will make myself clearer. Of course, it is incompetent testimony before the jury. The only reason I am allowing this to go in at all is that they may have it in the appellate court as showing what the affidavit would be.

Bryan—The reason I am answering is not for the benefit of the superior court. It is to keep these gentlemen from saying I was afraid to meet them and let them question me, and I want the Christian world to know that any atheist, agnostic, unbeliever, can question me anytime as to my belief in God, and I will answer him.

Darrow—I want to take an exception to this conduct of this witness. He may be very popular down here in the hills. . . .

Bryan—Your honor, they have not asked a question legally and the only reason they have asked any question is for the purpose, as the question about Jonah was asked, for a chance to give this agnostic an opportunity to criticize a believer in the word of God; and I answered the question in order to shut his mouth so that he cannot go out and tell his atheistic friends that I would not answer his questions. That is the only reason, no more reason in the world.

Malone—Your honor on this very subject, I would like to say that I would have asked Mr. Bryan—and I consider myself as good a Christian as he is—every question that Mr. Darrow has asked him for the purpose of bring [sic] out whether or not there is to be taken in this court a literal interpretation of the Bible, or whether, obviously, as these questions indicate, if a general and literal construction cannot be put upon the parts of the Bible which have been covered by Mr. Darrow's questions. I hope for the last time no further attempt will be made by counsel on the other side of the case, or Mr. Bryan, to say the defense is concerned at all with Mr. Darrow's particular religious views or lack of religious views. We are here as lawyers with the same right to our views. I have the same right to mine as a Christian as Mr. Bryan has to his, and we do not intend to have this case charged by Mr. Darrow's agnosticism or Mr. Bryan's brand of Christianity. (A great applause.)

Mr. Darrow:

Q—Mr. Bryan, do you believe that the first woman was Eve?

A—Yes.

Q—Do you believe she was literally made out of Adams's rib?

A—I do.

Q—Did you ever discover where Cain got his wife?

A—No, sir; I leave the agnostics to hunt for her.

Q—You have never found out?

A—I have never tried to find

Q—You have never tried to find?

A—No.

Q—The Bible says he got one, doesn't it? Were there other people on the earth at that time?

A—I cannot say.

Q—You cannot say. Did that ever enter your consideration?

A—Never bothered me.

Q—There were no others recorded, but Cain got a wife.

A—That is what the Bible says.

Q—Where she came from you do not know. All right. Does the statement, "The morning and the evening were the first day," and "The morning and the evening were the second day," mean anything to you?

A— I do not think it necessarily means a twenty-four-hour day.

Q—You do not?

A—No.

Q—What do you consider it to be?

A—I have not attempted to explain it. If you will take the second chapter—let me have the book. (Examining Bible.) The fourth verse of the second chapter says: "These are the generations of the heavens and of the earth, when they were created in the day that the Lord God made the earth and the heavens," the word "day" there in the very next chapter is used to describe a period. I do not see that there is any necessity for construing the words, "the evening and the morning," as meaning necessarily a twenty-four-hour day, "in the day when the Lord made the heaven and the earth."

Q—Then, when the Bible said, for instance, "and God called the firmament heaven. And the evening and the morning were the second day," that does not necessarily mean twenty-four hours?

A—I do not think it necessarily does.

Q—Do you think it does or does not?

A—I know a great many think so.

Q—What do you think?

A—I do not think it does.

Q—You think those were not literal days?

A—I do not think they were twenty-four-hour days.

Q—What do you think about it?

A—That is my opinion—I do not know that my opinion is better on that subject than those who think it does.

Q—You do not think that?

A—No. But I think it would be just as easy for the kind of God we believe in to make the earth in six days as in six years or in 6,000,000 years or in 600,000,000 years. I do not think it important whether we believe one or the other.

Q—Do you think those were literal days?

A—My impression is they were periods, but I would not attempt to argue as against anybody who wanted to believe in literal days.

Q—I will read it to you from the Bible: "And the Lord God said unto the serpent, because thou hast done this, thou art cursed above all cattle, and above every beast of the field; upon thy belly shalt thou go and dust shalt thou eat all the days of thy life." Do you think that is why the serpent is compelled to crawl upon its belly?

A—I believe that.

Q—Have you any idea how the snake went before that time?

A—No, sir.

Q—Do you know whether he walked on his tail or not?

A—No, sir. I have no way to know. (Laughter in audience).

Q—Now, you refer to the cloud that was put in heaven after the flood, the rainbow. Do you believe in that?

A—Read it.

Q—All right, Mr. Bryan, I will read it for you.

Bryan—Your Honor, I think I can shorten this testimony. The only purpose Mr. Darrow has is to slur at the Bible, but I will answer his question. I will answer it all at once, and I have no objection in the world, I want the world to know that this man, who does not believe in a God, is trying to use a court in Tennessee—

Darrow—I object to that.

Bryan—(Continuing) to slur at it, and while it will require time, I am willing to take it.

Darrow—I object to your statement. I am exempting you on your fool ideas that no intelligent Christian on earth believes.

The Court—Court is adjourned until 9 o'clock tomorrow morning.

Source: *The State of Tennessee v. John Thomas Scopes (1925),* Day 7. See Douglas Linder's transcript of the trial at: http://www.famous-trials.com/scopesmonkey/2124-day7.

Further Reading

Adair, James. 2008. *Introducing Christianity.* New York: Routledge.

Armitage, Angus. 1951. *The World of Copernicus.* New York: Mentor Books.

Barbour, Ian G. 1997. *Religion and Science: Historical and Contemporary Issues.* New York: HarperCollins.

Barbour, Ian G. 2000. *When Science Meets Religion.* New York: HarperSanFrancisco.

Calvin, John. (c. 1555) 1980. *Sermon on the Ten Commandments.* Grand Rapids, MI: Baker Book House.

Chryssides, George D. 2010. *Christianity Today.* New York: Continuum.

Cohen, I. Bernard. 1985. *Revolution in Science.* Cambridge, MA: Belknap.

Colish, Marcia L. 1997. *Medieval Foundations of the Western Intellectual Tradition, 400–1400.* New Haven, CT: Yale University Press.

Collins, Francis. 2006. *The Language of God.* New York: Free Press.

Crosby, Alfred W. 1997. *The Measure of Reality.* Cambridge: Cambridge University Press.

Danielson, Dennis Richard. 2000. *The Book of the Cosmos.* Cambridge, MA: Perseus Publishing.

Darwin, Charles. (1859) 2003. *The Origin of Species and the Voyage of the Beagle.* New York: Knopf.

Darwin, Francis, and A. C. Sewards, eds. 1903. *More Letters of Charles Darwin.* 2 vols. New York: Appleton.

Dembski, William. 1999. *Intelligent Design: The Bridge between Science and Theology*. Downers Grove, IL: Intervarsity Press.

Dowe, Phil. 2005. *Galileo, Darwin, and Hawking: The Interplay of Science, Reason, and Religion*. Grand Rapids, MI: Eerdmans.

Draper, John William. 1874. *History of the Conflict between Religion and Science*. New York: Appleton.

Ferngren, Gary B., ed. 2002. *Science and Religion: A Historical Introduction*. Baltimore: Johns Hopkins University Press.

Finocchiaro, Maurice A. 1989. *The Galileo Affair: A Documentary History*. Berkeley: University of California Press.

Fyfe, Aileen. 2004. *Science and Salvation: Evangelical Popular Science Publishing in Victorian Britain*. Chicago: University of Chicago Press.

Gingerich, Owen. 2006. *God's Universe*. Cambridge, MA: Belknap Press.

Gould, Stephen Jay. 1999. *Rocks of Ages: Science and Religion in the Fullness of Life*. New York: Ballantine.

Grant, Edward. 1971. *Physical Science in the Middle Ages*. New York: Wiley.

Grant, Edward. 1994. *Planets, Stars, and Orbs: The Medieval Cosmos, 1200–1687*. Cambridge: Cambridge University Press.

Grant, Edward. 1996. *The Foundations of Modern Science in the Middle Ages: Their Religious, Institutional, and Intellectual Contexts*. Cambridge: Cambridge University Press.

Jaki, Stanley. 2000. *The Savior of Science*. Grand Rapids, MI: Eerdmans.

Johanson, Donald, and Blake Edgar. 2006. *From Lucy to Language*. Rev. ed. New York: Simon and Schuster.

Larson, Edward. 1997. *Summer for the Gods: The Scopes Trial and America's Continuing Debate over Science and Religion*. Cambridge, MA: Harvard University Press.

Lyell, Charles. (1830–1833) 1997. *Principles of Geology*. London: Penguin.

Margenau, Henry, and Roy Abraham Varghese. 1992. *Cosmos, Bios, Theos: Scientists Reflect on Science, God, and the Origins of the Universe, Life, and Homo Sapiens*. La Salle, IL: Open Court.

Mason, Stephen E. 1962. *A History of the Sciences*. Rev. ed. New York: Macmillan.

Miller, Kenneth R. 1999. *Finding Darwin's God*. New York: Cliff Street Books.

Numbers, Ronald. 2007. "Vulgar Science." In *Modern Christianity: To 1900*, edited by Amanda Porterfield. Minneapolis, MN: Fortress Press.

Olson, Steve. 2003. *Mapping Human History*. Boston, MA: Houghton Mifflin.

Park, Katharine, and Lorraine Daston. 2001. *Wonders and the Order of Nature, 1150–1750*. Rev. ed. Brooklyn, NY: Zone Books.

Polkinghorne, John. 2000. *Faith, Science and Understanding*. New Haven, CT: Yale University Press.

Porter, Roy. 1998. *The Greatest Benefit to Mankind*. New York: W. W. Norton.

Rosenberg, Charles E. 1997. *No Other Gods: On Science and American Social Thought*. 2nd ed. Baltimore: Johns Hopkins University Press.

Russell, Jeffrey Burton. 1997. *Inventing the Flat Earth: Columbus and Modern Historians*. Westport, CT: Praeger.

Sobel, Dava. 1999. *Galileo's Daughter*. London: Penguin.

Stark, Rodney. 2003. *For the Glory of God: How Monotheism Led to Reformations, Science, Witch-Hunts, and the End of Slavery*. Princeton, NJ: Princeton University Press.

Stark, Rodney. 2005. *The Victory of Reason: How Christianity Led to Freedom, Capitalism, and Western Success*. New York: Random House.

Stark, Rodney. 2011. *The Triumph of Christianity*. New York: HarperOne.

Tattersall, Ian. 1998. *Becoming Human*. San Diego, CA: Harcourt Brace.

Thomas, Keith. 1971. *Religion and the Decline of Magic*. New York: Scribners.

White, Andrew Dickson. 1896. *A History of the Warfare of Science with Theology in Christendom*. New York: D. Appleton.

Whitehead, Alfred North. (1925) 1967. *Science and the Modern World*. New York: Free Press.

8

The United States Is
Abandoning Christianity

What People Think Happened

It is common to read headlines announcing the decline of religion in the United States. It is a trope in U.S. history that reappears fairly regularly, both in the distant past as well as more recently. For example, in 1966, *TIME* magazine resurrected this narrative by famously asking "Is God Dead?" on its ominous-looking red and black cover. That iconic issue—about the declining relevance of Christianity in the United States—is often cited as one of the most impactful magazine covers in U.S. journalistic history. It was very effective in its ability to capture the zeitgeist of the counterculture movement that was so vibrant during the era.

Since then, journals, books, and surveys routinely declare Christianity's steep decline in the United States. Some have even claimed "the end of Christian America" (notably without a question mark) as Jon Meacham did in his 2009 *Newsweek* magazine article. Drawing from surveys, trends, and reports, Meacham argued that Americans are walking away from faith. This trope continues with books such as *The End of White Christian America* (2016) by Robert Jones, and the scholarly treatise *The Secular Landscape: The Decline of Religion in America* (2017) by Kevin McCaffree. Scholars such as Phil Zuckerman have made their careers by arguing secularization is coming to the United States, just as it has in Europe, and we should welcome it. Zuckerman is part of "The New Atheism" movement that is usually headlined by the so-called Four Horsemen: Sam Harris,

Christopher Hitchens (1949–2011), Richard Dawkins, and Daniel Dennett. These thinkers have pushed the narrative that religion is dying, and it is a most welcomed development.

It is common to think of the United States as a nation that began with extremely religious people. The Puritans are usually associated with religious zealotry, as they came to the United States for religious freedom. While the Founding Fathers supposedly separated church from state, the religious impulse in the United States continued . . . until the late nineteenth and early twentieth century. That is when scientific thinking started making its mark on U.S. educational institutions. Darwin's legacy started winning the battle against Christian fundamentalism in education, prayer was forced out of public schools, the Swinging Sixties liberated everybody, and the great process of secularization in the United States hit its stride.

According to this story, by the late twentieth century, religion was no longer a major force in the United States. Christian institutions were declining; God had been forced out of schools, courts, and most other public institutions. The tables had turned in many ways: it used to be the case that evolution could not be taught in public schools, but by the late twentieth century, it was illegal to teach *creationism* to public school kids.

Thus, while the United States began as a religious nation, this was no longer the case. Christian denominations were in rapid decline. An increasing number of people were declaring themselves to be "not religious" on surveys. Gone were the days when everyone went to church, and God was proclaimed everywhere: from the Pledge of Allegiance to the prayer before Friday-night football at high school stadiums across the nation. In the days of old, all hotels had Bibles in the rooms, and Billy Graham's sermons were a constant presence on national television. But those were the 1950s, when virtually everybody was religious. By the twenty-first century, those days were long gone.

The United States had abandoned Christianity. Its future was a secular one. Or such is what people thought. Both the extremely religious and the extremely non-religious made these proclamations, albeit with very different motives.

How the Story Became Popular

Perhaps the best place to start would be that 1966 *TIME* magazine cover that asked "Is God Dead?" That magazine cover was a game-changer, as it was cutting edge, even shocking, to many. Up to that point, Americans thought of themselves as the antithesis to Communist China and the atheistic Soviet Union. Americans were the Christians, and the Soviets and other Communists were victims of their own success. They pushed God out of their nations, but at a terrible price: their freedoms. Those "godless" cultures were not us. The United States was a religious nation, as Jesus claimed, a "city on a hill," letting its light shine over the entire world.

The "Christian America" idea has ebbed and flowed throughout history. The writers of the U.S. Constitution (authored in 1787) represent a low point, as they seem to have consciously kept any mention of God or the divine out of the document. However, the Declaration of Independence writers, in 1776, utterly championed the role of the divine, as they boldly referred to God four times: (1) the "laws of nature and of nature's God"; (2) men are "endowed by their Creator with certain unalienable rights"; (3) Congress appeals "to the Supreme Judge of the world for the rectitude of our intentions"; and (4) the signers, "with a firm reliance on the protection of divine Providence," pledged to each other their lives, fortunes, and sacred honor.

Another example here is the U.S. Pledge of Allegiance. While it was written in 1892 by Francis Bellamy, it was not formally adopted by Congress until 1942. The original version of the Pledge did not have the words "under God" in it. In 1954, however, due largely to the United States' long and protracted conflict with the atheist Communists, President Eisenhower supported a bill that enshrined "under God" into the Pledge. In his speech on Flag Day, June 14, 1954, while signing the bill to include "under God" in the Pledge, Eisenhower said these two words would be like a "spiritual weapon," and "millions of our school children will daily proclaim in every city and town, every village and rural school house, the dedication of our nation and our people to the Almighty."

The Soviet Union fell apart, however, in 1989. The Berlin Wall was pummeled by Germans celebrating their reunion as a nation. Over the next couple of years, nation after nation in the Soviet Union, declared independence and began their attempts at democracy, some more effective than others. And what was perhaps most surprising was that Soviet atheism was a sham. It was a policy that was brutally enforced over the years since Vladimir Lenin (a convinced atheist) tried to supplant Orthodox Christianity with Marxism in his realm of influence. Joseph Stalin and Nikita Khrushchev continued the radically atheistic policies from the 1920s through the 1960s. By that time, religion had been effectively purged from the land. What few religious believers remained tended to practice privately or underground.

Since 1989, the United States' chief political enemy has changed dramatically. For much of the twentieth century, U.S. ideology defined itself against the USSR's unbelief. However, after September 11, 2001, the United States entered a new war against extreme belief, in the form of radical Islamic groups such as the Taliban, Hezbollah, and the Islamic State. This change was profound and impacted U.S. politicians in ways both subtle and profound. Instead of championing its national religious ideology, Americans tended to favor the "separation of church and state" ideals of the nation's founders such as Thomas Jefferson. No longer was it fashionable to fuse God and politics, as was so common in the 1950s and in the Cold War era overall. These political changes set the background for a secularization thesis that would gain much steam at the end of the twentieth century.

More recently, however, the primary engine pushing the story that the United States is abandoning Christianity is the field of social science. This is not at all to say that social scientists are collectively responsible. Rather, it is to say that since the 1960s there has been a major, complicated idea called the "secularization thesis." To simplify, this is a notion—often with Marxist assumptions—that religion will wither away, as Karl Marx famously predicted. Religion will one day be eclipsed by science and rational thinking. Fanaticism of all kinds will lose ground as humans evolve and learn more about our world and about ourselves. We will have no need for religion, since, instead of investing into gods and afterlife, we will invest into humans, and we will invest ourselves into improving this life. As science answers the questions that have vexed us for centuries, we will have no need for the God hypothesis.

Social science is an extremely useful tool. Both quantitative surveys and qualitative interviews are methods used by virtually all academicians in the humanities and social sciences, helping educators understand what is happening in society and providing insights into how to respond. One problem, however, is that social science is often hyper-focused on the present and future rather than the past. There is a tendency to focus on one moment in time, without evaluating the larger social context. Another problem with social science is that its predictions about the future are precarious. An obvious example is the 2016 U.S. presidential election. The social science—virtually all of it—predicted a Clinton landslide. But that didn't happen.

When the results of social science are combined with larger historical awareness, however, ideas that appear revolutionary or unprecedented come back down to earth. "History repeats itself" is a cliché that gets overused. It is not a precise statement, really. In a way, it is an absurd notion—that reality is on a cycle, on a loop, and everything simply gets repeated. Nevertheless, despite its obvious deficiencies, there is great truth to the idea that much of what we experience as a society has parallels in the events of our collective past.

In regard to Christianity, social science has been having a field day proclaiming the decline of Christianity in the United States. Pew Forum has declared that Christianity will decline substantially over the coming decades, with no rebound in sight. In their book *American Secularism* (2015), sociologists Joseph Baker and Buster Smith declare that the United States is a "nation of nonbelievers" (Baker and Smith 2015, 1). They base their research on a major database called the World Values Survey, which records that 28 percent of Americans are atheists or "not religious." The religiously based Barna Group regularly decries the "post-Christian" status of many Americans as well as many U.S. cities. Robert Putnam's important "Faith Matters" survey informs us that there are more religiously unaffiliated Americans than there are mainline Protestants today (Putnam 2010, 17).

Popular media outlets such as CNN, USA Today, and Fox often jump onto one or two statistics from the research without putting them into proper context. Results of a survey can be very misleading without a responsible historical or sociological explanation. For example, studies in Europe by Abby Day and Grace Davie have shown that many people who say they are not religious actually are. In the surveys, they will tick a box that says they have "no religious affiliation." The media then jumps all over the results of those surveys. But when those same people are questioned in a qualitative environment (rather than the quantitative survey), they admit to praying, believing in miracles, divine healing, talking with ancestors, belief in guardian angels, and all manner of religious beliefs. They just don't consider themselves religious. They often respond that they are "spiritual but not religious." In the eyes of a religious studies researcher, these people are actually religious. They just don't know it. There exists a disconnect between the person who designed the survey and the people being surveyed.

PRIMARY DOCUMENTS

VLADIMIR LENIN'S "SOCIALISM AND RELIGION" (1905)

Vladimir Lenin (1870–1924) was the most important early leader of the Bolshevik ("majority") movement in Russia in the early twentieth century. He served as the head of Soviet Russia and later the Soviet Union from 1917 until his death in 1924. Lenin was an ardent Marxist, in the sense that he thought religion was complicit in the exploitation of the masses. Committed to what he called the "scientific world-outlook," he agreed with Marx that religion is oppressive and therefore should be abandoned. In this reading, we see Lenin's deep disdain for religion. After his death, his ideas on religion became more radicalized, leading to the mass murder of clergy and religious sympathizers in Russia after the Bolsheviks attained full control. In the twentieth century, most Americans detested the Soviet Union's stance on religion, leading to a national pro-religious sentiment in the 1950s that lasted at least to the demise of the USSR. With the fall of the Soviet Union in 1989, the heavy social pressure on Americans to publicly support religion began to lift somewhat.

Present-day society is wholly based on the exploitation of the vast masses of the working class by a tiny minority of the population, the class of the landowners and that of the capitalists. It is a slave society, since the "free" workers, who all their life work for the capitalists, are "entitled" only to such means of subsistence as are essential for the maintenance of slaves who produce profit, for the safeguarding and perpetuation of capitalist slavery. The economic oppression of the workers inevitably calls forth and engenders every kind of political oppression and social humiliation, the coarsening and darkening of the spiritual and moral life of the masses. The workers may secure a greater or lesser degree of political liberty to fight for their economic emancipation, but no amount of liberty will rid them of poverty, unemployment, and oppression until the power of capital is overthrown. Religion is one of the forms of spiritual oppression which everywhere weighs down heavily upon the masses of the people, over burdened by their perpetual work for others, by want and isolation. Impotence of the exploited classes in their struggle against the exploiters just as inevitably gives rise to the belief in a better life after death as impotence of the savage in his battle with nature gives rise to belief in gods, devils, miracles, and the like. Those who toil and live in want all their lives are taught by religion to be submissive and patient while here on earth, and to take comfort in the hope of a heavenly reward. But those who live by the labor of others are taught by religion to practice charity while on earth, thus offering them a very cheap way of justifying their entire existence as exploiters and selling them at a moderate price tickets to well-being in heaven. Religion is opium for the people. Religion is a sort of spiritual booze, in which the slaves of capital drown their human image, their demand for a life more or less worthy of man.

But a slave who has become conscious of his slavery and has risen to struggle for his emancipation has already half ceased to be a slave. The modern class-conscious worker, reared by large-scale factory industry and enlightened by urban life, contemptuously casts aside religious prejudices, leaves heaven to the priests and bourgeois bigots, and tries to win a better life for himself here on earth. The proletariat of today takes the side of socialism, which enlists science in the battle against the fog of religion, and frees the workers from their belief in life after death by welding them together to fight in the present for a better life on earth.

Religion must be declared a private affair. In these words, socialists usually express their attitude towards religion. But the meaning of these words should be accurately defined to prevent any misunderstanding. We demand that religion be held a private affair so far as the state is concerned. But by no means can we consider religion a private affair so far as our Party is concerned. Religion must be of no concern to the state, and religious societies must have no connection with governmental authority. Everyone must be absolutely free to profess any religion he pleases, or no religion whatever, i.e., to be an atheist, which every socialist is, as a rule. Discrimination among citizens on account of their religious convictions is wholly intolerable. Even the bare mention of a citizen's religion in official documents should unquestionably be eliminated. No subsidies should be granted to the established church nor state allowances made to ecclesiastical and religious societies. These should become absolutely free associations of like-minded citizens, associations independent of the state. Only the complete fulfilment of these demands can put an end to the shameful and accursed past when the church lived in feudal dependence on the state, and Russian citizens lived in feudal dependence on the established church, when medieval, inquisitorial laws (to this day remaining in our criminal codes and on our statute-books) were in existence and were applied, persecuting men for their belief or disbelief, violating men's consciences, and linking cozy government jobs and government-derived incomes with the dispensation of this or that dope by the established church. Complete separation of Church and State is what the socialist proletariat demands of the modern state and the modern church.

The Russian revolution must put this demand into effect as a necessary component of political freedom. In this respect, the Russian revolution is in a particularly favorable position, since the revolting officialism of the police-ridden feudal autocracy has called forth discontent, unrest and indignation even among the clergy. However abject, however ignorant Russian Orthodox clergymen may have been, even they have now been awakened by the thunder of the downfall of the old, medieval order in Russia. Even they are joining in the demand for freedom, are protesting against bureaucratic practices and officialism, against the spying for the police imposed on the "servants of God." We socialists must lend this movement our support, carrying the demands of honest and sincere members of the clergy to their conclusion, making them stick to their words about freedom, demanding that they should resolutely break all ties between religion and the police. Either you are sincere, in which case you must stand for the complete separation of Church and State and of School and Church, for religion to be declared wholly and absolutely a private affair. Or you do not accept these consistent demands for freedom, in which case you evidently are still held captive by the traditions of the inquisition, in which case you evidently still cling to your cozy government jobs and government-derived incomes, in which case you evidently do not believe in the spiritual power of your weapon and continue to take bribes from the state. And in that case the class-conscious workers of all Russia declare merciless war on you.

So far as the party of the socialist proletariat is concerned, religion is not a private affair. Our Party is an association of class-conscious, advanced fighters for the emancipation of the working class. Such an association cannot and must not be indifferent to lack of class-consciousness, ignorance or obscurantism in the shape of religious beliefs. We demand complete disestablishment of the Church so as to be able to combat the religious fog with purely ideological and solely ideological weapons, by means of our press and by word of mouth. But we founded our association, the Russian Social-Democratic Labor Party, precisely for such a struggle against every religious bamboozling of the workers. And to us the ideological struggle is not a private affair, but the affair of the whole Party, of the whole proletariat.

If that is so, why do we not declare in our Program that we are atheists? Why do we not forbid Christians and other believers in God to join our Party?

The answer to this question will serve to explain the very important difference in the way the question of religion is presented by the bourgeois democrats and the Social-Democrats.

Our Program is based entirely on the scientific, and moreover the materialist, world-outlook. An explanation of our Program, therefore, necessarily includes an explanation of the true historical and economic roots of the religious fog. Our propaganda necessarily includes the propaganda of atheism; the publication of the appropriate scientific literature, which the autocratic feudal government has hitherto strictly forbidden and persecuted, must now form one of the fields of our Party work. We shall now probably have to follow the advice Engels once gave to the German Socialists: to translate and widely disseminate the literature of the eighteenth-century French Enlighteners and atheists.

But under no circumstances ought we to fall into the error of posing the religious question in an abstract, idealistic fashion, as an "intellectual" question unconnected with the class struggle, as is not infrequently done by the radical-democrats from among the bourgeoisie. It would be stupid to think that, in a society based on the endless oppression and coarsening of the worker masses, religious prejudices could be dispelled by purely propaganda methods. It would be bourgeois narrow-mindedness to forget that the yoke of religion that weighs upon mankind is merely a product and reflection of the economic yoke within society. No number of pamphlets and no amount of preaching can enlighten the proletariat, if it is not enlightened by its own struggle against the dark forces of capitalism. Unity in this really revolutionary struggle of the oppressed class for the creation of a paradise on earth is more important to us than unity of proletarian opinion on paradise in heaven.

That is the reason why we do not and should not set forth our atheism in our Program; that is why we do not and should not prohibit proletarians who still retain vestiges of their old prejudices from associating themselves with our Party. We shall always preach the scientific world-outlook, and it is essential for us to combat the inconsistency of various "Christians." But that does not mean in the least that the religious question ought to be advanced to first place, where it does not belong at all; nor does it mean that we should allow the forces of the really revolutionary economic and political struggle to be split up on account of third-rate opinions or senseless ideas, rapidly losing all political importance, rapidly being swept out as rubbish by the very course of economic development.

Everywhere the reactionary bourgeoisie has concerned itself, and is now beginning to concern itself in Russia, with the fomenting of religious strife—in order thereby to divert the attention of the masses from the really important and fundamental economic and political problems, now being solved in practice by the all-Russian proletariat uniting in revolutionary struggle. This reactionary policy of splitting up the proletarian forces, which today manifests itself mainly in Black-Hundred pogroms, may tomorrow conceive some more subtle forms. We, at any rate, shall oppose it by calmly, consistently and patiently preaching proletarian solidarity and the scientific world-outlook—a preaching alien to any stirring up of secondary differences.

The revolutionary proletariat will succeed in making religion a really private affair, so far as the state is concerned. And in this political system, cleansed of medieval mildew, the proletariat will wage a broad and open struggle for the elimination of economic slavery, the true source of the religious humbugging of mankind.

Source: Marxists Internet Archive. Originally published by Lenin in *Novaya Zhizn*, No. 28, December 3, 1905. Available at https://www.marxists.org/archive/lenin/works/1905/dec/03.htm.

What Really Happened

The truth is that Americans have always been religious, and there is no significant downward trend when looking at the evidence in a larger historical context. In 1776, "only about 17 percent of those living in one of the thirteen colonies actually belonged to a religious congregation." In a newly independent United States, over one-third of all first births occurred "after less than nine months of marriage." Thus, Rodney Stark points out, "Single women in Colonial New England were more likely to engage in premarital sex than to attend church." So much for the "puritanism" we tend to associate with that era. In reality, Puritans accounted for less than half of those aboard the *Mayflower* in 1620. And once the Puritans established a colony, only about 22 percent of the colonists belonged to a church (Stark 2011, 353–354). Most early Americans were not as religious as we tend to think.

Nevertheless, Europeans have always been somewhat perplexed by the high rates of U.S. religiosity that they encounter when they visit. This has been the case since very early on, most famously in the wonderfully insightful observations of Alexis de Tocqueville (1805–1859), who wrote in the aftermath of his 1831 visit, "There is no country in the world where the Christian religion retains a greater influence over the souls of men than in America." Like Tocqueville, European travelers to the United States routinely noticed high levels of religious participation, as well as the sincerity and intensity of their faith (Huntington 2004, 98).

In contrast, Americans who traveled to Europe, such as the religious historian Robert Baird, noted that "nowhere in Europe did church attendance come close to the level taken for granted by Americans." Baird made this observation in 1844, after spending eight years traveling in Europe (Stark 2011, 354).

Over the few centuries that the United States has existed, Christianity has remained a critical part of the society. It might ebb and flow in intensity, but it is always there. The fluctuations have little bearing on the fact that the United States is, by and large, a Christian nation. There are more Christians in the United States than in any other nation in the world. And Americans have always been rather religious when compared with other peoples, especially in the West. In fact, according to distinguished Harvard professor Samuel Huntington, "Little or no evidence exists of a downward trend in American religiosity." Americans are, literally, "a Christian people" overall (Huntington 2004, 98–102).

In 1811, the Supreme Court declared "We are a Christian people." The Senate Judiciary Committee said the exact same thing in 1853. President Lincoln used the same phrase "We are a Christian people" during the Civil War. In 1892 the Supreme Court declared "this is a Christian nation," as did the House of Representatives in 1908. Similar pronouncements were made at the highest levels of U.S. government in 1917 (the Congress), 1931 (the Supreme Court), and in 1954 when President Eisenhower orchestrated that the phrase "under God" would be said each day in U.S. schools (Huntington 2004, 98).

U.S. religious history is a story of revival. In the 1600s, the Puritans were excited about their faith, so much so that they were willing to cross the Atlantic in a perilous journey and begin new lives in a foreign land. In the 1700s, America was home to the First Great Awakening, led by Jonathan Edwards and the extremely popular Wesleyan preacher from England, George Whitefield. Mark Noll estimates that "Whitefield may have been heard by half of the inhabitants of the seven American colonies he visited during his initial 10-week tour." Whitefield's Christianity was based on a personal decision that one would make to follow Jesus Christ as Lord. It was often associated with a "warming of the heart" that led the believer to repentance. Tens of thousands of Americans were revived in their Christian faith due to the First Great Awakening (Daughrity 2010, 144–145).

U.S. religious life in the 1800s was dominated by what is known as the Second Great Awakening, which began with the Cane Ridge Revival in Kentucky in 1801. Led by Barton Stone, this revival attracted more than 25,000 people. Through the revivalist campaigns of Charles Finney, the revival morphed into a nationwide movement that birthed several important denominations that still exist in the United States today: Disciples of Christ, Seventh-Day Adventists, Jehovah's Witnesses, Church of Christ Scientists, and the Mormons.

Perhaps the most important revival in U.S. history took place in the 1900s, and that is the Azusa Street Revival, which first broke out in 1906 in Los Angeles, and lasted for several years. That revival gave birth to what we now call the Pentecostal movement, which has impacted hundreds of millions of people over its one-hundred-plus years of existence. Led by William Seymour, a son of freed slaves who had only one good eye, the 1906 revival changed the contours of world Christianity in remarkable ways. Los Angeles has always been a very multiracial city, and at the Azusa Street Revival it was famously said that "the color line was washed away in the blood of the lamb." It has been claimed that the Pentecostal movement is now five-hundred-million people strong, making it probably the fastest growing religious movement in human history (Daughrity 2015, 82–95).

In the 1960s and 1970s, some of the United States' leading scholars predicted that Americans would eventually secularize, much as Europeans seem to be doing. Now, that theory has been thrown out the window. Peter Berger (1929–2017), one of the foremost sociologists in the United States, held to the secularization theory in the 1960s, but by the end of his career he had completely changed his mind, conceding that the United States is as religious today as it ever has been.

The United States is not turning secular. It was a false alarm. Americans are today far more religious than they were at the founding of the nation. The United States has a history of revivalism that keeps it religious, and its religious plurality seems to keep churches on their toes, competing against each other, unlike the nations of Europe—where one church often monopolizes religion. This is one reason religious innovation rarely comes out of Finland (Lutheran), Spain (Catholic), or Greece (Orthodoxy). Europe's religious history is one of religious monopolization. But the opposite is true in the United States. Religious pluralism has led to religious vibrancy among the churches. As some churches lose relevance, they decline and eventually die. But new movements—such as Pentecostalism—are always waiting in the wings in the United States, ready to meet the needs of the people (Daughrity 2018, 67).

Samuel Huntington puts U.S. Christianity into perspective: "The proportion of Christians in America rivals or exceeds the proportion of Jews in Israel, of Muslims in Egypt, of Hindus in India, and of Orthodox believers in Russia." There are those who argue that as immigration increases, Christianity will decline in the United States. But the vast majority of immigrants to the United States are already Christian (e.g., Latin Americans and Filipinos). However, research shows that even immigrants from non-Christian nations tend to be Christians themselves. Or, they often become Christian after they arrive in the United States. For example, around 44 percent of Asian Americans are Christians, and for many years, somewhere around two-thirds of Arab immigrants to the United States were actually Christians (Daughrity 2018, 194; Huntington 2004, 99–100).

Thus, while headlines declare the end of Christianity in the United States, the truth is very different. In 1940, around 37 percent of Americans claimed to have gone to church in the previous week; in 2002, it was at 43 percent. In 1944, around 96 percent of Americans said they believe in God; in 1995, it was the same: 96 percent. In 2017, only 3 percent of Americans claim to be atheists. In 2017, the U.S. Congress was 91 percent Christian, and that number has hardly changed over the last few generations. Indeed, "if America doesn't qualify as a Christian nation, then it would be hard to find one that does" (Daughrity 2018, 85–86).

Perhaps Huntington said it best, "At the start of the twenty-first century, Americans were no less committed and quite possibly were more committed to their Christian identity than at any time in their history" (Huntington 2004, 103).

PRIMARY DOCUMENTS

REACTION TO THE AZUSA STREET REVIVAL
(APRIL 18, 1906)

The Azusa Street Revival was a major turning point in U.S. Christianity, and indeed in world Christianity. It launched the Pentecostal movement, which has exploded in size and has touched hundreds of millions of people all over the globe. It is by far the most significant religious movement born in the United States.

Weird Babel of Tongues
New Sect of Fanatics Is Breaking Loose.
Wild Scene Last Night on Azusa Street.
Gurgle of Wordless Talk by a Sister.

Breathing strange utterances and mouthing a creed which it would seem no sane mortal could understand, the newest religious sect has started in Los Angeles. Meetings are held in a tumble-down shack on

Azusa street, near San Pedro street, and the devotees of the weird doctrine practice the most fanatical rites, preach the wildest theories and work themselves into a state of mad excitement in their peculiar zeal. Colored people and a sprinkling of whites compose the congregation, and night is made hideous in the neighborhood by the howlings of the worshipers, who spend hours swaying forth and back in a nerve-racking attitude of prayer and supplication. They claim to have "the gift of tongues," and to be able to comprehend the babel. Such a startling claim has never yet been made by any company of fanatics, even in Los Angeles, the home of almost numberless creeds. Sacred tenets, reverently mentioned by the orthodox believer, are dealt with in a familiar, if not irreverent, manner by these latest religionists.

Stony Optic Defies

An old colored exhorter, blind in one eye, is the major-domo of the company. With his stony optic fixed on some luckless unbeliever, the old man yells his defiance and challenges an answer. Anathemas are heaped upon him who shall dare to gainsay the utterances of the preacher. Clasped in his big fist the colored brother holds a miniature Bible from which he reads at intervals one or two words—never more. After an hour spent in exhortation the brethren present are Invited to join in a "meeting of prayer, song and testimony." Then it is that pandemonium breaks loose, and the bounds of reason are passed by those who are "filled with the spirit," whatever that may be. "You-oo-oo gou-loo-loo come under the bloo-oo-oo boo-Ioo," shouts an old colored "mammy," in a frenzy of religious zeal. Swinging her arms wildly about her she continues with the strangest harangue ever uttered. Few of her words are intelligible, and for the most part her testimony contains the most outrageous jumble of syllables, which are listened to with awe by the company.

"Let Tongues Come Forth"

One of the wildest of the meetings was held last night, and the highest pitch of excitement was reached by the gathering, which continued in "worship" until nearly midnight. The old exhorter urged the "sisters" to let the "tongues come forth" and the women gave themselves over to a riot of religious fervor. As a result, a buxom dame was overcome with excitement and almost fainted. Undismayed by the fearful attitude of the colored worshiper, another black woman jumped to the floor and began a wild gesticulation, which ended in a gurgle of wordless prayers which were nothing less than shocking. "She's speakin' in unknown tongues," announced the leader, in an awed whisper. "Keep on, sister." The sister continued until it was necessary to assist her to a seat because of her bodily fatigue.

Gold among Them

Among the "believers" is a man who claims to be a Jewish rabbi. He says his name is Gold, and claims to have held positions in some of the largest synagogues in the United States. He told the motley company last night that he is well known to the Jewish people of Los Angeles and San Francisco, and referred to prominent local citizens by name. Gold claims to have been miraculously healed and is a convert of the new sect. Another speaker had a vision in which he saw the people of Los Angeles flocking in a mighty stream to perdition. He prophesied awful destruction to this city unless its citizens are brought to a belief in the tenets of the new faith.

> **Source:** *Los Angeles Daily Times*, Wednesday Morning, April 18, 1906. Photocopy available at https://www.newspapers.com/clip/9928151/azusa_street_weird_babel _tongues/.

THE APOSTOLIC FAITH, "PENTECOST HAS COME"

The Apostolic Faith *was the publication of William Seymour and the people first involved in the Azusa Street Revival. It was extremely successful in distributing the new message of these "Pentecostal" Christians. This reading is from the first issue of that paper. It is important to note that the revival began in April 1906, and by September of 1906 this paper was being published. It shows that the Pentecostal movement began with a surge of energy, powerfully impacting those who joined the revival during those early, frenetic months.*

The Apostolic Faith
Vol. I. No. 1.
Los Angeles, Cal.
September, 1906
Subscription Free

Pentecost Has Come

Los Angeles Being Visited by a Revival of Bible Salvation and Pentecost as Recorded in the Book of Acts

The power of God now has this city agitated as never before. Pentecost has surely come and with it the Bible evidences are following, many being converted and sanctified and filled with the Holy Ghost, speaking in tongues as they did on the day of Pentecost. The scenes that are daily enacted in the building on Azusa street and at Missions and churches in other parts of the city are beyond description, and the real revival has only started, as God has been working with His children mostly, getting them through to Pentecost, and laying the foundation for a mighty wave of salvation among the unconverted.

The meetings are held in an old Methodist church that had been converted in part into a tenement house, leaving a larger unplastered, barn-like room on the ground floor. Here about a dozen congregated each day, holding meetings on Bonnie Brae in the evening. The writer attended a few of these meetings and being so different from anything he had seen and not hearing any speaking in tongues, he branded the teaching as third-blessing heresy, and thought that settled it. It is needless to say the writer was compelled to do a great deal of apologizing and humbling himself to get right with God. In a short time God began to manifest His power and soon the building could not contain the people. Now the meetings continue all day and into the night and the fire is kindling all over the city and surrounding towns. Proud, well-dressed preachers come in to "investigate." Soon their high looks are replaced with wonder, then conviction comes, and very often you will find them in a short time wallowing on the dirty floor, asking God to forgive them and make them as little children.

It would be impossible to state how many have been converted, sanctified, and filled with the Holy Ghost. They have been and are daily going out to all points of the compass to spread this wonderful gospel.

Bro. Seymour's Call

Bro. W. J. Seymour has the following to say in regard to his call to this city:"It was the divine call that brought me from Houston, Texas, to Los Angeles. The Lord put it in the heart of some of the saints in Los Angeles to write to me that she felt the Lord would have me come over here and do a work, and l came, for I felt it was the leading of the Lord.

The Lord sent the means, and I came to take charge of a mission on Santa Fe Street. . . . The beginning of the Pentecost started in a cottage prayer meeting at 214 Bonnie Brae."

The Old-Time Pentecost

. . .

The meetings in Los Angeles started in a cottage meeting, and the Pentecost fell there three nights. The people had nothing to do but wait on the Lord and praise Him, and they commenced speaking in tongues, as they did at Pentecost, and the Spirit sang songs through them.

The meeting was then transferred to Azusa Street, and since then multitudes have been coming. The meetings begin about ten o'clock in the morning and can hardly stop before ten or twelve at night, and sometimes two or three in the morning, because so many are seeking, and some are slain under the power of God. People are seeking three times a day at the altar and row after row of seats have to be emptied and filled with seekers. We cannot tell how many people have been saved, and sanctified, and baptized with the Holy Ghost, and healed of all manner of sicknesses. Many are speaking in new tongues, and some are on their way to the foreign fields, with the gift of the language. . . .

Many have laid aside their glasses and had their eyesight perfectly restored. The deaf have had their hearing restored. A man was healed of asthma of twenty years standing. Many have been healed of heart trouble and lung trouble. A little girl who walked with crutches and had tuberculosis of the bones, as the doctors declared, was healed and dropped her crutches and began to skip about the yard.

The Lord has given the gift of writing in unknown languages, also the gift of playing on instruments. . . .

The secular papers have been stirred and published reports against the movement, but it has only resulted in drawing hungry souls who understand that the devil would not fight a thing unless God was in it. So they have come and found it was indeed the power of God.

Jesus was too large for the synagogues. He preached outside because there was not room for him inside. This Pentecostal movement is too large to be confined in any denomination or sect. It works outside, drawing all together in one bond of love, one church, one body of Christ.

A Mohammedan, a Soudanese by birth, a man who is an interpreter and speaks sixteen languages, came into the meetings at Azusa Street and the Lord gave him messages which none but himself could understand. He identified, interpreted and wrote a number of the languages.

A brother who had been a spiritualist medium and who was so possessed with demons that he had no rest, and was on the point of committing suicide, was instantly delivered of demon power. He then sought God for the pardon of his sins and sanctification, and is now filled with a different spirit.

. . .

In the meetings, it is noticeable that while some in the rear are opposing and arguing, others are at the altar falling down under the power of God and feasting on the good things of God. The two spirits are always manifest, but no opposition can kill, no power in earth or hell can stop God's work. . . .

Many have received the gift of singing as well as speaking in the inspiration of the Spirit. The Lord is giving new voices, he translates old songs into new tongues, he gives the music that is being sung by the angels and has a heavenly choir all singing the same heavenly song in harmony. It is beautiful music; no instruments are needed in the meetings.

The gift of languages is given with the commission, "Go ye into all the world and preach the gospel to every creature." The Lord has given languages to the unlearned, Greek, Latin, Hebrew, French, German, Italian, Chinese, Japanese, Zulu and languages of Africa, Hindu and Bengali and dialects of India, Chippewa and other languages of the Indians, Esquimaux, the deaf mute language and, in fact the Holy Ghost speaks all the languages of the world through His children. . . .

Not only old men and old women, but boys and girls, are receiving their Pentecost. Viola Price, a little orphan colored girl eight years of age, has received the gift of tongues.

Mrs. Lucy F. Farrow, God's anointed handmaid, who came some four months ago from Houston, Texas, to Los Angeles, bringing the full Gospel, and whom God has greatly used as she laid her hands on many who have received the Pentecost and the gift of tongues, has now returned to Houston, en route to Norfolk, Va. This is her old home which she left as a girl, being sold into slavery in the south.

The Precious Atonement
Children of God, partakers of the precious atonement, let us study and see what there is in it for us. First. Through the atonement we receive forgiveness of sins.

Second. We receive sanctification through the blood of Jesus

. . .

Third. Healing of our bodies. Sickness and disease are destroyed through the precious atonement of Jesus. . . . Sickness is born in a child just as original sin is born in the child. . . . Every sickness is of the devil. . . . Thank God, we have a living Christ among us to heal our diseases. He will heal every case.

Fourth. And we get the baptism with the Holy Ghost and fire upon the sanctified life.

From a Missionary to Africa

Bro. S. J. Mead, who was sent to Africa by Bishop Taylor in 1885, has been attending the meetings for several weeks. . . . God called Bro. Mead and wife from the Central part of Africa to Los Angeles to get their Pentecost. They recognize some of the languages spoken as being dialects of Africa. When God has fully equipped them they will return to their labor of love.

The Same Old Way

It has been said of the work in Los Angeles that He was "born in a manger and resurrected in a barn." Many are praising God for the old barn-like building on Azusa street, and the plain old plank beside which they kneeled in the sawdust when God saved, sanctified and baptized them with the Holy Ghost. . . .

The work began among the colored people. God baptized several sanctified wash women with the Holy Ghost, who have been much used of Him. The first white woman to receive the Pentecost and gift of tongues in Los Angeles was Mrs. Evans who is now in the work in Oakland. Since then multitudes have come. God makes no difference in nationality, Ethiopians, Chinese, Indians, Mexicans, and other nationalities worship together.

Pentecostal Faith Line

There are a dozen or more Christian workers who are devoting their time to the salvation of souls, having been called of God from other lines of employment to devote their time in praying with the sick, preaching, working with souls at the altar, etc. We believe in the faith line for

Christian workers, and no collections are taken. During the four months, meetings have been running constantly, and yet with working day and night and without purse or scrip, the workers have all been kept well and provided with food and raiment. Workers who have received calls to foreign lands are going out, the Lord providing the means with no needs being presented.

The Millennium

All these 6,000 years, we have been fighting against sin and Satan. Soon we shall have a rest of 1,000 years. We are going to rest from our 6,000 years of toil in a reign of 1,000 years. That will be the millennial age. (Jude 14,15). The saints who have part in the first resurrection will return with Jesus and reign over unglorified humanity. (Rev. 20:4). Our place will be higher than the angels, because we are partakers of His divine nature and His immortality, and angels are simply pure spirits. We can go and come, just as Jesus did when He rose from the dead. We can vanish out of sight and go millions of miles in a second. . . .

At the beginning of the Eighteenth century, among the French Protestants, there were wonderful manifestations of the Spirit power accompanied by the Gift of Tongues. The early Quakers received the same powerful religious stimulus and had the Gift of Tongues. The Irvingite church, about 1830, had the baptism with the Holy Ghost, and spoke in other tongues. In the Swedish revival in 1841–43 there were the same manifestations of the Spirit and also the Gift of Tongues. In the Irish revival of 1859 there is the record of the power of the Spirit in winning souls and the speaking in tongues by Spirit filled men and women. (For the above facts, my authority is Bishop Hurst's History of the Christian Church, Vol. 1).

Sample Copies

If you receive a sample copy of this paper and wish it continued, send your name and address to The Apostolic Faith, 312 Azusa Street, Los Angeles, Cal. Subscription free. If you know of any hungry souls to whom you wish the paper sent, send in their addresses and as the Lord permits we will send the paper. We are having 5,000 of this issue printed. The money came in answer to prayer. The next issue will come out as He permits. . . .

A baptismal service was held at Terminal Island, one of the beaches near Los Angeles. One hundred and six persons were baptized in the ocean. Bro. Seymour performed the baptismal services. All were immersed.

Missionaries to Jerusalem

A band of three missionaries, Bro. Andrew Johnson and Sisters Louisa Condit and Lucy M. Leatherman, who have been baptized with the Holy Ghost and received the gift of languages, have left for Jerusalem, going by way of Oakland, leaving there Aug. 10th. . . .

This is a worldwide revival, the last Pentecostal revival to bring our Jesus. The church is taking her last march to meet her beloved. . . .

He gave the former rain moderately at Pentecost, and he is going to send upon us in these last days the former and latter rain. There are greater things to be done in these last days of the Holy Ghost.

> **Source:** *The Apostolic Faith* 1:1 (September 1906). For the original version, see http://apostolicfaith.org/library/historical/azusa-originals/Azusa-Paper-Original-01.pdf. For an easier to read transcript, see http://www.azusabooks.org/af/LA01.shtml.

Further Reading

Aikman, David. 2012. *One Nation Without God? The Battle for Christianity in an Age of Unbelief.* Grand Rapids, MI: Baker.

Allen, John, Jr. 2009. *The Future Church: How Ten Trends Are Revolutionizing the Catholic Church.* New York: Doubleday.

Bailey, Julius. 2016. *Down in the Valley: An Introduction to African American Religious History.* Minneapolis, MN: Fortress.

Baker, Joseph, and Buster Smith. 2015. *American Secularism: Cultural Contours of Nonreligious Belief Systems.* New York: New York University Press.

Berger, Peter, Grace Davie, and Effie Fokas. 2008. *Religious America, Secular Europe? A Theme and Variations.* Farnham, UK: Ashgate.

Brown, Candy Gunther, ed. 2011. *Global Pentecostal and Charismatic Healing.* Oxford: Oxford University Press.

Bruce, Tricia Colleen. 2017. *Parish and Place: Making Room for Diversity in the American Catholic Church.* Oxford: Oxford University Press.

Calhoun, Craig, Mark Juergensmeyer, and Jonathan Van Antwerpen. 2011. *Rethinking Secularism.* Oxford: Oxford University Press.

Case, Jay Riley. 2012. *An Unpredictable Gospel: American Evangelicals and World Christianity, 1812–1920*. Oxford: Oxford University Press.

Chaves, Mark. 2011. *American Religion: Contemporary Trends*. Princeton, NJ: Princeton University Press.

Connor, Phillip. 2014. *Immigrant Faith: Patterns of Immigrant Religion in the United States, Canada, and Western Europe*. New York: New York University Press.

Corbett, Michael, Julia Corbett-Hemeyer, and Matthew Wilson. 2014. *Politics and Religion in the United States*. 2nd ed. New York: Routledge.

Daughrity, Dyron. 2010. *The Changing World of Christianity: The Global History of a Borderless Religion*. New York: Peter Lang.

Daughrity, Dyron. 2015. *To Whom Does Christianity Belong? Critical Issues in World Christianity*. Minneapolis, MN: Fortress.

Daughrity, Dyron. 2018. *Rising: The Amazing Story of Christianity's Resurrection in the Global South*. Minneapolis, MN: Fortress.

Davie, Grace. 1994. *Religion in Britain since 1945: Believing without Belonging*. Oxford: Wiley-Blackwell.

Day, Abby. 2011. *Believing in Belonging: Belief and Social Identity in the Modern World*. Oxford: Oxford University Press.

Gardella, Peter. 2014. *American Civil Religion: What Americans Hold Sacred*. Oxford: Oxford University Press.

Huntington, Samuel. 2004. *Who Are We? The Challenges to America's National Identity*. New York: Simon & Schuster.

Jones, Robert. 2016. *The End of White Christian America*. New York: Simon & Schuster.

Lane, Christopher. 2016. *Surge of Piety: Norman Vincent Peale and the Remaking of American Religious Life*. New Haven, CT: Yale University Press.

Marsden, George. 2014. *The Twilight of the American Enlightenment*. New York: Basic Books.

Martin, David. 2011. *The Future of Christianity: Reflections on Violence and Democracy, Religion and Secularization*. Farnham, UK: Ashgate.

Micklethwait, John, and Adrian Wooldridge. 2009. *God Is Back: How the Global Revival of Faith Is Changing the World*. New York: Penguin.

Miller, Donald, Kimon Sargeant, and Richard Flory. 2013. *Spirit and Power: The Growth and Global Impact of Pentecostalism*. Oxford: Oxford University Press.

Miller, Donald, and Tetsunao Yamamori. 2007. *Global Pentecostalism: The New Face of Christian Social Engagement*. Berkeley: University of California Press.

Noll, Mark. 2002. *America's God: From Jonathan Edwards to Abraham Lincoln*. Oxford: Oxford University Press.

Putnam, Robert. 2010. *American Grace: How Religion Divides and Unites Us*. New York: Simon & Schuster.

Schaeffer, Francis. 1976. *How Should We Then Live? The Rise and Decline of Western Thought and Culture*. Wheaton, IL: Crossway.

Setzer, Claudia, and David Shefferman, eds. 2011. *The Bible and American Culture: A Sourcebook*. New York: Routledge.

Shelton, Jason, and Michael Emerson. 2012. *Blacks and Whites in Christian America: How Racial Discrimination Shapes Religious Convictions*. New York: New York University Press.

Spickard, Paul, ed. 2012. *Race and Immigration in the United States: New Histories*. New York: Routledge.

Stark, Rodney. 2011. *The Triumph of Christianity*. New York: Harper Collins.

Sutton, Matthew Avery. 2007. *Aimee Semple McPherson and the Resurrection of Christian America*. Cambridge, MA: Harvard University Press.

Synan, Vinson. 1997. *The Holiness-Pentecostal Tradition: Charismatic Movements in the Twentieth Century*. Grand Rapids, MI: Eerdmans.

Synan, Vinson. 2001. *The Century of the Holy Spirit: 100 Years of Pentecostal and Charismatic Renewal*. Nashville, TN: Thomas Nelson.

Weigel, George. 2013. *Evangelical Catholicism: Deep Reform in the 21st Century Church*. New York: Basic Books.

Wuthnow, Robert. 2009. *Boundless Faith: The Global Outreach of American Churches*. Berkeley: University of California Press.

Zuckerman, Phil. 2015. *Faith No More: Why People Reject Religion*. Oxford: Oxford University Press.

Christianity Is Currently in Decline

What People Think Happened

It is fairly common to hear about Christianity's downward trend. Media outlets often report on the decline of various churches and the rise of "the nones"—people who claim to have "no religion." Denominations are shrinking and scaling back their budgets. Many of them survive on endowments built up by generations past. The Catholic Church is mired in scandals and its future appears bleak. Big name pastors are skewered in the headlines because of their very public misdeeds. Christianity seems to be losing its place in the public square as the courts rule in favor of "separation" of church from state. Seemingly, in court case after court case, prayer is removed from public schools, the Bible is under fire, Christianity is losing its cultural relevance, and a new age—a very secular one—seems to have dawned.

Even the social scientists present bleak news, especially in their analyses of the so-called Millennial generation—those born between 1982 and 2004. That generation is said to be losing its religion fast. According to some, Millennials are the least religious generation that the United States has ever seen. They go to church less, they pray or meditate less, they resist marriage for casual romantic relationships, and their values vary considerably from biblical norms.

While Christianity's decline is supposedly well established in the United States, anecdotal evidence from around the world suggests this is a global trend. Europeans are routinely described as being largely secularized. Their churches are closing, the state churches have lost their political power, and very few Europeans seem to care about Christianity at all. Media reports from Northern Europe indicate that church attenders are a rare breed. Religious adherence in Eastern Europe tends to get conflated with Communism, leaving Westerners with the impression that the former Soviet realm of influence is a rather godless place.

Meanwhile, Islam is on the rise, with some predicting that by the end of the twenty-first century, there will be far more Muslims than Christians in the world. Some even argue that one day Muslims will outnumber Christians in Western Europe—a land formerly known as Christendom. Some theorize that migration will continue to erode Christian hegemony in the West. Fertility rates among Western people are so low that they virtually have to support migration programs in their homelands, leading to a double whammy: migrants move to the West, and they have more kids than Westerners. Many scholars are already speaking of a "post-Christian America" or of "secular Europe."

There is a sense that religion may have lost its once-favored place in the world. With ideas more suited for a medieval understanding of reality, there are those who think Christianity has probably outlived its usefulness. No longer do clergy hold the influence they once did. Seminaries are closing, and the study of theology has given way to a more social-scientific orientation as evidenced in religious studies departments. Fewer college students aspire to be ministers, as their denominations are on the brink of collapse and will hardly be able to support them once they graduate.

How the Story Became Popular

Secularization is a sociological theory that religion will eventually recede as humans continue to learn more about their surroundings, and eventually realize the truth of materialism. The word "secularization" was probably coined by Max Weber (1864–1920), a German sociologist. He argued that as humans became more rational, they would become "disenchanted" with the world. They would stop thinking in theological terms and would think more in economic or materialistic terms. Religion placed conscious and unconscious restrictions on people that would fade as they gained knowledge about things normally associated with God. This has often been referred to as a "god of the gaps" mentality, meaning that as human knowledge deepens and expands, belief in gods would diminish. The "gaps" in human knowledge would be progressively filled by modern science and the discovery of facts. Eventually, there would be far fewer gaps in human knowledge because humans would understand the way things work. Mystery, superstition, and supernaturalism would simply fade away. As the gaps in our collective knowledge get filled, humans will call religion's bluff and have no need for the answers that religion provides.

The architects of this theory lived in the late nineteenth and early twentieth centuries: Weber, Karl Marx, Émile Durkheim, and Sigmund Freud. These theorists surmised that religion was on a fast track to extinction because it was false. Borrowing from the ideas of Ludwig Feuerbach, Sigmund Freud famously referred to religion as an "illusion" in his book *The Future of an Illusion* (1927).

Secularization theory progressed rapidly throughout the twentieth century and came to be an assumed doctrine in the secular academy. Late-twentieth-century theorists such as Peter Berger, Thomas Luckmann, and Bryan Wilson argued that Christianity's influence was obviously waning, and the rest of the world would follow the path that Western Europe had taken: they would forsake religion (Wuthnow 2009, 47).

Secularization theory is predicated on several key ideas such as urbanization, modernization, rationalism, and scientific advance. As humans urbanize, they become more secular because they are exposed to what more intelligent people have to say. They are exposed to rational explanations rather than traditional ideas they inherited from their parochial communities. As people became educated in the relatively secular academies pervasive across Europe and North America, their exposure to modern scientific theories would dislodge their religious inheritance and undermine their personal faith.

One important theorist in the study of secularization who has a different take on all this is Christian Smith. He argues that secularization actually arises out of academia. Society's elites—those who are highly educated in the secular academy—tend to have a critical view toward their own societies and thus want to mold society in their own image. What the intellectual class really wants is power, and by abandoning religion, or arguing against it, they are essentially undermining the historic institutions that were almost always affiliated with religion. Smith's chief contribution to the field is this notion that secularization is not so much about modernization and scientific progress; rather, it is about power. Intellectuals want to be the authors of society's great narrative. Thus, what students receive in the secular academy is a potent argument for why traditional—of course, religious—institutions are false. This allows the academy to shape society using new ideas and paradigms that will benefit itself, as well as those who invest in it.

Secularization theory became virtually unquestioned dogma in the Western academy, as well as educational institutions all over the world that borrowed from Western approaches to education. Religion's days were numbered. The elites of society—not just in the Western world but all over the world—were in on a secret. And that secret was that religion would eventually be eclipsed by other grand narratives that were predicated on Western, scientific ways of thinking. A widespread crisis of belief was thought to have occurred in the twentieth century, as committed Christians who entered the academy were philosophically undermined by the power of the secularization thesis. This is part of the backstory to the *TIME* magazine article, which asked, "Is God Dead?" in 1966. Unsuspecting university students were often confronted with an idea that seemed virtually unchallenged: the world was becoming secular.

Even church leaders have been impacted by the social doctrine of secularization, causing two types of response: a deeper entrenchment into fundamentalism or an attempt to align church doctrine with contemporary ideas about religion. There is a reason the Roman Catholic Church called for a Second Vatican Council during the 1960s—that decade caused it to question virtually every aspect of its history and institution. Similarly, many Protestant leaders applauded John Shelby Spong's conclusion that Christianity "must change or die." And by change, Spong meant the church should essentially discard anything that did not align with ideological currents propounded in the secular academy.

The impact on Evangelicals has been delayed, but it is finally happening. Evangelicals tended to resist the secularization thesis, but in the early twentieth century, this began to change, notably with the writings of Brian McLaren and Rob Bell. These two writers and others like them spawned an "emerging church movement," which was essentially a dissident Evangelical movement coming to terms with the social and theological conclusions of liberal Protestantism. Thus, many assumed that the path to secularization looked something like this: fundamentalists evolve into evangelicals who evolve into liberal Protestants who evolve into post-Christian humanists.

Some conservative churches positioned themselves as the last place where Christianity was faithfully preached without the infiltrations of secularization theory. Others, however, lost confidence and had to "look for a silver lining." In the words of sociologist Robert Wuthnow, churches often recast the situation as "a great opportunity" for people of faith. As secularization continued to spread, new possibilities would merge, allowing Christians to share their faith with people who had little knowledge of Christianity or why in the world it was still taken seriously by people in the modern world (Wuthnow 2009, 48).

There was an arrogant assumption in the late twentieth century that the rest of the world would follow the path predicted by the architects of secularization theory—everyone would secularize. Religion would go the way of the dinosaur. And as the European nations left their treasured colonies in the 1940s, 1950s, and 1960s, Christianity would collapse globally. A secular worldview would triumph in the postcolonial age. And Christianity would—as Marx and his ilk predicted—simply wither away.

PRIMARY DOCUMENT

LUDWIG FEUERBACH, *THE ESSENCE OF CHRISTIANITY* (1854)

Ludwig Feuerbach (1804–1872) is one of the most important thinkers at the root of modern humanism, materialism, and secularization theory. A burst of scholarship coming out of Germany in the nineteenth century was due largely to his pioneering work. The great theorists who are often associated with secularization theory are Karl Marx, Max Weber, Émile Durkheim, and Sigmund Freud. Their ideas, however, are firmly grounded in Feuerbach, in particular his groundbreaking work The Essence of Christianity, *first published in German in 1841. Feuerbach's key idea is that "the secret of theology is anthropology." He asserts that belief in God is illusory, and he goes to great lengths to show theology is actually an act of projection, or self-aggrandizement. Humans project their greatest desires and aspirations onto a god and then allow that god to rule over themselves. Thus, God becomes omnipotent, omnipresent, and omniscient. Humans thus deprive themselves by giving to God the attributes that are actually within their own capabilities. Feuerbach's ideas are, in many ways, still with us, as they greatly informed the fields of sociology, anthropology, and psychology. In this reading, we see Feuerbach's conviction that Christianity is not only fabricated but also malignant. Feuerbach's ideas set in motion a grand theory that religion, Christianity in particular, is contrived and will eventually give way to materialism and secularization. After a paragraph from the Preface, there is a long section dealing with faith and love in Christianity. Then we encounter Feuerbach's remedy to the situation: "We should raise ourselves above Christianity."*

[Preface] Religion is the dream of the human mind. But even in dreams we do not find ourselves in emptiness or in heaven, but on earth, in the realm of reality; we only see real things in the entrancing splendor of imagination and caprice, instead of in the simple daylight of reality and necessity. Hence I do nothing more to religion—and to speculative philosophy and theology also—than to open its eyes, or rather to turn its gaze from the internal towards the external, i.e., I change the object as it is in the imagination into the object as it is in reality.

[chapter 26] The essence of religion, its latent nature, is the identity of the divine being with the human.

. . .

Now, that which reveals the basis, the hidden essence of religion, is Love; that which constitutes its conscious form is Faith. Love identifies man with God and God with man, consequently it identifies man with man; faith separates God from man, consequently it separates man from man, for God is nothing else than the idea of the species invested with a mystical form,—the separation of God from man is therefore the separation of man from man, the unloosening of the social bond. By faith religion places itself in contradiction with morality, with reason, with the unsophisticated sense of truth in man; by love, it opposes itself again to this contradiction. Faith isolates God, it makes him a particular, distinct being: love universalizes; it makes God a common being, the love of whom is one with the love of man. Faith produces in man an inward disunion, a disunion with himself, and by consequence in outward disunion also; but love heals the wounds which are made by faith in the heart of man. Faith makes belief in its God a law: love is freedom,—it condemns not even the atheist, because it is itself atheistic, itself denies, if not theoretically, at least practically, the existence of a particular, individual God, opposed to man. Love has God in itself: faith has God out of itself; it estranges God from man, it makes him an external object. . . .

Faith discriminates thus: This is true, that is false. And it claims truth to itself alone. Faith has for its object a definite, specific truth, which is necessarily united with negation. Faith is in its nature exclusive. One thing alone is truth, one alone is God, one alone has the monopoly of being, the Son of God; all else is nothing, error, delusion. Jehovah alone is the true God; all other gods are vain idols. . . .

Faith gives man a peculiar sense of his own dignity and importance. The believer finds himself distinguished above other men, exalted above the natural man; he knows himself to be a person of distinction. In the possession of peculiar privileges; believers are aristocrats, unbelievers ple-beians. God is this distinction and pre-eminence of believers above unbe-lievers, personified. . . .

The Church was perfectly justified in adjudging damnation to heretics and unbelievers, [to faith, so long as it has any vital heat, any character, the heretic is always on a level with the unbeliever, with the atheist] for this condemnation is involved in the nature of faith. Faith at first appears to be only an unprejudiced separation of believers from unbelievers; but this separation is a highly critical distinction. The believer has God for him, the unbeliever, against him;—it is only as a possible believer that the unbeliever has God not against Him;—and therein precisely lies the ground of the requirement that he should leave the ranks of unbelief. But that which has God against it is worthless, rejected, reprobate; for that which has God against it is itself against God. To believe, is synonymous with goodness; not to believe, with wickedness. Faith, narrow and preju-diced refers all unbelief to the moral disposition. In its view the unbeliever is an enemy to Christ out of obduracy, out of wickedness. [Already in the New Testament the idea of disobedience is associated with unbelief. "The cardinal wickedness is unbelief."—Luther (xiii. p. 647).] Hence faith has fellowship with believers only; unbelievers it rejects. It is well-disposed towards believers, but ill-disposed towards unbelievers. In faith there lies a *malignant* principle. . . .

It is owing to the egoism, the vanity, the self-complacency of Christians, that they can see the motes in the faith of non-Christian nations, but cannot perceive the beam in their own. It is only in the mode in which faith embodies itself that Christians differ from the followers of other religions. The distinction is founded only on climate or on natural tem-perament. A warlike or ardently sensuous people will naturally attest its distinctive religious character by deeds, by force of arms. But the nature of faith as such is everywhere the same. It is essential to faith to con-demn, to anathematise. All blessings, all good it accumulates on itself, on its God, as the lover on his beloved; all curses, all hardship and evil it casts on unbelief. The believer is blessed, well-pleasing to God, a par-taker of everlasting, felicity; the unbeliever is accursed, rejected of God and abjured by men: for what God rejects man must not receive, must not indulge;—that would be a criticism of the divine judgment. The Turks exterminate unbelievers with fire and sword, the Christians with the flames of hell. . . .

To be a Christian is to be beloved by God; not to be a Christian is to be hated by God, an object of the divine anger. The Christian must therefore love only Christians—others only as possible Christians; he must only love what faith hallows and blesses. . . .

Thus faith is essentially a spirit of partisanship. He who is not for Christ is against Him. [Historically considered, this saying, as well as the others cited on pages 384 and 385, may be perfectly justified. But the Bible is not to be regarded as an historical or temporal, but as an eternal book.] Faith knows only friends or enemies; it understands no neutrality; it is preoccupied only with itself. Faith is essentially intolerant. . . .

Therefore, faith postulates a future, a world where faith has no longer an opposite, or where at least this opposite exists only in order to enhance the self-complacency of triumphant faith. Hell sweetens the joys of happy believers. "The elect will come forth to behold the torments of the ungodly, and at this spectacle they will not be smitten with sorrow; on the contrary, while they see the unspeakable sufferings of the ungodly, they, intoxicated with joy, will thank God for their own salvation.". . .

Faith is the opposite of love. . . .

Faith necessarily passes into hatred, hatred into persecution. . . .

[I]n Christianity love is tainted by faith, it is not free, it is not apprehended truly. A love which is limited by faith is an untrue love. . . .

[W]e should raise ourselves above Christianity, above the peculiar standpoint of all religion. We have shown that the substance and object of religion is altogether human; we have shown that divine wisdom is human wisdom; that the secret of theology is anthropology . . .

To place anything in God, or to derive anything from God, is nothing more than to withdraw it from the test of reason, to institute it as indubitable, unassailable, sacred, without rendering an account why. Hence self-delusion, if not wicked, insidious design is at the root of all efforts to establish morality. . . .

We need no incitement or support from above. We need no Christian rule of political right: we need only one which is rational, just, human. . . .

Thus the work of the self-conscious reason in relation to religion is simply to destroy an illusion:—an illusion, however, which is by no means indifferent, but which, on the contrary, is profoundly injurious in its effect on mankind. . . .

Think, therefore, with every morsel of bread which relieves thee from the pain of hunger, with every draught of wine which cheers thy heart, of the God who confers these beneficent gifts upon thee,—think of man! But in thy gratitude towards man forget not Gratitude towards holy Nature! Forget not that wine is the blood of plants, and flour the flesh of plants, which are sacrificed for thy well-being! Forget not that the plant typifies to thee the essence of Nature, which lovingly surrenders itself for thy enjoyment. . . .

Therefore let bread be sacred for us, let wine be sacred, and also let water be sacred! Amen.

Source: Ludwig Feuerbach, *The Essence of Christianity*, Preface to the 2nd ed.; Chapter 26, "The Contradiction of Faith and Love"; and Chapter 27, "Concluding Application." Originally published in German in 1941; translated into English in 1854. Full text available at https://www.marxists.org/reference/archive/feuerbach /works/essence/.

What Really Happened

One of the greatest "about-face" flip-flops in the history of the social sciences occurred in 1999 when Peter Berger published a bombshell book titled *The De-Secularization of the World: Resurgent Religion and World Politics.* Berger (1929–2017) was one of the most influential scholars working in the field of sociology in the second half of the twentieth century. His writings in the field of sociology are considered classics, notably *The Social Construction of Reality* and *The Sacred Canopy.* For many sociologists, his ideas were considered dogma. Berger was the key sociologist responsible for articulating the secularization thesis for generations of students and scholars alike.

This is precisely why Berger's 1999 book caused such a stir. In that book, he confessed that he had been proven wrong. His prediction that secularization was the future of humanity had been irreparably damaged. He stated in the introduction, "My point is that the assumption that we live in a secularized world is false. The world today, with some exceptions . . . is as furiously religious as it ever was, and in many places more so than ever." Near the end of his career, Berger was forced to recant one of the great theories that had made him such a celebrated academic. He flatly stated, "secularization theory is essentially mistaken." He provided example after example to substantiate his theory:

- The Islamic world is definitely not secularizing. It is notably more religious today than it was before the Islamic Revolution in 1979.
- Latin America is becoming more religious than ever as Protestants and Catholics struggle to win converts or maintain their adherents. In some nations, Pentecostalism is on pace to surpass Catholicism's once untested hegemony, especially in Central America.
- Sub-Saharan Africa has become the real heartland of Christianity. Northern Africa is fiercely Islamic.
- Eastern Europe, in the aftermath of the Soviet Union, is showing a massive openness to religion again. Churches are popping up all over, with the strong support of the government. This development would have been unimaginable in the 1960s.
- In China, strict Marxism is lifting; there is a renewed interest in religion. Some sociologists predict that by 2025, China will surpass the United States as the nation with the most Christians in the world. And with the current annual growth rate (7 percent) of Christians in China, by 2040 there could be nearly 600 million Christians there (Stark and Wang 2015, xi, 115).
- Pentecostalism is probably the fastest growing religious movement in the world and may have as many as 600 million adherents in the world today.
- India has proven not to be the "secular democracy" that Nehru envisioned. The Hindu nationalist party (BJP) is more powerful than ever in India.
- The United States remains strongly religious, a fact that puzzles sociologists who confidently predicted the recession of Christianity in the 1960s and 1970s.

Indeed, the news of the death of religion has been greatly exaggerated. Secularization theory was proven questionable if not false. Many people bought into the idea that whatever Western Europe did, the rest of the world would follow. The reality of the situation was very different and was aptly summarized in the title of a fascinating 2009 book: *God Is Back: How the Global Revival of Faith Is Changing the World.*

Of all faiths, it appears that Christianity's growth and fervor is second to none. At no other time in human history has a religion become so globally widespread. Christianity is today the largest religion in the world and claims around 33 percent of the world's population. That's around

2.5 billion people. And what is unique about Christianity is that it seems uniquely positioned to fit the social context of its host. Of the world's eight cultural blocks, Christianity is the largest religion in six of them:

- Latin America and the Caribbean (93 percent Christian)
- North America (81 percent Christian)
- Eastern Europe (80 percent Christian)
- Oceania (80 percent Christian)
- Western Europe (78 percent Christian)
- Africa (47 percent Christian, 41 percent Muslim)
- Asia (9 percent Christian)
- Middle East (2 percent Christian)

It would be no exaggeration to say we are living in the heyday of Christianity (Daughrity 2010, 3).

Christianity is booming globally. The largest churches in the world are in South Korea. One Pentecostal church in Seoul has over 800,000 members! In a generation or two, China could conceivably surpass the United States as the nation with the most Christians. People are turning to Christ there in numbers rarely seen in history. India is now home to megachurches, one boasting over 150,000 members. The city of Moscow currently has two hundred new churches under construction. Hillsong, a Pentecostal church in Sydney, Australia, reaches over 100,000 people weekly through its music and media ministry. Even traditionally Muslim nations such as Indonesia and Malaysia are home to rapid Christian growth.

Some of the most interesting developments in global Christianity have to do with Western denominations that are now primarily rooted in the Global South. For instance, the Anglican Church has far more members in Africa than in the entire Western world. The Roman Catholic Church is now anchored in the Global South. The top three Catholic nations in the world are Brazil, Mexico, and the Philippines. But the fastest growing Catholic populations are in Africa. For example, the population of the DR Congo is over 80 million souls—and half of them are Roman Catholic.

Some people have argued that global migration will affect Christianity adversely, but nothing could be further from the truth. Latin America is almost entirely Christian; therefore, virtually all Latino immigrants to the United States are Christians—and strengthen the U.S. churches with their presence. Another fascinating statistic is that Asian Americans often convert to Christianity once they immigrate to the United States. While only 10 percent of Asians are Christian, fully 44 percent of Asian Americans are Christians. Western Europe's case will be very interesting in the future, as so many of its migrants are from Christian nations. While the mass immigration of 2015–2017 stole the headlines, the more common immigrant to Western Europe is English-speaking and Christian. Immigrants from the Caribbean, Africa, and Eastern Europe are far more likely to be Christian than any other religion (Daughrity 2018, 221).

Another important story that gets little notice is that the Western world is today being evangelized by Christians from other lands. For example, African Christians not only establish large churches in the West designed for Africans but also have a knack for reaching the local people, too. In London, for every Anglican church that closes, three Pentecostal churches—usually led by African pastors—open. The Kingsway International Christian Centre in London now has over 12,000 members. The largest church in all of Europe, the Blessed Kingdom of God for All Nations in Kiev, has more than 25,000 members. And the problem of the Roman Catholic Church's shortage of priests is now being ameliorated by priests from India, the Philippines, and Africa.

It is no secret that the Roman Catholic Church is a behemoth, both in sheer numbers and in influence. Around 17 percent of the world's population is Roman Catholic. Over a billion people look to the bishop of Rome as their authority in matters pertaining to religion and morality. No other person in the world has that level of influence. The Roman Catholic Church may be the largest human institution to have ever existed. And while some people predict the downfall of the Catholic Church, the reality is that it is growing steadily due to much higher fertility rates in the places where Catholicism is strong. For example, between 2006 and 2011, the Catholic Church grew 22 percent in Africa, 12 percent in Asia, and 6 percent in the Americas.

Christianity is experiencing staggering growth in Africa today. Already around 20 percent of the world's Christians live in Africa, and that number is sure to increase. African Pentecostalism has taken the continent by storm, and there is no telling how much growth is in store. Huge churches are emerging from the context of African Pentecostalism, such as Winner's Chapel and Deeper Life Bible Church in Nigeria. Ghana is home to International Central Gospel Church, which owns a highly respected university. Synagogue of All Nations church in Nigeria claims to reach a million subscribers on YouTube (Daughrity 2018, 142ff).

Christianity has a history of surprising growth at various times in its history. From a tiny Jewish sect in the first century, it survived Roman persecution and eventually converted the emperor in the 300s. Nearly the entire Russian people converted to Christianity around the turn of the millennium, beginning in 988. The Protestant Reformation birthed more Christian groups than can be counted. The Azusa Street Revival gave birth to Pentecostal Christianity that has taken the world by storm. Now, the former colonies of Christendom are grabbing hold of Christianity and even bringing it back to the secularizing nations of the West.

It is an amazing story that has no end. Christianity is not in decline. Its future is well endowed. If anything, it appears that secularization's days may be numbered. The predictions of Christianity's demise in the 1960s were ill-advised. The more pertinent question today is not whether Christianity will survive, but rather how high will it soar.

PRIMARY DOCUMENT

JOHN MOTT, *THE EVANGELIZATION OF THE WORLD IN THIS GENERATION* (1900)

John Mott (1865–1955) was an American Methodist who became one of the most important Christian leaders of his time. He converted from agnosticism to Christian faith while an undergraduate at Cornell. He joined the Student Volunteer Movement in his twenties and pledged to become a missionary. He became well known through his work with the Young Men's Christian Association (YMCA) in various capacities for forty-four years, rising to the top position of general secretary. His famous catch phrase was to "evangelize the world in this generation," through mission work, and he is said to have inspired over twenty thousand college students to become missionaries. He led the World's Student Christian Federation from 1895 to 1928. He is considered the most well-traveled Christian of his time (estimated at 1.7 million miles). Mott became famous all over the Western World for his leadership of the Edinburgh World Mission Conference in 1910, which he organized and chaired. He was a strong advocate for missionizing India and China, the most populous nations on earth. He founded and chaired the International Missionary Council (IMC) in 1921, arguing for collaboration between churches for the purpose of worldwide evangelism. He is often called the father of the World Council of Churches, which finally formed in 1948. He was honored by President Woodrow Wilson for his peace work in Russia and Mexico during

World War I. He received the Nobel Peace Prize in 1946. He is buried in the Washington, D.C., Episcopal Cathedral Church of Saints Peter and Paul.

The book this excerpt comes from became the rallying cry of tens of thousands of Christians as they gave themselves to foreign missionary service. Its message and urgency still reverberate in the hearts of those who commit to the task of Christian evangelism.

Chapter II
The Obligation to Evangelize the World

It Is Our Duty to Evangelize the World Because All Men Need Christ

The Christian Scriptures and the careful and extended observation of earnest men the world over agree that with respect to the need of salvation all nations and races are alike. The need of the non-Christian world is indescribably great. Hundreds of millions are today living in ignorance and darkness, steeped in idolatry, superstition, degradation and corruption. Reflect on the desolating and cruel evils which are making such fearful ravages among them. See under what a burden of sin and sorrow and suffering they live. Can any candid person doubt the reality of the awful need after reviewing the masterly, scientific survey by Dr. Dennis of the social evils of the non-Christian world? No one who has seen the actual conditions can question that they who are without God are also without hope. The non-Christian religions may be judged by their fruits. While they furnish some moral principles and precepts of value, they do not afford adequate standards and motives by which rightly to guide the life, nor power to enable one to take the step between knowing duty and doing it. Though there are among the followers of these religions men of high and noble lives, in the sight of God all have sinned and stand in need of the Divine forgiveness and of Christ the Savior. All other religions have failed to do what Christianity has done and is doing as a regenerating power in the individual and as a transforming force in society. It is a significant fact that the thousands of missionaries scattered throughout the world, face to face with heathenism and thus in the best position to make a scientific study of the problem, bear such a unanimous testimony as to the practical results of the non-Christian religions as should forever banish any doubt or reservation regarding their inadequacy to meet the world's need. The Scriptures clearly teach that if men are to be saved they must be saved through Christ. He alone can deliver them from the power of sin and its penalty. His death made salvation possible. The Word of

God sets forth the conditions of salvation. God has chosen to have these conditions made known through human agency. The universal capability of men to be benefited by the Gospel, and the ability of Christ to satisfy men of all races and conditions, emphasize the duty of Christians to preach Christ to every creature. The burning question for every Christian then is, "Shall hundreds of millions of men now living, who need Christ and are capable of receiving help from Him, pass away without having even the opportunity to know Him?" It is not necessary that we go to the Scriptures, or to the ends of the earth, to discover our obligation to the un-evangelized. A knowledge of our own hearts should be sufficient to make plain our duty. We know our need of Christ. How unreasonable, therefore, for us to assume that the nations living in sin and wretchedness and bondage can do without Him whom we so much need even in the most favored Christian lands.

It Is Our Duty to Evangelize the World Because We Owe All Men the Gospel

We have a knowledge of Jesus Christ, and to have this is to incur a responsibility toward every man who has it not. To have a Savior who alone can save from the guilt and power of sin imposes an obligation of the most serious character. We received the knowledge of the Gospel from others, but not in order to appropriate it for our own exclusive use. It concerns all men. Christ tasted death for every man. He wishes the good news of His salvation made known to every creature. All nations and races are one in God's intention, and therefore equally entitled to the Gospel. The Christians of today are simply trustees of the Gospel and in no sense sole proprietors. Every Indian, every Chinese, every South Sea Islander has as good a right to the Gospel as anyone else; and, as a Chinese once said to Robert Stewart, we break the eighth commandment if we do not take it to him. In the words of Mr. Eugene Stock, "Bring me the best Buddhist or Mohammedan in the world, the most virtuous, the most high-minded, and I think that man has a right to hear of the tremendous fact that a Divine Person came into the world to bring blessing to mankind. Whether he needs it or no, I will not stop to argue. I think he has a claim upon Christian people to tell him of that fact." What a wrong against man- kind to keep the knowledge of the mission of Christ to men from two-thirds of the race!

Our sense of obligation must be intensified when we ask ourselves the question, "If we do not preach Christ where He has not been named, who will?"

God has committed unto us the word of reconciliation, and from whom shall the heathen now living ever hear that word, if the Christians of the present day fail to discharge the debt? We know their need; we know the only remedy; we have access to them; we are able to go. The claims of humanity and universal brotherhood prompt us to make Christ known to those who live in darkness and in misery. The Golden Rule by which we profess to live impels us to it. The example of Christ, who was moved with compassion to meet even the bodily hunger of the multitudes, should inspire us to go forth with the Word of life to the millions who are wandering in helplessness in the shadow of death. "Give me Thy heart, O Christ! Thy love untold That I like Thee may pity, like Thee may preach. For round me spreads on every side a waste drearer than that which moved thy soul to sadness; No ray hath pierced this immemorial gloom; And scarce these darkened toiling myriads taste even a few drops of fleeting earthly gladness; As they move on, slow, silent, to the tomb."

The evangelization of the world in this generation is to Christians no self-imposed task; it rests securely upon Divine commandment. The Great Commission of Christ given by Him in the upper room in Jerusalem on the night after the resurrection, again a little later on a mountain in Galilee, and yet again, on the Mount of Olives, just before the ascension clearly expresses our obligation to make Christ known to all men. While this command was given to the disciples of Christ living in the first generation of the Christian era, it was intended as well for all time and for each Christian in his own time. That the command was not intended for the Apostles alone is seen from the promise with which it is linked, "Lo I am with you alway, even unto the end of the age." The practice of the Church in the Apostolic Age and Sub-Apostolic Age shows that the command was regarded as binding not only upon the Apostles but also upon all Christians. It was addressed to all in every place and throughout every generation who should call upon the name of the Lord Jesus Christ. It is true there is no express command to evangelize the world in this generation; but, as Mr. Stock has pointed out, "If we have a general command to make the Gospel known to those who know it not, there seems no escape from the conclusion that the duty to make it known to all—that is, all now alive—lies in the nature of the case." Thus the expression, the evangelization of the world in this generation, simply translates Christ's last command into terms of obligation concerning our own lifetime. In this command of our Lord we have "a motive power sufficient to impel disciples always with uniform force; which will survive romance; which will outlive excitement; which is independent of experiences and emotions;

which can surmount every difficulty and disappointment; which burns steadily in the absence of outward encouragement, and glows in a blast of persecution; such a motive as in its intense and imperishable influence on the conscience and heart of a Christian shall be irrespective at once of his past history, of any peculiarities in his position, and of his interpretation of prophecy." This command has been given to be obeyed. It is operative until it is repealed. The execution of it is not optional but obligatory. It awaits fulfilment by a generation that shall have courage and consecration enough to attempt the thing commanded. It should move to action all real Christians; for, in the words of Archbishop Whately, "If our religion is not true, we ought to change it; if it is true, we are bound to propagate what we believe to be the truth." "Why call ye me, Lord, Lord, and do not the things which I say?" "If ye love me ye will keep my commandments."

It is our duty to evangelize the world because this is essential to the best life of the Christian Church. If all men need the Gospel, if we owe the Gospel to all men, if Christ has commanded us to preach the Gospel to every creature, it is unquestionably our duty to give all people in our generation an opportunity to hear the Gospel. To know our duty and to do it not is sin. Continuance in the sin of neglect and disobedience necessarily weakens the life and arrests the growth of the Church. Who can measure the loss of vitality and power that she has already suffered within our own day from her failure to do all in her power for the world's evangelization? The Christians of today need some object great enough to engage all the powers of their minds and hearts. We find just such an object in the enterprise to make Christ known to the whole world. This would call out and utilize the best energies of the Church. It would help to save her from some of her gravest perils—ease, selfishness, luxury, materialism and low ideals. It would necessitate, and therefore greatly promote, real Christian unity, thus preventing an immense waste of force. It would react favorably on Christian countries. There is no one thing which would do so much to promote work on behalf of the cities and neglected country districts of the home lands as a vast enlargement of the foreign missionary operations. This is not a matter of theory; for history teaches impressively that the missionary epochs have been the times of greatest activity and spiritual vigor in the life of the home Church. So the best spiritual interests of America, Great Britain, Germany, Australasia and other Christian lands are inseparably bound up with the evangelization of the whole wide world. The dictates of patriotism, as well as of loyalty to our Lord, thus call upon us to give ourselves to the world's evangelization. But the most serious and important consideration of all is that the largest manifestation of the presence of Christ with us as individual Christians, and with the Church at large, depends upon our obedience to His command. There is a most intimate and vital connection between "Go ye and make disciples of all the nations," and "Lo, I am with you alway." The gift of the Holy Spirit is associated in the New Testament with spreading the knowledge of Christ. More than that, the power of the Holy Spirit was bestowed for the express purpose of equipping Christians for the work of preaching the Gospel unto the uttermost parts of the earth, beginning from Jerusalem. If the Church of today, therefore, would have the power of God come mightily upon her—and is not this the great need?—she will necessarily receive it while in the pathway of larger obedience to the missionary command.

The Obligation to Evangelize the World Is an Urgent One

Every reason for doing this work of evangelizing at all demands that it be done not only thoroughly but also as speedily as possible. The present generation is passing away. If we do not evangelize it, who will? We dare not say the next generation will be soon enough. The Church has too long been in the habit of committing the heathen to the next generation. "It is not possible for the coming generation to discharge the duties of the present, whether it respects their repentance, faith, or works; and to commit to them our share of preaching Christ crucified to the heathen, is like committing to them the love due from us to God and our neighbor. The Lord will require of us that which is committed to us."

The present generation is one of unexampled crisis in all parts of the un-evangelized world. Missionaries from nearly every land urge that, if the Church fails to do her full duty in our lifetime, not only will multitudes of the present generation pass away without knowing of Christ, but the task of our successors to evangelize their generation will be much more difficult. Our generation is also one of marvelous opportunity. The world is better known and more accessible, its needs more articulate and intelligible, and our ability to go into all the world with the Gospel is much greater than in any preceding generation. All this adds to our responsibility. The forces of evil are not deferring their operations to the next generation. With world-wide enterprise and with ceaseless vigor they are seeking to accomplish their deadly work in this generation. This is true not only of the dire influences which have been at work in the un-evangelized nations for centuries, but also of those which have come from so-called Christian lands. By the liquor traffic, by the opium trade and by the licentious lives and gambling habits of some of our countrymen we have greatly increased the misery and woe of the heathen. All non-Christian nations are being brought under the influences of the material civilization of the West, and these may easily work their injury unless controlled by the power of pure religion. The evangelization of the world in this generation is not, therefore, merely a matter of buying up the opportunity, but of helping to neutralize and supplant the effects of the sins of our own peoples. Because of the infinite need of men without Christ; because of the possibilities of men of every race and condition who take Christ as the Lord of their lives; because of the command of our Lord which has acquired added force as a result of nineteen centuries of discovery, of opening of doors, of experience of the Christian Church; because of the shameful neglect of the past; because of the impending crisis and the urgency of the situation in all parts of the non-Christian world; because of the opportunity for a greatly accelerated movement in the present; because of the danger of neglecting to enter upon a great onward movement; because of the constraining memories of the Cross of Christ and the love wherewith He loved us, it is the solemn duty of the Christians of this generation to do their utmost to evangelize the world.

Source: John R. Mott, *The Evangelization of the World in This Generation* (New York: Student Volunteer Movement for Foreign Missions, 1900), chapter 2.

Further Reading

Aikman, David. 2012. *One Nation Without God? The Battle for Christianity in an Age of Unbelief.* Grand Rapids, MI: Baker.

Allen, John, Jr. 2009. *The Future Church: How Ten Trends Are Revolutionizing the Catholic Church.* New York: Doubleday.

Anderson, Gerald, ed. 1998. *Biographical Dictionary of Christian Missions.* Grand Rapids, MI: Eerdmans.

Banchoff, Thomas, and Jose Casanova. 2016. *The Jesuits and Globalization: Historical Legacies and Contemporary Challenges.* Washington, D.C.: Georgetown University Press.

Berger, Peter. 1999. *The Desecularization of the World: Resurgent Religion and World Politics.* Grand Rapids, MI: Eerdmans.

Brown, Candy Gunther, ed. 2011. *Global Pentecostal and Charismatic Healing.* Oxford: Oxford University Press.

Case, Jay Riley. 2012. *An Unpredictable Gospel: American Evangelicals and World Christianity, 1812–1920.* Oxford: Oxford University Press.

Christerson, Brad, and Richard Flory. 2017. *The Rise of Network Christianity: How Independent Leaders Are Changing the Religious Landscape.* Oxford: Oxford University Press.

Connor, Phillip. 2014. *Immigrant Faith: Patterns of Immigrant Religion in the United States, Canada, and Western Europe.* New York: New York University Press.

Daughrity, Dyron. 2010. *The Changing World of Christianity: The Global History of a Borderless Religion.* New York: Peter Lang.

Daughrity, Dyron. 2015. *To Whom Does Christianity Belong? Critical Issues in World Christianity.* Minneapolis, MN: Fortress.

Daughrity, Dyron. 2018. *Rising: The Amazing Story of Christianity's Resurrection in the Global South.* Minneapolis, MN: Fortress.

Gornik, Mark. 2011. *Word Made Global: Stories of African Christianity in New York City.* Grand Rapids, MI: Eerdmans.

Granberg-Michaelson, Wesley. 2011. *Unexpected Destination: An Evangelical Pilgrimage to World Christianity.* Grand Rapids, MI: Eerdmans.

Granberg-Michaelson, Wesley. 2013. *From Times Square to Timbuktu: The Post-Christian West Meets the Non-Western Church.* Grand Rapids, MI: Eerdmans.

Hanciles, Jehu. 2008. *Beyond Christendom: Globalization, African Migration, and the Transformation of the West.* Maryknoll, NY: Orbis.

James, Jonathan. 2015. *A Moving Faith: Mega Churches Go South.* Thousand Oaks, CA: Sage.

Jenkins, Philip. 2011. *The Next Christendom: The Coming of Global Christianity.* 3rd ed. Oxford: Oxford University Press.

Micklethwait, John, and Adrian Wooldridge. 2009. *God Is Back: How the Global Revival of Faith Is Changing the World.* New York: Penguin.

Miller, Donald, Kimon Sargeant, and Richard Flory. 2013. *Spirit and Power: The Growth and Global Impact of Pentecostalism.* Oxford: Oxford University Press.

Miller, Donald, and Tetsunao Yamamori. 2007. *Global Pentecostalism: The New Face of Christian Social Engagement.* Berkeley: University of California Press.

Putnam, Robert. 2010. *American Grace: How Religion Divides and Unites Us.* New York: Simon & Schuster.

Sanneh, Lamin, and Michael McClymond, eds. 2016. *The Wiley Blackwell Companion to World Christianity.* Chichester, UK: Wiley Blackwell.

Sharkey, Heather, ed. *Cultural Conversations: Unexpected Consequences of Christian Missionary Encounters in the Middle East, Africa, and South Asia.* Syracuse, NY: Syracuse University Press.

Shaw, Mark. 2010. *Global Awakening: How 20th Century Revivals Triggered a Christian Revolution.* Downers Grove, IL: IVP Academic.

Smith, Christian. 2003. *The Secular Revolution: Power, Interests, and Conflict in the Secularization of American Public Life.* Berkeley: University of California Press.

Stanley, Brian. 2018. *Christianity in the Twentieth Century: A World History.* Princeton, NJ: Princeton University Press.

Stark, Rodney. 2011. *The Triumph of Christianity.* New York: HarperCollins.

Stark, Rodney, and Xiuhua Wang. 2015. *A Star in the East: The Rise of Christianity in China.* West Conshohocken, PA: Templeton Press.

Sunquist, Scott. 2015. *The Unexpected Christian Century: The Reversal and Transformation of Global Christianity, 1900–2000.* Grand Rapids, MI: Baker.

Weigel, George. 2013. *Evangelical Catholicism: Deep Reform in the 21st Century Church.* New York: Basic Books.

Wuthnow, Robert. 2009. *Boundless Faith: The Global Outreach of American Churches.* Berkeley: University of California Press.

Zuckerman, Phil. 2015. *Faith No More: Why People Reject Religion.* Oxford: Oxford University Press.

Bibliography

Aikman, David. 2012. *One Nation Without God? The Battle for Christianity in an Age of Unbelief.* Grand Rapids, MI: Baker.

Allen, John, Jr. 2009. *The Future Church: How Ten Trends Are Revolutionizing the Catholic Church.* New York: Doubleday.

Anderson, Gerald, ed. 1998. *Biographical Dictionary of Christian Missions.* Grand Rapids, MI: Eerdmans.

Baker, Joseph, and Buster Smith. 2015. *American Secularism: Cultural Contours of Nonreligious Belief Systems.* New York: New York University Press.

Banchoff, Thomas, and José Casanova. 2016. *The Jesuits and Globalization: Historical Legacies and Contemporary Challenges.* Washington, D.C.: Georgetown University Press.

Berger, Peter. 1999. *The Desecularization of the World: Resurgent Religion and World Politics.* Grand Rapids, MI: Eerdmans.

Berger, Peter, Grace Davie, and Effie Fokas. 2008. *Religious America, Secular Europe? A Theme and Variations.* Farnham, UK: Ashgate.

Boak, Arthur E. R. 1955. *Manpower Shortage and the Fall of the Roman Empire in the West.* Ann Arbor: University of Michigan Press.

Bornstein, Daniel E., ed. 2009. *Medieval Christianity.* Minneapolis, MN: Fortress.

Brown, Candy Gunther, ed. 2011. *Global Pentecostal and Charismatic Healing.* Oxford: Oxford University Press.

Brown, Peter. 1995. *Authority and the Sacred: Aspects of the Christianization of the Roman World.* Cambridge: Cambridge University Press.

Brown, Peter. 1996. *The Rise of Western Christendom: Triumph and Diversity, A.D. 200–1000*. Chichester, UK: John Wiley.

Brown, Peter. 2015. *The Ransom of the Soul: Afterlife and Wealth in Early Western Christianity*. Cambridge, MA: Harvard University Press.

Bruce, Tricia Colleen. 2017. *Parish and Place: Making Room for Diversity in the American Catholic Church*. Oxford: Oxford University Press.

Calhoun, Craig, Mark Juergensmeyer, and Jonathan Van Antwerpen. 2011. *Rethinking Secularism*. Oxford: Oxford University Press.

Christerson, Brad, and Richard Flory. 2017. *The Rise of Network Christianity: How Independent Leaders Are Changing the Religious Landscape*. Oxford: Oxford University Press.

Daughrity, Dyron B. 2010. *The Changing World of Christianity: The Global History of a Borderless Religion*. New York: Peter Lang.

Daughrity, Dyron B. 2012. *Church History: Five Approaches to a Global Discipline*. New York: Peter Lang.

Daughrity, Dyron B. 2015. *To Whom Does Christianity Belong? Critical Issues in World Christianity*. Minneapolis, MN: Fortress.

Daughrity, Dyron B. 2016. *Roots: Uncovering Why We Do What We Do in Church*. Abilene, TX: Leafwood.

Daughrity, Dyron B. 2018. *Rising: The Amazing Story of Christianity's Resurrection in the Global South*. Minneapolis, MN: Fortress.

Davie, Grace. 1994. *Religion in Britain since 1945: Believing without Belonging*. Oxford: Wiley-Blackwell.

Day, Abby. 2011. *Believing in Belonging: Belief and Social Identity in the Modern World*. Oxford: Oxford University Press.

Deanesley, Margaret. 1925. *A History of the Medieval Church 590–1500*. London: Routledge.

Digeser, Elizabeth DePalma. 1999. *The Making of a Christian Empire: Lactantius and Rome*. Ithaca, NY: Cornell University Press.

Dowe, Phil. 2005. *Galileo, Darwin, and Hawking: The Interplay of Science, Reason, and Religion*. Grand Rapids, MI: Eerdmans.

Drake, H. A. 2000. *Constantine and the Bishops: The Politics of Intolerance*. Baltimore: Johns Hopkins University Press.

Duffy, Eamon. 1997. *Saints and Sinners: A History of Popes*. New Haven, CT: Yale University Press.

Ehrman, Bart, and Zlatko Plese. 2013. *The Other Gospels: Accounts of Jesus from Outside the New Testament*. Oxford: Oxford University Press.

Eire, Carlos M. N. 2016. *Reformations: The Early Modern World, 1450–1650*. New Haven, CT: Yale University Press.

Esler, Philip E., ed. 2000. *The Early Christian World*. Vol. 2. London: Routledge.

Ferguson, Everett, ed. 1999. *The Encyclopedia of Early Christianity*. 2nd ed. New York: Routledge.

Finocchiaro, Maurice A. 1989. *The Galileo Affair: A Documentary History*. Berkeley: University of California Press.

Frend, W. H. C. 1984. *The Rise of Christianity*. Philadelphia: Fortress Press.

Gorman, Michael J. 1982. *Abortion and the Early Church*. Downers Grove, IL: InterVarsity.

Gornik, Mark. 2011. *Word Made Global: Stories of African Christianity in New York City*. Grand Rapids, MI: Eerdmans.

Gould, Stephen Jay. 1999. *Rocks of Ages: Science and Religion in the Fullness of Life*. New York: Ballantine.

Granberg-Michaelson, Wesley. 2013. *From Times Square to Timbuktu: The Post-Christian West Meets the Non-Western Church*. Grand Rapids, MI: Eerdmans.

Hanciles, Jehu. 2008. *Beyond Christendom: Globalization, African Migration, and the Transformation of the West*. Maryknoll, NY: Orbis.

Hillenbrand, Carole. 1999. *The Crusades: Islamic Perspectives*. Edinburgh: Edinburgh University Press.

Huntington, Samuel. 2004. *Who Are We? The Challenges to America's National Identity*. New York: Simon & Schuster.

James, Jonathan. 2015. *A Moving Faith: Mega Churches Go South*. Thousand Oaks, CA: Sage.

Jenkins, Philip. 2011. *The Next Christendom: The Coming of Global Christianity*. 3rd ed. Oxford: Oxford University Press.

Johanson, Donald, and Blake Edgar. 2006. *From Lucy to Language*. Rev. ed. New York: Simon and Schuster.

Kertzer, D. I., and R. P. Sallers. 1991. *The Family in Italy from Antiquity to the Present*. New Haven, CT: Yale University Press.

Kraemer, Ross Shepard. 1992. *Her Share of the Blessings: Women's Religions among Pagans, Jews, and Christians in the Greco-Roman World*. Oxford: Oxford University Press.

Larson, Edward. 1997. *Summer for the Gods: The Scopes Trial and America's Continuing Debate over Science and Religion*. Cambridge, MA: Harvard University Press.

Lefkowitz, Mary R., and Maureen B. Fant. 2005. *Women's Life in Greece and Rome: A Source Book in Translation*. 3rd ed. Baltimore: Johns Hopkins University Press.

Leithart, Peter J. 2010. *Defending Constantine*. Downers Grove, IL: IVP Academic.

Madden, Thomas. 1999. *A Concise History of the Crusades*. Lanham, MD: Rowman & Littlefield.

Madigan, Kevin. 2015. *Medieval Christianity: A New History*. New Haven, CT: Yale University Press.

Marsden, George. 2014. *The Twilight of the American Enlightenment*. New York: Basic Books.

Martin, David. 2011. *The Future of Christianity: Reflections on Violence and Democracy, Religion and Secularization*. Farnham, UK: Ashgate.

Meeks, Wayne. 1983. *The First Urban Christians: The Social World of the Apostle Paul*. New Haven, CT: Yale University Press.

Michaud, Joseph. 1999. *The History of the Crusades*. Vol. 3. Cambridge: Cambridge University Press.

Micklethwait, John, and Adrian Woolridge. 2009. *God Is Back: How the Global Revival of Faith Is Changing the World*. New York: Penguin.

Miller, Donald, Kimon Sargeant, and Richard Flory. 2013. *Spirit and Power: The Growth and Global Impact of Pentecostalism*. Oxford: Oxford University Press.

Miller, Donald, and Tetsunao Yamamori. 2007. *Global Pentecostalism: The New Face of Christian Social Engagement*. Berkeley: University of California Press.

Moffett, Samuel Hugh. 1998. *A History of Christianity in Asia*. Vol. 1, *Beginnings to 1500*. Maryknoll, NY: Orbis.

Myers, Eric M., and Mark A. Chancey. 2012. *Alexander to Constantine: Archaeology of the Land of the Bible*. New Haven, CT: Yale University Press.

Parkin, Tim G. 1992. *Demography and Roman Society*. Baltimore: Johns Hopkins University Press.

Pelikan, Jaroslav. 1985. *Jesus through the Centuries*. New Haven, CT: Yale University Press.

Percival, Henry. 1900. "First Council of Nicaea, A.D. 325." In *Nicene and Post-Nicene Fathers*, edited by Philip Schaff and Henry Wace. Buffalo, NY: Christian Literature Publishing.

Polkinghorne, John. 2000. *Faith, Science and Understanding*. New Haven, CT: Yale University Press.

Pomeroy, Sarah B. 1975. *Goddesses, Whores, Wives, and Slaves: Women in Classical Antiquity*. New York: Schocken Books.

Putnam, Robert. 2010. *American Grace: How Religion Divides and Unites Us*. New York: Simon & Schuster.

Rawson, Beryl, ed. 1986. *The Family in Ancient Rome*. Ithaca, NY: Cornell University Press.

Richard, Jean. 1999. *The Crusades, c. 1071–c. 1291*. Cambridge: Cambridge University Press.

Riddle, John M. 1994. *Contraception and Abortion from the Ancient World to the Renaissance*. Cambridge, MA: Harvard University Press.

Riley-Smith, Jonathan. 2005. *The Crusades: A History*. 2nd ed. London: Continuum.

Riley-Smith, Jonathan. 2011. *The Crusades, Christianity, and Islam*. New York: Columbia University Press.

Runciman, Sir Steven. 1951. *A History of the Crusades*. 3 vols. Cambridge: Cambridge University Press.

Russell, Jeffrey Burton. 1997. *Inventing the Flat Earth: Columbus and Modern Historians*. Westport, CT: Praeger.

Sanders, E. P. 1993. *The Historical Figure of Jesus*. London: Penguin.

Sanneh, Lamin, and Michael McClymond. 2016. *The Wiley Blackwell Companion to World Christianity*. Chichester, UK: Wiley Blackwell.

Setzer, Claudia, and David Shefferman, eds. 2011. *The Bible and American Culture: A Sourcebook*. New York: Routledge.

Sharma, Arvind, and Katherine Young, eds. 1999. *Feminism and World Religions*. Albany, NY: SUNY Press.

Spickard, Paul, ed. 2012. *Race and Immigration in the United States: New Histories*. New York: Routledge.

Stanley, Brian. 2018. *Christianity in the Twentieth Century: A World History*. Princeton, NJ: Princeton University Press.

Stark, Rodney. 1996. *The Rise of Christianity*. San Francisco: HarperCollins.

Stark, Rodney. 2009. *God's Battalions: The Case for the Crusades*. San Francisco: HarperOne.

Stark, Rodney. 2011. *The Triumph of Christianity*. New York: HarperOne.

Stark, Rodney, and Xiuhua Wang. 2015. *A Star in the East: The Rise of Christianity in China*. West Conshohocken, PA: Templeton Press.

Strauss, Gerald. 1978. *Luther's House of Learning: Indoctrination of the Young in the German Reformation*. Baltimore: Johns Hopkins University Press.

Sutton, Matthew Avery. 2007. *Aimee Semple McPherson and the Resurrection of Christian America*. Cambridge, MA: Harvard University Press.

Synan, Vinson. 2001. *The Century of the Holy Spirit: 100 Years of Pentecostal and Charismatic Renewal*. Nashville: Thomas Nelson.

Tyerman, Christopher. 2006. *God's War: A New History of the Crusades*. Cambridge, MA: Belknap.

Tyerman, Christopher. 2011. *The Debate on the Crusades, 1099–2010.* Manchester: Manchester University Press.

Vermes, Geza. 1981. *Jesus the Jew.* Minneapolis, MN: Fortress.

Von Harnack, Adolf. 1908. *The Mission and Expansion of Christianity in the First Three Centuries.* Vol. 2. 2nd ed. New York: G. P. Putnam's Sons.

Weigel, George. 2013. *Evangelical Catholicism: Deep Reform in the 21st Century Church.* New York: Basic Books.

Wright, N. T. 1996. *Jesus and the Victory of God.* Minneapolis, MN: Fortress.

Wuthnow, Robert. 2009. *Boundless Faith: The Global Outreach of American Churches.* Berkeley: University of California Press.

Zuckerman, Phil. 2015. *Faith No More: Why People Reject Religion.* Oxford: Oxford University Press.

Index

Abelard, 106; letters of, 108–111
Abin, Jose ben, 16
Abortion, 61
Acts, Book of: early Christians living
    socialist utopian existence, 24; Jesus
    as meek, 4–5; Jesus's teachings as
    universal, 3; Paul as rich and liter-
    ate, 35; role of women, 53, 58
Adam and Eve, 46, 47, 49–51, 107,
    169
Adultery, 60
Aegyptius, 75
Africa, 209, 210
Agassiz, Louis, 156
"Age of Faith," 104
Ambrose, St., 80
Angels, 100–104
Anna, 57
Apollonius, 41
Apollos, 36, 58
Apologeticus (Tertullian), 38–40
Apostolic Faith (Seymour), 189–195
Aquila, 36, 58
Aristotle, 100, 101, 103
Arius, 87
Arnulf, 144
Atheism, 156

Augustine, 80, 100, 102, 133
Aulus Plautius, 32
Azusa Street Revival, 186, 187–189

Bacon, Francis, 122, 159
Baird, Robert, 184
Baker, Joseph, 179
Baldwin, 131
Barna Group, 179
Barnabas, 36
Barnes, Timothy, 81, 82
Basil the Great, 80
Beatitudes: early Christians as poor
    and marginalized, 21; Jesus as
    meek, 27
Bede, Venerable, 160
Bell, Rob, 202
Bellamy, Francis, 177
Benedict XVI, Pope, 48
Berger, Peter, 186, 201; The
    De-Secularization of the World:
    Resurgent Religion and World
    Politics, 207–208
Bird, Robert, 2
Bishop of Le Puy, 139–140
Blandina, 58, 63–65
Boethius, 101

Bohemund, 139
Bongars, Jacques, 123
Borg, Marcus, 2
Brewer, Michael, 2
Brown, Antoinette, 62
Brown, Dan, 72
Brown, Peter, 33
Bryan, William Jennings, 161,
    162–171
Buchanan, George Wesley, 5–6
Burckhardt, Jacob, 73–74

Caesar Augustus, 28, 36, 41
The Caesars (Julian the Apostate), 74
Cane Ridge Revival, 185
Cautinus, 106
Celibacy, 55
Charles Martel, 133
Chasing of the Temple, 17
Chi-Rho symbol, 4
Child exposure, 59, 65–66
Christianity, supposed decline of,
    199–203, 207–211; The Essence of
    Christianity (Feuerbach), 203–207;
    The Evangelization of the World in
    This Generation (Mott), 211–217.
    See also Early Christianity; Religion
Chuza, 34
Cicero, 95
Clare, St., 97
Classical antiquity, 93
Claudius, 36
Clement, 41
Clinton, Bill, 120
Clinton, Hillary, 178
Columbus, Christopher: flat earth
    argument, 147, 149–150, 160
Commodus, 41
Communism, 176–177
Comnenus, Alexius, 129, 130, 136
Condit, Louisa, 195
Constantine, 4, 26, 33, 41; baptism
    of, 80–81, 87–89; The Caesars

(Julian the Apostate), 74; conver-
    sion to Christianity, 81–82; death
    of, 89; Edict of Milan (Constantine
    and Licinius), 83–85; The History
    of the Decline and Fall of the Roman
    Empire (Gibbon), 76–80; Life of
    Constantine (Eusebius), 85–89;
    New History (Zosimus), 75–76;
    and sincerity of his Christian faith,
    69–74
Constantinople, fall of, 133, 135
Copernicus, 159
Corinthians: defiling temple of God,
    82; divisions in the church, 37–38;
    early Christians as social rejects,
    22; humility of Christians, 27, 29;
    Jesus as wealthy, 34; marriage, 46;
    role of women, 50–51, 52–53, 57
Cornell, Ezra, 155, 156
Count of St.-Gilles, 139–140, 143
Creationism, 148, 151, 161–162,
    169–171
Crispus, 35, 75, 79
Crusades, 119–121; as defensive wars,
    133–136; An Essay on Universal
    History, the Manners, and Spirit of
    Nations, from the Reign of Char-
    lemagne to the Age of Lewis XIV
    (Voltaire), 128–132; Gesta Fran-
    corum (The Deeds of the Franks),
    137–144; historiography of,
    121–125; History of England
    (Hume), 125–128; Pope Urban
    II's speech at Council of Clermont,
    135–137, 138
Curbara, 141
Cursing of the Fig Tree, 17

Damascene, 102
Dark Ages, 93, 95, 147, 159
Darrow, Clarence, 161, 162–171
Darwin, Charles, 156
Davie, Grace, 179

Dawkins, Richard, 150, 176

Day, Abby, 179

The De-Secularization of the World: Resurgent Religion and World Politics (Berger), 207–208

Deaconess, 47–48

Deborah, 57

Decius, 22

Declaration of Independence, 177

Deissmann, Adolf, 22, 37

Dennett, Daniel, 176

Dennis, Dr., 212

Descartes, René, 159

Didache, 61

Diderot, Denis, 123

Diocletian, 22, 41, 42

Dionysius the Areopagite, 40

Divorce, 60

Domitian, 32

Dorylaeum, Battle of, 139–141

Dowd, Maureen, 119

Draper, John William: *History of the Conflict between Religion and Science*, 150, 151–154, 157

Dupuy, Raymond, 131

Durant, Will, 104

Durkheim, Émile, 201, 203

Early Christianity: *Apologeticus* (Tertullian), 38–40; Christians as poor and marginalized, 21–22; Christians as social rejects, 22–23; exceptions to poor and marginalized stereotype, 32; *Foundations of Christianity* (Kautsky), 30–31; *On the History of Early Christianity* (Engels), 29–30; *History of the Christian Church* (Schaff), 31–32; *On the Inward Spread of Christianity* (von Harnack), 40–42; middle and upper class, 32–37; middle and upper-class, 40–42; women in, 57–62. *See also*

Christianity, supposed decline of; Religion

Earth: age of, 168; and sun orbiting, 165–166

Eastern Orthodox church: and women priests, 45, 48

Eaton, Elizabeth, 48

Edict of Milan (Constantine and Licinius), 83–85

Edwards, Jonathan, 185

Einstein, Albert, 162

Eisenhower, Dwight D., 177, 185

Engels, Friedrich, 23–25; *On the History of Early Christianity*, 29–30

Enlightenment, 94, 96–97, 148

Ephesians: on marriage, 60; role of women, 52

Erastus, 35, 36

An Essay on Universal History, the Manners, and Spirit of Nations, from the Reign of Charlemagne to the Age of Lewis XIV (Voltaire), 128–132

The Essence of Christianity (Feuerbach), 203–207

Euodia, 35, 58

Eusebius, 83, 87; *Life of Constantine*, 85–89

Eustace, Count, 143

Evangelicals, 202

The Evangelization of the World in This Generation (Mott), 211–217

"Evangelize the world" (Mott), 211–217

Evolution, 151, 162, 169–171

Faith, 204–206

Farrow, Lucy F., 192

Fausta, 75

Felicitas, 58

Fell, Margaret, 61–62, 66–67

Feuerbach, Ludwig, 150, 201; *The Essence of Christianity*, 203–207

Finney, Charles, 185

First Great Awakening, 185
Flavia Domitilla, 32, 41
Flood, biblical, 166
Foundations of Christianity (Kautsky), 30–31
Fox, George, 61
Francis, Pope, 48
Francis of Assisi, 72, 96
French Revolution, 95–96
Freud, Sigmund, 150, 201, 203
Fuller, Thomas, 123

Gabriel, 9
Gaius, 35
Galatians: apostles as being from higher class, 33; role of women, 46, 61, 63
Galileo, 159; sun at center of cosmos argument, 147–148, 154, 160–161
Gamaliel, 35
Gaston of Beert, 144
Gautier sans Argent, 129
Genesis: role of women, 49–50
Genghis Khan, 132
"Gentle Jesus, Meek and Mild" (Wesley), 5, 12
Gesta Francorum (The Deeds of the Franks), 137–138; Battle of Dorylaeum, 139–141; defeat of Kerbogha, 141–142; fall of Jerusalem, 143–144; Franks' victory at Nicaea, 138–139; Urban II's speech at Clermont, 138; vision of peace, 144
Gibbon, Edward, 73, 76–80, 123, 128, 148, 150
Gibson, Mel, 2
Gift of Tongues, 194
"God of the gaps" mentality, 200–201
Godfrey, Duke of Boüillon, 127, 131, 139–140, 143, 144
Godfrey of Monte-Scaglioso, 140
Good Shepherd, 4, 11
Gould, Stephen Jay, 150, 162

Graham, Billy, 176
Greco-Roman era, 93
Greek Orthodox church: *History of the Conflict between Religion and Science* (Draper), 151, 153
Greeley, Horace, 157
Gregory of Nazianzus, 80
Gregory of Nyssa, 80
Gregory VII, Pope, 126
Gregory X, Pope, 106
"Guilt of Exposing Children" (Justin Martyr), 65–66
Guy of Lufignan, 131–132

Harnack, Adolf von, 40–42
Harris, Sam, 150, 175
Hebrews, Book of: adultery, 60
Helena, 75, 81
Heloise, 106; letters of, 108–111
Henry IV, 130
Herlwin, 142
Hermas, 41
Herod, 8, 9
Herod Antipas, 34
Histoire des croisades (Michaud), 122
History of England (Hume), 125–128
The History of Joseph the Carpenter, 6–10
History of the Christian Church (Schaff), 31–32
History of the Conflict between Religion and Science (Draper), 150, 151–154, 157
The History of the Decline and Fall of the Roman Empire (Gibbon), 73, 76–80
A History of the Warfare of Science with Theology in Christendom (White), 150, 154–159
Hitchens, Christopher, 150, 176
Holy Orders, sacrament of, 54–55
Hugh, Count of Vermandois, France, 127, 139–140

Huldah, 57
Hume, David, 123, 125–128
Huntington, Samuel, 185, 186
Hus, Jan, 72

Iliad (Homer), 5
Immigration and Christianity, 186–187
Infertility, 61
Inter Insigniores: On the Question of Admission of Women to the Ministerial Priesthood (Roman Catholic Church), 55–57
Irving, Washington, 150
"Is God Dead?" cover, *TIME* magazine, 175, 176, 202
Islam: during Crusades, 123–124, 126, 133–136; radical groups, 178; rise of, 200, 208

Jacob, 10
James, Apostle, 34
James, Book of: prejudice against poor in early church, 38
James, brother of Jesus, 61
James the Less, 8
Jason, 36
Jefferson, Thomas, 178
Jerome, 6
Jerusalem: during Crusades, 120, 123, 125–126, 130–135, 138; fall of, 143–144; Jesus in temple, 3, 16, 17, 21, 34
Jesus Christ: answers question with a question, 19; as carpenter, 2, 5–6, 14; conversation with Joseph, 7; crucifixion, 4–5; emotional personality, 13–14, 16–19; God of the Chi-Rho, 81, 85, 86; Good Shepherd and His Sheep, 11; in *The History of Joseph the Carpenter,* 9; as illiterate, 16; in Jerusalem temple, 3; meek depiction of, 1–12, 27–29;

Parable of the Lost Sheep, 10–11; as rabbi, 14–15, 16–19, 33–34; and women, 57, 66–67
Joanna, 34
Joel, 57
John, Apostle, 34
John, Gospel of: Cleansing of the Temple, 17; Jesus as good shepherd, 4, 11; Jesus as rabbi, 14–15, 16; sorrowful Jesus, 13
John Chrysostom, 80
John Paul II, Pope, 48, 54
Johnson, Andrew, 195
Jonah and whale story, 164–165
Jones, Robert, 175
Joseph: birth of Jesus, 28–29; as carpenter, 5–6; conversation with Jesus, 7; *The History of Joseph the Carpenter,* 7–10; as poor, 21–22
Joseph of Arimathea, 34
Judge, E. A., 36
Julian the Apostate, 74
Junia, 58
Justin Martyr, 59, 65–66

Kautsky, Karl, 30–31
Kerbogha, defeat of, 141–142
Khrushchev, Nikita, 177

Lactantius, 76, 82, 83
Lazarus, 13, 31
Leatherman, Lucy M., 195
Leithart, Peter, 70, 82
Lenin, Vladimir, 177; "Socialism and Religion," 179–184
Leviticus: bleeding women, 57; poor people offering two doves or pigeons instead of lamb, 21–22
Licinius, 77; *Edict of Milan,* 83–85
Life of Constantine (Eusebius), 85–89
Lincoln, Abraham, 185
The Little Flowers of St. Francis, 97–100

Locke, John, 159
Lord's Supper, 37–38
Love, 204–206
Luckmann, Thomas, 201
Luke, Apostle, 35
Luke, Gospel of: birth of Jesus, 28–29; bleeding women, 57; early Christians as poor and marginalized, 21; Jesus and family, 14; Jesus as carpenter, 6; Jesus as good shepherd, 4; Jesus as meek, 27, 28–29; Jesus as rabbi, 14–15, 16; Jesus in Jerusalem temple, 3; Lazarus, 31; Parable of the Lost Sheep, 10–11; role of women, 57, 63
Luther, Martin, 107; *Small Catechism*, 111–115
Lydia, 35

Mahomet, 125
Malherbe, Abe, 37
Manchester, William, 94
Marcion, 41
Mark, Apostle, 36
Mark, Gospel of: angry Jesus, 13; apostles as rich, 34; Cursing of the Fig Tree, 17; Jesus and family, 14; Jesus as carpenter, 5, 6, 14; Jesus as rabbi, 14–15
Marriage, 60
Martha, 57, 63, 66
Martyrdom, 58, 63–65
Marx, Karl, 23–25, 29, 150, 178, 180, 201, 203
Mary, 57, 63, 66; birth of Jesus, 28–29; as poor, 21–22; virginity of, 6, 7–8, 9
Mary Magdalene, 15, 66
Matthew, Apostle, 34
Matthew, Gospel of: adultery, 60; apostles as rich, 34; divorce, 60; early Christians as poor and marginalized, 21; Jesus against divorce, 62; Jesus and family, 14; Jesus answers question with a question, 19; Jesus as carpenter, 5, 6, 14; Jesus as meek, 27–28; Jesus as rabbi, 14–15; Jesus's Seven Woes speech, 13; not "peace, but a sword," 18–19; Sermon on the Mount, 13; Seven Woes against the Religious Teachers, 17–18; sorrowful Jesus, 13
Maxentius, 69, 78, 81, 83
Maximilla, 57
McCaffree, Kevin, 175
McDowell, Josh, 2
McLaren, Brian, 202
Meacham, Jon, 175
Mead, S. J., 193
Medieval Christianity, 93–97, 104–107; letters of Heloise and Abelard, 108–111; *The Little Flowers of St. Francis*, 97–100; *Small Catechism* (Luther), 111–115; *Summa Theologiae* (Thomas Aquinas), 100–104
Meeks, Wayne, 35–36
Mehmed II, 135
Michael, 9
Michaud, Joseph François, 122, 124
Millennial generation, 199
Miller, Ron, 2
Mills, Charles, 122, 124
Milton, John, 161
Milvian Bridge, Battle of, 69–70, 76, 82, 83, 85
Minucius Felix, 41
Miriam, 57
Mission work, 211–217
Moses, 62
Mott, John: *The Evangelization of the World in This Generation*, 211–217
Muhammad, 133

Narcissus, 36
Nero, 22

New History (Zosimus), 75–76
Newton, Isaac, 159
Nicaea, 138–139
Nicanor, 53
Nicolas from Antioch, 53
Noll, Mark, 185
Noradin, 132

Obama, Barack, 120
On the History of Early Christianity (Engels), 24, 29–30
On the Inward Spread of Christianity (von Harnack), 40–42
Ordination, 54–55
Ordination of women, 45, 48
Origen, 41
Owens, Teresa Hord, 48

Paganism, 105
Parable of the Lost Sheep, 3–4, 10–11
Parmenas, 53
Pascal, Blaise, 159
The Passion of the Christ (2004), 2
Patriarch of Alexandria, 48
Paul, Apostle, 3–4, 32; on marriage, 60; ministry of, 3–4; patriarchal views of, 45–46; as rich and literate, 35; role of women, 50, 52–53, 57, 58, 61, 63; treatment of women, 61
Paul VI, Pope, 55
Pelikan, Jaroslav, 15
Pentecostal movement, 186, 187, 189–195, 209, 210
Perpetua, 58
Peter, Apostle, 57, 141
Peter, Book of: crucifixion of Jesus, 5
Peter the Hermit, 127, 129, 130, 142
Petrarch, 95, 148
Pharisees, 17–18
Philemon, 36
Philip, 53
Philip the Arabian, 42

Philippians: gentility of Jesus, 3–4; humility of Jesus, 11; role of women, 58
Phoebe, 36, 47–48, 53, 58
Pledge of Allegiance, 177
Pliny, 40
Pomponia Graecina, 32, 40
Pontius Pilate, 34
Price, Viola, 192
Prisca, 36
Priscilla, 57, 58
Procorus, 53
Protestant Christians: *History of the Conflict between Religion and Science* (Draper), 151, 153
Protestant Reformation, 111, 211
Protestantism, 45, 48, 202
Puritanism, 184
Putnam, Robert, 179

Quakers, 61
Quirinius, 28

Rainaud de Chatillon, 131–132
Raymond, Count of Toulouse, 127, 143, 144
Reconciliation Walk, 119–120
Reign of Terror, 95–96
Religion: critique by Marx and Engels, 23–25; *The Essence of Christianity* (Feuerbach), 203–207; evolution from sects to churches, 25–27; "Socialism and Religion" (Lenin), 179–184. *See also* Christianity, supposed decline of; Early Christianity
Roman Catholic church, 209, 210; Enlightenment, 96–97; French Revolution, 95–96; *History of the Conflict between Religion and Science* (Draper), 151, 153–154; *Inter Insigniores: On the Question of Admission of Women to the Ministerial Priesthood*, 55–57; Sacrament

Roman Catholic church (*cont.*)
  of Holy Orders, 54–55; Second
  Vatican Council, 202; and women
  priests, 45, 48
Romans, Book of: deaconess, 47; role
  of women, 58
Rousseau, Jean-Jacques, 123
Runciman, Steven, 124
Russell, Bertrand, 150

Sacrament of Holy Orders: Roman
  Catholic church, 54–55
Saladin, 129, 131–132, 135
Schaff, Philip, 31–32, 105
Schori, Katharine Jefferts, 48
Science versus religion: Columbus and
  flat earth argument, 147, 149–150,
  160; Dark Ages, 147, 148–149,
  159; Galileo and sun at center
  of cosmos argument, 147–148,
  154, 160–161; *History of the Con-
  flict between Religion and Science*
  (Draper), 150, 151–154, 157; *A
  History of the Warfare of Science with
  Theology in Christendom* (White),
  150, 154–159; Scopes monkey
  trial, 148, 150–151, 161–171
Scopes, John, 151
Scopes monkey trial, 148, 150–151,
  161–171
Scott, Walter, 124
Second Great Awakening, 185
Secularization thesis, 178, 200–203,
  207–208
Sergius Paulus, 40
Sermon on the Mount, 26
"Seven Woes" speech (Jesus Christ),
  13, 17–18
Severus, 22
Seymour, William, 186, 189–195
Shaw, Brent, 59
Small Catechism (Luther), 111–115
Smith, Buster, 179

Smith, Christian, 201
Smith, Goldwin, 156
Social morality, 105–106
"Socialism and Religion" (Lenin),
  179–184
Soviet Union, 177–178; "Socialism
  and Religion" (Lenin), 179–184
Spong, John Shelby, 202
Stalin, Joseph, 177
Stark, Rodney, 60, 80, 81, 149, 184
Stephen, 53
Stephen, Count of Blois, 127
Stewart, Robert, 213
Stock, Eugene, 213, 214
Stone, Barton, 185
Summa Theologiae (Thomas Aquinas),
  100–104
Sun and earth orbiting, 165–166
Susanna, 34
Syntyche, 35, 58

Tancred, 144
Taylor, Bishop William, 193
Tekton, 5
Teradion, Haninah ben, 16
Tertius, 35
Tertullian, 41, 47; *Apologeticus,* 38–40
Theodosius, 105
Theology, 24
Thomas, Keith, 107
Thomas Aquinas, 96, 160; *Summa
  Theologiae,* 100–104
TIME magazine, "Is God Dead?"
  cover, 175, 176, 202
Timon, 53
Timothy, Letter to: role of women,
  50; treatment of women, 61
Titus Flavius Clemens, 32, 41
Tocqueville, Alexis de, 184
Trajan, 22, 40
Troeltsch, Ernst, 25–26
Tyerman, Christopher, 124
Tyndall, John, 157

United States, status of Christianity, 175–179, 184–187; *Apostolic Faith* (Seymour), 189–195; Azusa Street Revival, 186, 187–189
Urban II, Pope, 130, 134; speech at Council of Clermont launching First Crusade, 135–137, 138

Valerian, 22, 41
Voltaire, 72, 123, 148, 150; on Crusades, 128–132; *An Essay on Universal History, the Manners, and Spirit of Nations, from the Reign of Charlemagne to the Age of Lewis XIV,* 128–132

Walter the Moneyless, 127
Watkins, Sharon, 48
Weber, Max, 200, 201, 203
Wesley, Charles, 5, 12
Whately, Archbishop Richard, 215
White, Andrew Dickson: *A History of the Warfare of Science with Theology in Christendom,* 150, 154–159
Whitefield, George, 185
Wilken, Friedrich, 122, 124

William, son of Marquis and brother of Tancred, 140
Wilson, Bryan, 201
Wilson, Woodrow, 161, 211
Women, ordination of, 45, 48
Women, role of, 46–49, 57–62; Acts, Book of, 53; Blandina, 63–65; Corinthians, 50–51, 52–53; Ephesians, 52; Galatians, 63; Genesis, 49–50; Luke, Gospel of, 63; in priesthood, 55–57; Timothy, Letter to, 50; "Womens Speaking Justified, Proved and Allowed of by the Scriptures" (Fell), 66–67
"Womens Speaking Justified, Proved and Allowed of by the Scriptures" (Fell), 62, 66–67
Woolsey, Theodore Dwight, 157
Wuthnow, Robert, 202
Wycliffe, John, 72

Yoder, John Howard, 72

Zacchaeus, 34
Zakkai, Yohanan ben, 14, 16
Zosimus, 72, 75–76, 105
Zuckerman, Phil, 175

About the Author

Dyron B. Daughrity is professor of religion at Pepperdine University in Malibu, California. He has written nine books on the history of Christianity and world religions. In 2017, he published *Martin Luther: A Biography for the People* and in 2018 published *Rising: The Amazing Story of Christianity's Resurrection in the Global South*. Both books, as well as his others, are available on his Amazon.com page. He is currently involved in a research project in India, sponsored by the John Templeton Foundation. He does editorial work with Fortress Press (USA), Bloomsbury Publications (UK), and De Gruyter Press (Germany). Daughrity is an ordained minister and currently pastors the Pasadena Church of Christ in California. When not engaged in scholarship, he is likely with family, traveling for work, on the basketball court, or plopped down in front of the TV watching the NFL. (Go Cowboys!) Daughrity grew up in New Mexico and loves to return as often as possible. If you would like to request Daughrity for a speaking engagement, please reach out to him directly at: Dyron.daughrity@pepperdine.edu

Now unto him that is able to do exceeding abundantly above all that we ask or think, according to the power that worketh in us, Unto him be glory in the church by Christ Jesus throughout all ages, world without end. Amen (Ephesians 3:20–21, KJV).